I0563866

Women
vs.
Women

OFFICIALLY DISCARDED BY
UNIVERSITY OF PITTSBURGH LIBRARY

WOMEN vs. WOMEN

The Uncivil Business War

Tara Roth Madden

amacom

American Management Association

This book is available at a special
discount when ordered in bulk quantities.
For information, contact Special Sales Department,
AMACOM, a division of American Management Association,
135 West 50th Street, New York, NY 10020.

Library of Congress Cataloging-in-Publication Data

Madden, Tara Roth.
    Women vs. women.

    Includes index.
    1. Sex role in the work environment. 2. Women—
Employment. 3. Women—Psychology. 4. Interpersonal
conflicts. I. Title. II. Title: Women versus women.
HD6060.M33 1987   658.4′095′088042   87-47701
ISBN 0-8144-5900-5

© 1987 Tara Roth Madden
All rights reserved.
Printed in the United States of America.

This publication may not be reproduced,
stored in a retrieval system,
or transmitted in whole or in part,
in any form or by any means, electronic,
mechanical, photocopying, recording, or otherwise,
without the prior written permission of AMACOM,
a division of American Management Association,
135 West 50th Street, New York, NY 10020.

Printing number

10 9 8 7 6 5 4 3 2 1

To my husband,
Ned,
who now understands why so many mates
are honored on a book's dedication page.

A6034

AKC 11.20.87

Acknowledgments

Women across the country participated in filling out the questionnaires that provided the basis for this book, sharing their personal and work lives. Although the request was informal, many not only responded, but copied the form and passed it on to others. Signed or unsigned, women took the time and energy to follow through and return the completed questionnaires within a four-week schedule. Thanks to all.

Through these questionnaires and personal contacts, many women volunteered for in-depth interviews about their own work lives to be used here in composite form. Their contributions provide a national scope of experiences.

Thanks to Dr. Joy Davidson. She gave her personal and professional time and talent as a friend and as a psychologist. She suggested the structure for the questionnaire.

Others contributed more than a little to the steps from thought to deed: editor Ron Mallis often suffered, but always with humor and understanding. Thanks also to Dr. Harold E. Wilson, Lary Bloom, the Costa Mesa branch of the Orange County Public Library, and special helpers Steve, Sue, Nick, Craig, and Chris Weissfeld, agent Sherry Robb, and Stan, Diana, Sally, Harv, Steffie, Lewis, Mark, Tracey Joan, and Thelma Jean.

Deep thanks to Leo, who may have been a writer in another time and place, and Char, who collected my early clippings and did the best she could. To Edward E. Madden, husband and nurturer, on the massive marriage tester that is a long tome on a short deadline.

Introduction

Why am I writing a book that blows the whistle on my own gender? Why, indeed, do I feel called upon to tell everyone why my fellow females aren't advancing all that far or fast in today's challenging work world? Why do I need to say there's a war going on among women in business that's keeping the majority from achieving leverage in the power structure?

What drove me to begin clipping pro and con articles on my theory that fighting among women is driven by their fear that they will fail and fall to a lower social and economic status? What compelled me to quit my managerial position and write a book to share my findings? And where did my own uncivil war begin?

Although I can't pinpoint the precise moment when I became consciously aware of Women vs. Women, I do recall the first time I did battle in the trenches.

At some moment in every female's life, she becomes aware of the inner chant she hears while interacting merrily with other females: "I hate her, I really hate her."

I remember that as a preschooler, I shared smiles, giggles, and a plate of cookies with my best girlfriend as we primly sat side by side on the top step of my front porch. We were both scrubbed and polished, and had new ribbons in our hair. My eye kept wandering toward her ribbon. It was wider than mine and trimmed with lace. I didn't want her ribbon; I didn't even like her ribbon. I just though that, in the eyes of the world, it might be considered a better ribbon.

The sweet little girl who was me turned to Suzee and giggled. "Your ribbon is fat," I said.

Seeing her smile fade slightly as she tugged the offending ornament into a wrinkled mess, I was gratified.

I remember thinking, "She shouldn't have done that. Now she has on a garbage-can ribbon." Whatever that might have meant to me at the time, I knew it resolved the question about who was sporting the better ribbon.

Treasuring my reputation for cleanliness, I carefully brushed the cookie crumbs off my lap. Suzee spontaneously hugged me, at the same time wiping her gooey hands on my shirt. As we joined hands and skipped away, the thought flashed across my mind: It's okay to hate her. Sometimes she hates me, too.

So we learn the business of life.

Relationships between females can flow along for years, happily bobbing up and down through school and career dreams amid seas of rivalry, envy, and competitive jealousy. It only takes a flashpoint—such as vying for the same date for the senior prom or a coveted promotion in a crowded job market—to produce real trouble. When the same method is used to solve both types of problems, the groundwork is laid for full-fledged warfare in the workplace.

Like most wars, there were years of undercover skirmishes before incendiary incidents formed a pattern. Young women, first tokens of the equal rights times, entered the work scene with entry-level expectations of learning and support service. How they behaved toward one another had little bearing on their ability to get their daily tasks completed.

Women weren't ready to go anywhere at the time. The perils of the Uncivil Business War looming in their futures was not foreseen. Getting in was the goal, not getting ahead.

I started my first, full-time, "real" job in 1970. I lived and worked near Kent State University, where the conservative midwestern influence was dimmed by the new talk of "peace and love." It permeated the behavior of campus students and lingered to influence grad students and hangers-on.

The young and the less young found fun and comfort in the

college atmosphere. It was great be a part of an era of equality with blue jeans for everyone, sincere contemplation of global problems—and a rock-n-roll good time. It was okay to advocate change, and even to protest. Girls as well as boys could speak up. March. Demand rights. Challenge authority.

Those particular notions came to an abrupt halt on May 4 of that year. Four students were shot, executed without a trial on a sunny hillside, primarily for the sin of being naive about the power of authority. Life was as real as bullets, and it wasn't wise to be found guilty of the fatal error of bad timing.

At Kent, one young woman was photographed sticking a flower in a young National Guardsman's rifle. Later, another was photographed screaming to the heavens as she hovered over the body of a dead student. The lesson was well learned. I had the unspoken, perhaps unshared, feeling that for females especially, it was safer to exist under the protective coloration of quiet "girldom."

I immersed myself in my new job with a passion, embracing the comfort of every rule and regulation. I was the public communications department for an entire small city school system. I was enthusiastic about the educational environment and the opportunity to use my skills to help the community and schools understand one another—and pass necessary school bond issues. Salary didn't matter, hours didn't matter. The only thing that mattered was to do the best job I could, every single day. I basked in approval for the next eight years as I proudly did my job and produced good results.

Next to my father, the man I most respected was my boss. His Navy background and doctorate brought authority to his position as superintendent of schools. He was fair and just. He allowed me the right to think, question, and grow. I seldom took him up on the privilege. Generally, going along seemed more safe and secure.

Actually, one time I did take him up on the privilege, and we both nearly died of the shock. For two entire years I had watched the closed door of the Friday principals' meeting held in the administrative office next to mine. Behind that door every principal in the district strutted his stuff about plans and activities, and I, whose job it was to communicate it all to the eager public, was on the outside.

Following those meetings, it would take me hours to quiz individual principals about what went on in the inner sanctum. I had hoped, in vain, to be invited to join them. Finally, after much deliberation and postponement, I decided to take action.

I planned, reasoned, and bought a new outfit. After staying awake for two nights, I clutched an index card of notes and made an appointment to see my open-door, shirt-sleeved boss. I trembled as I explained the merits of my attending the principals' meetings. The good doctor was contemplative, his hands folded prayer-style. "They're all men, you know."

I didn't comment, but I had noticed that most teachers were female and *all* principals were male. He continued, "And they work hard." I nodded. No argument there. "And the meetings are long and tense." My head went up and down again, in serious agreement.

His gaze was just as serious. He cleared his throat. "So at the end of each meeting, I, uh, break the tension with a little risqué joke."

I had heard raucous laughter, sure enough. He continued, "The joke is usually of the men's variety and I wouldn't want you to be, you know, embarrassed." His smile was gentlemanly.

Oh, God, being a woman was sometimes a heavy career burden. What to do? What to do? It came to me in a flash. Brightly, I chirped a suggestion. "I could attend the meeting and leave *before* the joke."

The superintendent smiled, seeming relieved. "Fine. I'll say, 'Is there anything for the good of the order?' right at the end, and you can slip out then."

The good man shook his head in gentle wonder as his liberated, braless employee clutched a notebook in front of her—and backed out his office door.

After five years or so, as principals died and moved and times and laws changed, a woman joined their group. Since no one had the courage to tell her they felt the need to relax by saying "son-uv-a-bitch" or some such after each meeting, the custom faded.

All I had to put up with was an occasional put-down from the secretaries for my boldness as I took my seat in the rear of the room each week. Looking back, I must admit that if I knew it would take only five years for another woman to join the ranks, I'd have been tempted to wait it out.

I share this story to illustrate that even as I became more confident and advanced in my career, I still had a great internal reservoir of "good girl" within me. Good girls, after all, wait patiently to be invited to the party. And, of course, girls watch and wait for an eternity before chancing rocking the boat.

You wouldn't doubt the word of a professional who waited two years to attend a meeting, and probably would have waited another five if necessary, right?

This experience was probably my first inkling of the frustration of being on the outside looking in and being unable to pinpoint the exact reason why. It was also the beginning of a pattern of shutting out unpleasant career truths.

It was sensible for me to attend principals' meetings, but there was another reason—in addition to the stated one—for my exclusion.

My attendance would set a precedent and create hard feelings. The hierarchy seemed to know that other women wouldn't "approve." Women who were invited to the conclave only to give special reports made their displeasure known in acts of subtle retaliation. My small success isolated me from my sisters. I wore the "S" for "showoff" on my forehead.

To return to female favor, I spearheaded the spreading of trendy rhetoric about the acceptable enemy, "male chauvinist pigs"—none we knew personally—who were holding us all back. The men we did know—daddy, boyfriends, husbands, bosses—were all "good guys," praised to the skies. We *expected* to work for—and adore—capable, caring men who would guide and lead.

More snide, personal remarks were directed toward the women who worked alongside us. Among women, the ones we didn't know were upheld and admired. With men, we hated the ones we didn't know and admired the ones we did know. Like high-schoolers, we deflected personal criticism by targeting someone else.

Women leaders, in the press or somewhere far away, were

admired. We were expected to admire them. The women at our own place of business, the ones we did know, were something else again. They were verbally hung out to dry for every misstep, from clothes to attitude. And God preserve us from the fate worse than death—working for a woman. But, despite this, we all strived to be the bosses none of us wanted.

Achieving the lofty level of middle management, I decided to work harder every day until I got promoted so that I could stand above the war between the sexes. I, like my ambitious and qualified female compatriots, wanted to be the unique exception to the rule of male dominance in the workplace hierarchy.

I tried to "network" with the few women in positions above my own. Buzzwords flew, but not much positive activity. They exhibited no distress that I and my vast sisterhood were not tapped to join their ranks. I vowed to do better than that.

Liberated, awakened, and certainly talented, I worked to help other women. I dutifully tried to hoist those below me. I ostentatiously schlepped secretaries and clerks to every "women in . . ." meeting.

Not many got better jobs as a result of my efforts, but that didn't seem to be the point. As the women above me had decided, the cream had risen to the top and the rest were destined for a watery bottom. I had done all I could.

As a self-designated leader of women, I always set a good example. The failure of others seemed to prove that I was probably exceptional.

I dressed for success, "did lunch," and worked late. I groomed myself to be the first perfect female executive ever in Western civilization, or at least where I worked.

I was only as strident and assertive as the rule books insisted I be. I read every trendy self-help business article and book written for women to be sure I got it just right. My eager face looked up from the front row of any new career course, seminar, or workshop for men, women, or fish that would accept me. If it was in, I was there.

Still, nothing much happened. Men continued to run the big time. They didn't keep me out. Men hired me, men promoted me, though they didn't vow to dedicate their careers to get me past middle management. It would have taken that. There was room only in the middle. As always, the men and I were "friends." They did their job, I did mine.

I applied my marketing and communications skills to a variety of corporations and institutions: schools, public service, utilities, computer manufacturers—nonprofit, little profit, dubious profit. During a ten-year period, I saw patterns emerging.

Women are bogged down in the lower echelon. More than fifty million are working, but only two-and-a-half million have made it to middle management. That breaks down to a puny, unimpressive .05 percent. For so many millions, there ought to be more women in positions of power.

Nationwide, women above middle management can be counted without getting out the calculator. Success articles always dredged up the same names, many of whom achieved their results through lucky encounters with fate.

If a high-echelon female executive fell from grace, she was replaced by a male. Checking public information profiles, I began to wonder. Consider media attractions of the calibre of "Bendix Mary" Cunningham, or the oft-touted May Company CEO Judi Hofer—a 43-year-old who took pride in lining the mirrored shelves of her office with dolls and teddy bears to express her inner self. She spoke with pride of being "one of only 15 women in the nation with jobs the size of mine." Both have been replaced by men and toil in other vineyards, largely unnoticed.

Could it be that the startling individuality of these women did not boost the idea to men in power of elevating more women? If their actions sometimes made me cringe, how did they affect *men* at top corporate levels? Did these stars make them think twice before inviting another woman executive to join the board? Or was I just being "witchy"?

Frustration began to take hold. Women seemed to be functioning in free-floating capsules of isolation, orbiting management without a glimmer that they were outside the center. I wondered, deep down, did the majority of women want others to rise on their own merits? Did they really want other women to move ahead? Did they deem this to be in their best mutual interests over the long term?

If large numbers of qualified women were working together to advance beyond tokenism, why didn't the statistics show significant inroads into senior management? Why did the higher echelons remain so solid a patriarchal man's world?

Women continued to seem more comfortable with a powerful "daddy" in firm control. No matter what they said, they continued to exhibit respect, rather than envy, for senior management's awesome male power in their work lives. Most evidenced few signs of trying to unseat him and fewer signs of supporting the singular women who dared try. For women, it continued to seem "unnatural" to defy "daddy."

"Daddy" had always told his little girl what to do. "Mommy," on the other hand, is a different story. "Mommy" is there to tell her little girl what *not* to do.

As girls, women learn the unforgettable lesson that you can go only so far in challenging daddy's power. In most households it's less dangerous to tangle with mommy.

As women grow to maturity, they learn that it is acceptable to challenge other women, at any level. Most carry this tactic into the workplace.

I forged ahead in my own career to middle management, only to stall there in neutral gear. I faced the fact that women were fighting women at work as they had at home and at school. Evidence was hard to pinpoint, and difficult to document.

Two male managers and I attended a daylong seminar. My subsequent paycheck was short a day's wages. When I asked, the payroll office explained, "We had calls that you were gone Friday." I traced this to the department clerk who turned in the time cards. She said, "Oh, I knew all three of you managers were going to a meeting, but I thought you'd want to use a vacation day." When questioned why, she offered a blank stare and a shrug. It happened again when I attended a two-day meeting.

I once took on an open-house project for a female director. She asked me to do without the auxiliary helper available to my male predecessor. "First," she said, "you have to prove yourself. I did it two years ago. I came in early and stayed late to get everything ready. We can save on budget if you write the invites at home and bake the cookies. You can do it. I did."

Women were definitely zeroing in on women. Having noticed, I was certain that some respected and knowledgeable authority would document it. Being patient, I waited a few good long years to hear someone else speak the truth about this fiasco. A doctor, an academic, a sociologist—someone to show us the error of our ways. It didn't happen.

As a woman, I had this great fear that a man—a credentialed expert, wise in the ways of women—would have to ride up on a white horse to save us from ourselves. But men tend to stay away from women's issues that don't interfere with their own well-being.

Uncivil female warfare was not a subject to bring up in casual conversation in the ladies' room. In a new world of women's equality, there seemed no demand for naysayers. I kept a low profile and watched, hoped, and waited for the problem to disappear.

During my working years, evergrowing numbers of women have entered the workplace. I saw it getting crowded at the bottom and the middle—because not many women were making room for others by moving on to the top. Whispers started: "What *can* the matter be?"

Women, qualified and ambitious, began questioning and looking around for culprits. They tended to blame groups: feminists, misogynists, chauvinists. That was safe territory; it didn't help, but it didn't hurt.

Other women appeared smiling and supportive. They may have pulled one another's ribbons and sullied one another's Ms. Clean reputations, but there were always plenty of hugs to compensate. So, women decided that men were barring them from top-level success.

The Uncivil Business War is going to let men off the hook for now. Since they have no apparent need to keep women from success, they're not working overtime to do a job that is being done for them.

The spoils go to the victor. Men are helping themselves to power positions, and getting them. In their careers, they're doing better than women. However the score is tallied, men are victors.

Women are helping men by covertly fighting one another. That invisible combat removes half the players from the game. In time-honored female fashion, our unacceptable behavior has remained hidden, not only from other women, but from ourselves as well.

Can a problem of this magnitude be solved? I believe it can be. Self-awareness is the first step on the road to change. Women are champions at accepting advice and being willing to re-evaluate their behavior. Recognizing that a crisis is immobilizing them, women seem ready to look inside themselves for solutions—*if* these are presented in a form they can identify with.

I read a lot, three to five books a week. All the best-sellers, fiction and nonfiction, find a spot by my chair.

I speed read naturally, and books clue me in on what's going on in the world and inside the authors' creative imaginations. I think about all the people reading these books and making them best-sellers. I contemplate how people choose to relax and what they want to learn in their leisure.

Believe me, it took a lot of thinking, from 1970 to 1986, before I decided to write a book. Yes, I'm a writer, but writing a book to provoke people to think in a new way would be a full-time project. It meant rocking the boat, possibly being very disliked, and giving up my toehold on the corporate ladder.

My growing stack of clippings that showed women were doing one another in—in politics, business, social causes, legal fights, and all of the personal areas—was becoming a library of material. Statistics showing women gaining significant personal and economic ground were few; articles about managerial women elevating other women above midlevel were almost nil.

The tail of the tiger was firmly in my hand. I decided to disclose my findings and ask other women to share their business experience with me. I met just the right psychologist at the time I was formulating the questionnaire. She was knowledgeable and worked with women in midlevel management who have business problems. She gave her seal of approval. Everything seemed to fall into place. The ideas had staying power. And you know me well enough to know I tried to wait them out.

Women vs. Women focuses on the personal work world of today's women. Shining a light on the many facets of this issue and the myriad ways that women are fighting women might lead to a truce.

Women vs. Women sounds a clarion call to women to pay attention. No individual or group can fix this problem affecting all women. This book is intended to begin the process of change.

It isn't necessary to call a halt to all aspects of the glorious battle women have grown to know and love. It's only urgent to keep the battle confined to leisure pursuits—and screen personal hatreds from wreaking havoc with women doing serious economic battle to survive in today's tough business world.

Contents

Part Four. Cease-Fire   219

PART ONE

Are You Dying for Joan of Arc's Sins?

Is there a problem here? Women vs. Women is the order of the business day. Today's modern working women are warriors in a civil war that has become decidedly uncivil. White-collar, middle-class women are engaged in a form of unacknowledged urban guerrilla warfare in the corporate business office. In addition to wage competition, the fighting is provoked by boredom, frustration, jealousy, and fear.

Those who have risen above middle management are singular tokens. And most, in their secret heart of hearts, prefer it that way. Their behavior toward one another serves to protect their preferred status as shining stars, the lone roses among thorns.

Rivalry, not cooperation, is the spirit among most women in today's corporate world. They undermine one another and go as far as lying, character assassination, back stabbing, and sabotage. Working women have a lot to worry about: themselves, their families, their personal lives, and the economic perils confronting them. They regard one another as adversaries in the quest for job security, promotions, mates, and more. What everyone wants is what everyone needs.

1

The Uncivil Business War is a multi-faceted socioeconomic class struggle among women—those vying to move up from the working and lower-middle classes are pitted against middle-class women trying to prevent a fall into poverty. The war is also a generational conflict between older and younger women who hold contrasting values, ambitions, expectations.

Despite all of the fire and fury, this war remains invisible because women have been socialized to hide their true feelings. They have especially learned to disguise their rivalries with their "girl-friends." Even when confronted with the evidence, women often automatically deny that they are acting as their own worst enemies.

Many upper-level businessmen are equally unwilling to confront the seriousness of the female/female conflict, although it results in loss of overall productivity. It is to their benefit to remain complacently aloof and label female office warfare as "girls will be girls" behavior. In many cases men admire the working women in their lives, but their admiration does not extend to the workplace. In the business world they still prefer to hire male colleagues to fill senior management positions.

Often in Women vs. Women, the question arises, "Don't men engage in these conflicts, too?" The answer, of course, is "They sure do." However, when two men fight, one wins. When two women fight, both lose.

This is because working women, despite their great numbers in the workplace, are in fact a minority in middle management and above. As such, they feel the bite of discrimination that all minorities experience—they are often prejudged as a group. Because men are not so judged when they behave ruthlessly, such behavior does not undermine all "working men." Women in upper management are so small in number that any damage done to one is damage done to all.

The dynamics of women holding back other women from professional success is best understood by sticking as closely as possible to that issue without falling back on, "Yes, but men . . ."

The Uncivil Business War springs from the realities of the workplace. Fully 70 percent of all American women aged 25–54 work for pay, or are actively seeking jobs. In 1985, a special U.S. Labor Department report on the female work force noted that women are "still concentrated in the lower paying industries and occupations." Reporting that the number of women in the civilian work force had risen, the report stated that "most were clustered in five occupations: secretaries, cashiers, bookkeepers, registered nurses, and waitresses—nearly the same grouping as ten years ago."

Except for income, things are only marginally better for the female executive elite. Whereas about 50 percent of today's entry-level managers are women, the figure diminishes by half at middle-management levels and to a tiny 2 percent at the highest levels. The *Washington Post*'s Katharine Graham, whose family controlled the business, is the only woman heading a Fortune 500 company.

Because women are not advancing in the corporate hierarchy, the office becomes a breeding ground for boredom, frustration, anger, resentment, jealousy, hostility, suspicion, insecurity, mistrust, and fear.

Millions of women are afraid of the next layoff or cutback, losing out to someone younger or prettier. They fear for their financial independence, home, and self-image. In the harsh arena of today's economy, fear is a compelling motivator. It provides a fertile ground for feelings of insecurity that are apt to lead to battle conditions.

Nature and society place dissimilar burdens on the sexes, which are reflected in the female business persona. There is a need to explore this ambivalence openly, because it holds career women back. Women demand both equality and priority treatment, while career goals remain gender-based.

This conflict is often just below the surface. It plays havoc as a typical midlevel working woman attempts to quell her fears of inadequacy by comparing her lot in life with other women's, only to feel that she "is coming up short." If she has fallen victim to believing the Big Lie—that most women approaching middle age have satisfying personal lives and are moving rapidly upward into senior management—she is especially frustrated by her own humble station.

Entry-level managers, the young and the qualified, are hot on their older sisters' heels. With full intentions of having it all, they wave their degrees and expect to be ushered forward. Positioning and networking, they move toward the "glass ceiling" already encountered by their more seasoned colleagues.

A New York management consultant explains why young women at their first or second jobs are unaware that there is a problem. "It often happens when a woman approaches a key managerial position where she'll affect company policy . . . well below boardroom level."

A program director at a New York women's research firm reports, "Up to a certain point, brains and competence work. But then, fitting in becomes very important. It's at that point that barriers against women set in."

Since most women are shut out of the climb to the top, the result is fighting among the few on the rise. Elbows out, women are using the weapons at their disposal to move into the comfort zones of some form of economic survival. Some assign theoretical blame to the male hierarchy, but in practice work hard and respectfully support male claims to sole leadership. Others attempt to marry the professed enemy and retreat to the home with honor.

For all who must work to eat, it's become the Uncivil Business War. Women fight one another without seeming to notice that the face of the enemy is so similar to their own. Because they do not trust one another, they do not accept women as leaders. As a result, they give silent confirmation to their own self-doubt.

In Part One we look at the historical precedent for this dilemma. Joan of Arc serves as a metaphor for the struggles of a woman among women. Although she eventually fell victim to the powers of war and men, her fate could have been altered had she allowed women, who might have offered her support and power, into her sphere. In the great saint's case, there may well have been less misery in more company. Joan accomplished much in her short life that not many women since have been able to emulate. Perhaps few have desired to give as much to reach a goal.

The Uncivil Business War is a harsh confrontation, deadly to many hopes and dreams. Acknowledging that it rages daily is the first step to slowing its body count. Harsh truth can be hard to take. Women may initially recoil at seeing their own faces mirrored back at them when they seek the source of their problems. However, the first step to truce may be a jolting dose of shock therapy.

There's no need for public confession. Each woman, in her heart of hearts, knows the score. Women are practical and capable. They may not enjoy airing their private wars, but they are strong enough to confront harsh problems—especially when faced with sheer necessity. The Uncivil Business War is one that today's working women cannot afford to lose.

1

Joan's Legacy— Female Leaders Born to Be Burned

What is the legacy of Joan of Arc? She was an inspired leader of men, but in pursuit of her cause, women were of little use to her.

The name Joan of Arc can be found on most Famous Women in History lists. Yet, Joan was hardly a woman's woman. Nor was she a woman who helped other women, served with them, or left women an easier path to follow. In her day most women were chattel. Joan was more comfortable in a man's world, where she could achieve what she wanted rather than manipulate others to provide it for her.

Joan dreamed her singular vision and fought her own fight. If career success can be measured by earning one's place in history through a life's work, Joan certainly was successful. If career failure can be measured by one's ineffectiveness in changing male power structure attitudes about females in positions of leadership, Joan certainly was a failure.

Joan claimed divine inspiration for her actions, otherwise why would anyone consider allowing a peasant girl to lead an army?

Religion was an effective rationale for her determination, a viable explanation for her motivation. Only because Joan invoked the name of God as the source of her claims to leadership was she acknowledged at all. Quite simply, women are seldom taken seriously, no matter how serious the situation they face.

As a religious saint, Joan represents an untouchable level of achievement. In the secular world, she stands as an example of the dangers awaiting women who would lead in the dominion of the male.

The modern Joans who anger their peers—women and men— by being "pushy," "aggressive," or "masculine" inevitably seem to be headed for the corporate stake. Creating a zone of discomfort for others around them, they often find themselves isolated from both the mainstream and the hierarchy. Few care to work for them; fewer still care to work with them.

With the onset of the Reagan 80s in the United States, middle-class women working in modern business environments have finally reached middle management and leadership jobs in appreciable numbers. Although not too many had set out to command armies or achieve martyrdom, a fair number had entered diverse careers with grand ambitions of personal and professional rewards.

There appeared to be an ever-increasing number of work choices beckoning these women. Qualified white-collar females entered the work force with every intention of beginning at lower-level "managerial-type" positions and rising to authority and leadership.

These aspirations were certainly far below Joan's lofty goal of attaining the highest level of command, but they would do for a start. The modern working woman's goal was a more modest version of having it all.

Of the millions of eligible women, only a few have actually arrived or are even within striking distance of major command posts. And given the current pace, even fewer appear to have a chance, statistically or otherwise, to move much further upward. In fact, one trend is to retreat, drop out of the job market, or stop short of any but the most modest goals.

Modern working women arrive at a crossroads in the late 1980s and fully experience the legacy of Joan of Arc. How would today's working women answer the question: Are you dying for Joan of Arc's sins?

Joan was in the business of war. Her greatest trespass against propriety was boldness, an unforgivable trait for a woman. Teenage girls like Joan, who run away from home to take on the world, find few in authority ready to hand over positions of leadership. Although neither women nor men lend much credence to inexperienced newcomers, women are especially unyielding to noncredentialed young "girls" moving out of line to the forefront.

Even today, women who act boldly in the workplace find themselves fighting not only the corporate hardball with men, but a war with women who neither accept nor condone traits they consider "overly masculine" in women. Many not only guard against these characteristics in themselves, but exhibit repugnance when they see them in other women. Uncompromising working women are often maligned by their peers and find little more acceptance now than they would have in male-dominated occupations in the 1400s.

Joan, in a common female pattern, gave as good as she got. Leaving her home and parents at an especially young age to begin her quest, she operated as an army of one. In early interactions with other women, she remained aloof. As her life unfolded, Joan did not allow other women to join her fight. In today's work world women also tend to maintain a solitary business stance, despite personal friendships.

Lone warriors all, modern women fight one another at every station along the power track. Until the 1980s, women had worked in clerical, support, and entry-level, white-collar management trainee jobs, more traditional bastions of preferred male-female and female-female relationships. But then, the Joans of the world made a grab for power and position. Battle lines were drawn. Women vs. Women.

The first Joan led men. Women do not traditionally take action by forming armies, and female generals are few. So the Joans who strive to serve as unique leaders face a lot of competition. But they have no one to fight except other women. Those who don't cut and run instead march to unplanned martyrdom.

Every time a woman has been burned at the stake, at war or

at work, other women have been near enough to hand over the torch and whisper words of encouragement to the executioner. At every point in history, women, fearful of a perceived inability to provide for themselves—emotionally as well as materially, have used every weapon available to keep the competition at bay.

Striving to be the singular success, the exception to the rule of their own perceived inferiority, women have, historically, done battle with other women. With women thus engaged, men have had less reason, desire, or need to contend with women over positions of power, leadership, and authority.

Throughout history, women have used charm, feminine wiles, and manipulation to achieve what they want from men. To get what they want from other women, they have used their common needs as a basis for friendship. But that friendship has always been subject to forces that could destroy it in an instant. When a woman gets in the way of what another woman wants, she's got to go.

The only group large and strong enough to keep women in their place or get them out of the way is other women. Whether through action or inaction, working women do not help other working women.

The story of Joan of Arc indicates that she didn't really understand the seriousness of her situation until it was too late. Her public life started with a dream, a fever-pitched vision that encompassed glory and power. As she moved unswervingly forward, Joan made no allowance for failure along the way. She knew where she was headed and seemed dismayed when others didn't follow her lead and see things her way.

Joan was captured in battle and imprisoned. But even when she was put on trial, she seemed so involved in proving her superiority that she gave little thought to proving her innocence, much less to defending her life.

Like many modern working women, she gave every sign of believing that she was so in command of her situation, that others could only follow her clear reasoning and agree with her thinking. She operated according to the "right is might" theory.

Only in the last days of her life did Joan appreciate the life-threatening nature of the testimony of her enemies. When this dawned on her, she stopped bragging and showing off and began to seriously consider the requests of her captors.

In her jail cell Joan changed from men's to women's clothing—a major source of contention—and recanted her position. She signed each formal paper her enemies put before her and agreed with every major issue on their agenda.

That she did this so casually, after a long period of repeated refusal, made both her friends and enemies consider that she didn't comprehend the import of the documents. In a complete turnaround, Joan even used tears and cajoling. She pleaded for help.

Later evidence shows that she indeed understood her every action. She had panicked when she realized these men were serious about burning her at the stake. Party time was over. There was a distinct possibility that her grandstanding posture would bring her life to an end.

When a series of happenstance events made Joan finally realize that all really was lost and that the situation was irreversible, she reverted to expected behavior.

Dressed once again in male garb, restating her former positions, she taunted, "I will change all only when you return me to my friends." This didn't happen.

When her last day on earth came, Joan's unexplained request was to be burned wearing a long dress. She was granted this wish. If she meant it as a symbol, or a subconscious wish that her life had been led in a less life-threatening path away from "womanhood," Joan chose not to say.

The saga of Joan of Arc is a sobering treatise on the perils of women in leadership roles. Women of promise move up to the challenge and back away again as they move closer to reaching their goals. Small wonder other women watch them with worry and dread. If their foray rocks the boat and is unsuccessful, all women may find themselves in unprotected peril. Hand in hand with leadership is the risk that men will be offended and withdraw their love, support, and protection, leaving women vulnerable and dependent on only their own kind.

Joan was in a position similar to that of women currently trying to unlock the secrets to recognition and success. Was she a victim, an innocent adolescent who pushed the older generation's hot buttons too long and too hard? Or was she a young woman with a mission that she believed in to the exclusion of caution? In showing many times that she felt the run of ordinary women to be far beneath her serious consideration, did she set herself up for a lonely fall?

Joan serves as an appropriate metaphor because she exhibited so much of the ambivalence of women today. A perpetual virgin— Joan offered to prove this point on many occasions as a badge of honor—she relied on the high morals of her male peers.

On the other hand, she was extremely macho as she played a man's games with the big boys. She was proud of her strength and dedication. Unrealistically, she persisted in thinking that because she considered herself under heavenly protection, all others would share her view and behave accordingly.

Joan exhibited disdain for other women, yet she expected their help and support. She pushed them away with one hand and later beckoned them with the other, surprised that there was no positive response. Despite reason, there is an emotional—she got what was coming to her—response to victims who unwittingly lay the groundwork for their eventual destruction. So it was with Joan; so it is for many others.

The best women in business often do an unconsciously superb job of performing as victims and victimizers, often at the same time. So did Joan.

The most effective working women—the Joans of Arc—will forever be consumed by the flames of women pretending these leaders don't exist. If women continue on these paths of war to keep one another in their place, they will indeed be dying for the sins of Joan of Arc.

2

Self-Image:
The Crack in the
Looking Glass

Did Joan of Arc ever look in the mirror with dread? Did she quake at the sight of her slight bone structure and plain features and feel . . . fear? Was she unsure about whether the rather ordinary image in the mirror could accomplish great deeds?

Did Joan ever think that she'd be caught at being just a girl with an extremely strange idea? Did she wonder if it was all right to be trodding a path so different from that of her childhood girl-friends?

Self-image is an individual's conception of herself and her own identity, abilities, and worth. Like many of today's successful women, Joan of Arc appeared to possess a sturdy self-image. She seemed impervious to uncertainty and fear, even under the most life-threatening conditions.

But could there have been an unsure side to Joan? One that kept her from getting too close to the more ordinary women of her time—those who were living out the expected role of wife and mother? Did she struggle against giving in to such mundane thoughts? Did she ever believe what her accusers said—that she might be nothing more than a great pretender?

Self-image is a crucial issue for women. When women at work fail to first believe in themselves, they tend to have little faith in the worth of female coworkers—and the trouble begins. Self-image problems, springing from an undercurrent of fear, plague almost every woman in today's work world.

Of course men, too, have their self-image problems. Most men would prefer to be tall and have a full head of dark and healthy hair. They would adore being virile and vigorous, highly paid, and commanding. Instead, many are short, bald, potbellied, over-weight, overtired, underpaid, and unappreciated.

The difference is that women are usually around to reassure men when they worry about their every flaw, to praise them when they humbly confess their imperfections, turning the negative to positive. Women consistently bolster the self-images of the men in their lives.

The woman reassures the man that the love handles on his waist are cute; she would enjoy taking a golf cart when he shows signs of becoming winded; his three-piece striped suit makes him look long and lean; bald men are the sexiest. Does he believe all this? What else could entice him to stroll the beach proudly with a huge gut hanging over his swim trunks?

Self-assurance, honed to believability by females, helps a man keep his fears in check. He believes that his woman believes what she tells him. The self-confidence of a successful businessman turns women on. Wrinkles, flab, fade away in the presence of the aura of power given off by successful male executives.

Girls and women are quick to criticize one another but bolster an important man's feeling of inner value. Only older men who are perceived as complete failures discover that their time-worn tales are boring.

Generally, when men turn gray, their worth in the market-place increases up to mandatory retirement time; wisdom is an assumed by-product of age. So, although their self-image some-times quavers—because of business deals gone sour, poor reviews, missed promotions, occasional impotence—if they've reached midlevel status or better, it almost never interferes with their success in the workplace.

Although a man's self-image can be nourished in the workaday world, the marketplace is not where a woman typically develops her own sense of self. For too many centuries, home and family have been the source of her identity. Nonetheless, today she finds herself by the millions at work in the offices of America—and she seldom has the support from other women in nurturing her self-image that men have come to expect.

Women seldom make much of an effort to support one another. They spot one another's idiosyncrasies, physical imperfections, and signs of aging—in women, a cause for ridicule and even banishment—with more glee than dismay.

In a spurt of negative sisterhood, they want other women to suffer the same sting of outrageous fortune. The self-image of millions of women is bolstered by the misery-loves-company theory.

Women without power of their own, without a working husband, a well-paying job, supportive children—a good number of women—are at everyone's mercy. In the office, when unknown women come onto the scene, men tend to watch and wait as stories beyond the scope of resumes are told. Men tend to stand back and, ultimately, accept the judgment women pass on one another. They adore the young and the pretty automatically; the others must prove their worthiness by exhibiting good humor and exceptional talent.

In modern society, a woman can easily come to believe that her looks determine her worth. Women peer into the looking glass for reassurance, but imagine a distorted, somehow flawed image. For some, this means unworthiness, incompleteness, and even failure. The seeds are planted at an early age, the fruit harvested in adulthood.

Sondra G., age 31, Corpus Christi office manager, says:

> Sometimes, when I'm doing my full-out professional bit at work, and put it all down at somewhere near three o'clock— no matter what—to refresh myself and my makeup, some part of me is embarrassed. I don't know if anyone notices, or cares,

but I feel that part of the daily game I play revolves around how I look as much as what I do. There's usually more than one woman in the rest room doing a similar drill while I'm in there.

You'll laugh, but it's the same routine I started when I played office as an eight-year-old in my backyard. I'd set up a card table and get some stray supplies and call the girl next door to come to business. Before we started, we'd devote a lot of time to dress up. In fact, I think we liked that part best. Dressing in our mom's odds and ends, and plastering on gobs of our kiddy set of organic makeup.

Then we'd work a bit, drink watered-down tea in tiny cups at our break time, and we'd go to get out the lipstick and comb again. Gad. I wonder if my friend is still into the routine. Then, we knew it was just pretend. Now, I'm not sure it was. I don't know where our glamour-as-necessity came from. . . .

I almost can hear my mother calling me to put it all away for the day and come in to set the dinner table.

A shaky—or even somewhat uncertain—self-image plays havoc with a woman's hopes and dreams. To the disinterested observer, a woman could appear normal and competent in her work. But in her mind, real or perceived flaws could threaten to keep her from the good life. She'll go out of her way to forestall criticism, over-compensate in some areas, and ignore others altogether. Such women are likely to feel that other women have succeeded better at the important things in life—thin thighs, good promotions, shining hair, longer vacations, better marriages, better job titles, better divorce settlements, the most glowing complexion.

Jelene J., age 27, Seattle executive secretary, says, "Other women seem to have figured life out better. Just better. I keep hearing that there's more than one right way to look. And act. But, then, at some level, everyone simultaneously believes in the superior merits of the same fabrics, and moves in some new direction. I'm always trying to figure out how they all know the best job field and the best shampoo—and then I try to catch up."

Pauline Clance, psychologist at Georgia State University and author of *The Impostor Phenomenon—Overcoming the Fear That*

Haunts Your Success, studied successful men and women who believe that they are fakes who have succeeded not on the merit of
talent or skill, but because of luck, charm, or the grace of God.
They fear they are in constant danger of being found out.

Joan C. Harvey, a clinical psychologist in Philadelphia and
author of *If I'm So Successful, Why Do I Feel Like a Fake?*, says,
"The imposter phenomenon is a facade people set up to protect
their true selves."

She notes that any of her clients who experience the imposter
phenomenon have a "horror of being average." What's a woman
to do when she lacks the self-confidence to think she can match
her sisters' positive adult accomplishments?

The psychologists point toward overdemanding parents as the
source of the problem. They instruct clients to overcome their
need for perfectionism, admit their limitations, visualize the worst
things that could happen, and calculate the odds of that happening. They also encourage their clients to overcome their fear of
failure.

Unfortunately, too many women don't even recognize that
there's a problem. When there's trouble at the office, it is likely
that the insecure child within that woman will draw from solutions
that originated at home, in babyhood. She may draw from the
approaches she perfected in adolescence for the sole purpose of
securing a suitable date for the prom.

The operative rule: Hold firm to your own small place in the
universe and fight off any rivals who dare to invade your turf.

Prom night is long past, but many women continue their constant struggle to shore up a fragile self-image. If a woman is afraid
she is losing her appeal, condescension toward others is a good
morale booster. There's always comfort in knowing another woman who's even worse off. Everyone laughed at the fat girl who
bought a dress for the prom but didn't go because her mysterious
boyfriend from out of town had to cancel at the last minute. Many
bring these adolescent attitudes into their adult lives, scorning the
working woman with the duffel-bag figure, horn-rimmed glasses,
and whiny voice who has little to recommend her but her business
competence.

How can intelligent women act and react this way? More to

the point, how can they not? Almost all women now in the white-collar work force are products of middle-class families who did not have role models who behaved differently.

And it continues. New trends don't fool at least one grand-parent from cooing into pink-shell ears: "Pretty, pretty girl. Smile pretty."

Whether a new generation of baby girls grows up to become rebels, housewives, doctors, or business people, they will be influenced by their early conditioning. Many strange beliefs are here to stay. The trouble is embedded in the female mind.

Dr. Wilder Penfield of McGill University explains that the brain plays back the events and feelings of our lives like a stereo system. Early childhood experiences are reheard in continuous sequence, even as we live our adult lives. Because of this, we are often literally in two places at one time.

One place is where our mind is now, the other years removed, replaying events as vividly as when they first happened. Dr. Wilder says that "we not only remember the past, we relive it . . . even what we don't remember."

In his study called *Memory Mechanisms*, Dr. Wilder reported on the experiences of hundreds of patients undergoing surgery. The evidence indicates that the prejudices of dislike and hatred begin in earliest memory and are impossible to dispel.

Dr. Wilder showed that a probe of a section of brain showed evidence that the past is recorded in time sequence and in detail. He explains, "There is one single recollection after another, not a mixture of memories or a generalization."

This is powerful testimony that there's little possibility that people can forget about early conditioning and get on with it. To this, men and women add ongoing cultural images that let them know if they're doing okay. For women, there is a wider swing between early input and adult expectations—especially in work situations—than there is for men. For females, what was acceptable then and what is expected now are eons apart; for males, the poles are closer and more compatible.

Girls were reared to expect to engage in feminine mischief that would evolve into Women vs. Women. Boys were reared to be held responsible for behavior, according to standards similar to the ones they would encounter in the world of commerce.

Heeding childhood memories of rewards not for what they did, but for how they behaved while doing it, women sometimes revert to nursery-rhyme conditioning to meet behavioral expectations. For example, "What are little girls made of?" was answered "sugar and spice and everything nice." In answer to "What are little boys made of?" boys were given some leeway to be obnoxious with the more earthy "snips and snails and puppy dog tails."

Sugar and spice toddlers learned to hide their natural feelings. They were conned into thinking that other little girls—also flashing big, lovable smiles—came by their sweetness naturally.

One ex-toddler, now age 38, verified this: "'Tis true. I might outthink 'em, outdunk 'em, or outrun 'em, but seldom could I 'outsweet' my mom's careful selections of 'nice' little girlfriends."

Other wrong-headed notions that have influenced normal growing female minds include commonly held ideas about the self-image of the body.

A 1984 update of the pace-setting *Our Bodies Ourselves*, first compiled by the Boston Women's Health Book Collective in 1969, reassured women yet again that healthy and natural bodies were beautiful. Saying that "women often feel negative about our physical selves," the book highlighted the parts deemed "not right." These included hair, nose, breast size, stomach, thigh size, bone structure, and body odors. "Fixing" these routinely involves surgery, cosmetics, vaginal deodorants, chemicals, hair dyes, clothes, and shoes that "seriously hamper freedom of movement."

Our Bodies cautions that "looking good is so narrow, few women feel they have made it. It's a profitable business to convince women that we don't look good enough."

Standards of beauty change as generations and cultures clash— over such "qualities" as breast size and figure shape. The feminists established their own "look," the "muscular, shapely Amazon-type." In contrast, "fat pride" is offered as a healthy and acceptable option. The book concludes: ". . . it's hard for nearly every woman to love and accept herself as she is."

A poor self-image plays a large part in the reasoning behind some women's need to bring others down as they struggle to define their own place in the work world. Jennie J., age 41, executive secretary, says:

> As a kid, I was always a few pounds overweight and not good at team sports. And both points still stand.
> I feel I've come to terms with it, but I still feel set apart from skinny women I work with now. Their attitude is like a silent criticism. They might say they're going to the gym on the way home and part of me thinks they could stay and finish their work instead. Even if that doesn't make total sense, it's how I react.

Body awareness probably predates history, but the current fixation began when most of today's working women were youngsters. Fitness first came to national attention in 1956 when President Dwight D. Eisenhower, distressed by a report showing the country's children were not fit, started the President's Council on Physical Fitness. It was a part of President John F. Kennedy's program, with gains finally reported for both boys and girls in President Lyndon B. Johnson's follow-up report in 1965.

The all-important fact is that, from the beginning, girls had a less "okay" attitude toward formal fitness than boys. Team sports were given less emphasis in girls' lives than almost all other physical considerations and activities.

Physical activity finally came into its own by the Baby Boomer 70s. Fit bodies for women were in. In the late 80s, although the adults still pound the pavement and squeeze the Nautilus, the trend is not taking hold among schoolchildren, who veer again toward the "indoor inactive" mode.

But for today's young women starting out in the workplace, self-image is still a problem. In the 80s, the struggle of health vs. acceptability sometimes sacrifices scholastic and athletic success for thinness. The emphasis on the slim and sleek look can bring on illness.

The fact that the severe eating disorders anorexia and bulimia are suffered, for the most part, by young middle- to upper-middle-class white females, attests that many modern women subscribe to fitting the mold at any cost. Even those not afflicted derive values from a peer-focused central "norm." They are willing to pay a high price not only to look good, but to look *better* than other girls.

Improving self-image requires expensive and tough tactics that invade the office. The cultural images that working women use to fashion their own business personas instill a sense of "buy up to go up." The beauty industry sells cosmetic skills and techniques touted to outdo female competition. (Men may buy and use various health and beauty products, but those products aren't as tied into an inner sense of male worth. At work, a male ego is tied more to earning power.)

In sophisticated adulthood, middle-class women know that new cosmetic products are mainly hype and that in all likelihood

hair conditioner is probably unable to condition each section differently when poured over the wet head;

lard is as good a moisturizer as any;

American mousses and gels are just as good as French ones;

the exotic tones of lip and cheek colorings are still based simply on red or orange;

and miracle ingredients are but a hope and empty promise of eternal youth.

The media—a large part of it advertising—has a strong hold on the female self-image. Slick four-color ads and fast-paced videos have great power over the American woman's mind. Preteens weaned on *Seventeen* magazine remain loyal to its basic products and to the notion that a magazine can be a savvy authority. Authoritative fashion magazines guide women through all levels of age and income.

Alayne K., age 47, says:

I hate to admit that I never kicked the *Cosmo* habit. I know they write for young, unmarried women and I'm not even one of the two. [She laughs.] Probably the only reader they have older than I am is the woman who owns it. I read Helen Gurley Brown's books, too. She's an inspiration as a smart businesswoman who's hangin' in there.

But, if I read the magazine in a restaurant at lunch, I hide it under something. The covers are an embarrassment with manipulative titles of how to get your own way. Maybe I buy *Cosmo* because I just want to see what my competition is doing. Or what they probably are trying to do to my husband. Or, then again, maybe I read it so I can try a few of the new tricks and see if they really work. I'm hangin' in there, too.

When the media does offer positive role models, their images are distorted. Do real women—as opposed to actresses playing a part—project a strong self-image on television? It seems that more attention is paid to the speech patterns of Barbara Walters than to her record-breaking annual salary.

Even Mary Tyler Moore—the fictional Mary of the often shaky but ever-enduring self-image—didn't make it big in sitcom land the second time around. She returned to a similar glamour job, but jettisoned some of her "cute" along the road to middle age. The show seemed to stall when women didn't enjoy identifying with her new, jaded, and earthy sidekick, who avoided the familiar "oh, Mary, help me" interactions remembered from the first show's characters. The new series offered a divorced, slightly less virginal Mary trading quips with a sexy, middle-aged boss, as opposed to the Mary who leaned on the comfortable fatherly shoulder of Mr. Grant.

If a woman has no means to bolster her self-image—which has diminished in stages from girlhood through adulthood—what hope can there be for her positive interaction with other, enviable women? How can she renew her own worth? What is the fate of women who are no longer "cute"?

In their own minds, as well as the minds of others, they may be failures. They could lose their jobs and the love of their families—and be cast aside, alone and penniless. This is a real fear for some women today, who see divorced husbands remarried and with new families. Self-image can take it on the chin when new wives offer to incorporate the offspring of the first marriage in their clan, rather than help subsidize old mom with child support payments.

What if the head-of-household mother suffers a long-term illness? Who will take care of her then?

Another deep fear came to light with a *Newsweek* report on the 1986 study, "Marriage Patterns in the United States," by Yale and Harvard experts. They concluded that "women who are single by 30 have only a 20 percent chance of marrying; by 35, the odds drop to 5 percent, and 40-year-olds are more likely to be killed by a terrorist (2.6 percent) . . ." than to waltz up the center aisle. Some women readers were vexed and pained by the prediction of spinsterhood. Several reported to *Newsweek* that, as a result of the report, they felt pressured to marry immediately. Whoever was available.

Those who didn't rush out to marry the first nerd to come forth on short notice were informed by an opposite report that it wasn't that bad, after all. A study prepared by U.S. Census demographer Jean Moorman disputes the findings of the Yale-Harvard paper. At age 25, for example, the Moorman data show an 85 percent chance of marriage (compared with Y-H's 50 percent).

For age 30, the Moorman data show a 65 percent chance of marriage, compared with 20 percent in the earlier survey. For age 35, the comparatives show 40 percent in Moorman to 5 percent in Y-H. Moorman's figures show a 22 percent chance of marriage for college-educated women at age 40, and 10 percent for those over 45.

"Those numbers are well beyond terrorist probabilities," writes syndicated columnist Ben Wattenberg.

The argument has now settled on the usefulness of rarified statistical projection techniques. Yet the furor over these numbers highlights an important aspect of female self-image. Wanting or not wanting a man in one's life is one thing; being unable to attract a mate is another. A woman who feels isolated by fears of making it on her own may base her self-image on her sense of financial well-being. Envisioning a need to be cared for until the grave, she imagines that other women are out to get what is rightfully hers.

Insecure women are likely to be ungenerous toward their sisters. This is expressed in their treatment of their status in the greater world. The title "Ms." was intended to give no more information than the male equivalent "Mr." The idea backfired most with those who didn't need this cloak of equality. Married women remain comforted by the title "Mrs." They feel that it advertises their worth. Many cling to it as their earned portion after divorce. Titles bestowed by men have historically soothed the female self-image.

In the 1600s, "Miss" was reserved for very young girls, and changed meaning when females wanted to identify older lasses who were, literally, the mistresses of men. The title "maid" was then used to cloak status; "Mrs." was used for both married and unmarried respectable women.

In seventeenth-century England, "spinster" was the title for women who earned their living working on crafts in the home. Because they didn't meet many men, they often remained unmarried, and that label expanded to include all unmarried women.

With self-worth often defined by the men, or lack of male attention, in their lives, women have jockeyed for titles in many ways.

Elizabeth B., divorcee, age 53, confides, "I've adjusted to single life in most ways. This sounds silly, but I do miss my physician husband's title as much as any single thing. I remember being in a department store once and the clerk was snippy, but when I took out my charge card with "Dr." on it, her attitude changed from night to day. His title belonged to me, too."

Sue M., age 26, a nurse married to a physician, says, "Staffs in hospitals tend to treat nurses like lesser beings. Like they're stupid and just there to wait on people. When I got married and I managed to someway drag my husband's name into the conversation, they listened to what I said. Suddenly, I was brilliant, and my opinion mattered. Maybe they thought if a doctor married me, I couldn't be too dumb. But I was the same person. They changed in how they respected my status."

Many women still seek to enhance their self-image through the status of others. Mrs. is better than Miss or Ms. in most opinions.

Then there are the "single-by-choice" women, some of whom are now changing their minds. After examining "roads untaken," some consider changing direction. Says a 38-year-old director of a temporary help service in Baltimore, "That stuff about the biological clock is finally getting to me. And the family inquiries almost have me going to Dear Abby for a snappy comeback. It used to be easier to answer when I was secure about my own life decisions. And I did reach each business goal to get to where I am. Now, part of my brain and body agrees with the promoters of women for home and motherhood. So I'm torn. I'm switching to the side I argued against for years and years."

Of course, the worst self-image possible is the Bag Lady. Phil Donahue did a show on the theme that up to half the women in this country have fears of "ending up in the streets at poverty level." Guests Gloria Steinem and Lily Tomlin shared personal fears about just such nightmares.

Steinem is a feminist leader and journalist, and Tomlin is a successful and popular entertainer; yet both fear that it might happen to them. For most women, becoming a destitute old hag of the streets is a "worst-case" scenario, no matter how unlikely.

The fear of becoming destitute and homeless—a ragged, stumbling scarecrow pushing a grocery cart containing all her worldly possessions—is a wide-awake nightmare for many women of all ages. At the root of this feeling is a fear of failure, of not being the beloved of anyone, particularly men, at home and at work. As women grow older and see how few women achieve high success by their own merits and toil, they strike out at female rivals with all of the means—subtle, inconspicuous, and overt—that have become a part of their learned behavior. Self-image tends to decline with age, especially for those with shaky lives at work and at home.

Is there a healthy self-image that would enable today's woman to relate—positively—to the women with whom she works? Men are reared to believe in their ability to lift themselves up by their own bootstraps. The heroes in the boyhood stories point the way. How about women?

The Baby Boomers' grandmothers reared their children during the Depression. This economic tragedy scarred more than one generation that followed. In the 30s, many a woman's self-image was shaken by the privations and humiliations of a hardscrabble life in a shattered economy. Their daughters inherited their pain, but repressed it in their search for security after World War II.

The 50s suburban mothers found their self-image in the family and the home, a life their mothers would have regarded as heaven on earth. Suburb moms reared their daughters to be strong and independent and to expect much of the world.

Those daughters, the educated, upwardly mobile, stylish mothers of the 80s, find being strong and independent nearly impossible, and have discovered that the promises of the good life are out of reach. They are a part of the first generation of Americans to achieve less than the generation preceding them. A few have achieved the dream, although at greater personal cost than they had imagined.

Other women of the 80s compromised before reaching their goal, somewhat surprised at the social and professional rejections they encountered in the workplace. Today, when these women gaze in the mirror for answers, their reflection is puzzled.

Who was able to make girlhood dreams the reality of adulthood? In *Women Like Us*, former *Wall Street Journal* reporter Liz Gallese interviewed women who "made the cut" and moved from the 10 percent female, Harvard Business School MBA program of 1975 to some degree of business success. Elite in both brains and ambition, these women were part of the first generation of women in management who thought they could have it all.

Their lives are different. Some are happily married and others divorced. There are women in therapy, mothers, battered wives, and victims of severe eating disorders among them. Two-fifths "pulled back" short of the top. But ten years after graduation, the 88 women shared some experiences in common.

In the hierarchy of business, Gallese notes, "By law, there is no discrimination at entry-level jobs." However, just beyond that first job and continuing thereafter, many hit a ceiling, particularly in the stage between upper-middle and senior management. They said they were not discriminated against, but a subtle inability to "create a comfort level with men" was the problem . Those who went highest, Gallese says, thought and acted on the job like . . . men.

She explains: "It is highly unlikely that these women—impersonal and ambitious—would pull a switch and become 'humanist' when reaching senior management . . . Corporations are run by men and to advance in that world, women have to be like those men, at least while they are at work."

Women with different value systems might have the roughest time balancing the described self-image of the Harvard MBAs with their own. Female behaviors are derived from matriarchal expectations. How far can an adult allow mother's "nice girl" to veer?

Mother's own self-image may inhibit ambitious women, causing them to falter before they can fully participate in the hardball of senior management.

Young women throughout the ages have learned to "read between the lines" when mother speaks. Many working women have mothers who wanted them to do better than they themselves could, but in the action-speaks-louder-than-words department, many exhibit pride in mom's we're-the-same, we're-just-like-sisters tone that showered approval on those who maintained the status quo.

Differences in achievements and career choices—often mother was a homemaker, part-time worker, or support-level office worker; daughter dreamed of an MBA position—could lead to differences in the primal relationship.

Helen J., age 46, homemaker, says:

> My attitude toward my daughter's career is similar to that of my lady friends who have college-age daughters. Work now, but don't rule out marriage.
>
> First of all, since Jill was little I've wanted her to be a happy and fulfilled person. Just as I've wanted for her brother. No one thing makes me happy. I like my life at home most of the time. Years ago, when the kids first went to school all day, I got a job. I liked to be with people and we didn't need the money, so I worked part time in my friends's macrame shop.
>
> It was okay, but I wanted to be home when the kids got there and it tied me down more than it was worth. Work can be just as boring as home. Jill will work, I know, but I'd like her to marry and have a family, too. Work fades away.

Jill, 22, a graduate student, speaks to the issue.

> Mom and I are close. She's proud of me being in grad school, I know. And brags about it to her friends; it's kind of a status

thing. But she doesn't ask many in-depth questions about my subjects and the kind of job they will lead to.

She asks more about my personal life—dates, and how many times the good ones ask me out. Would she be crushed if I decided to marry a doctor and stay home and raise babies? Surely, you jest. Those would be the glory days. To her, that would be the ultimate chance for my happiness and success—as much as it was grandma's choice for her.

I'm not sure about how happy and fulfilled that would make me. I want to try to see how high I can go in business. But I'm not shooting down mom's idea, either. If I can't do both, some part of me would like to flash a diamond engagement ring at my sorority sisters that would make their eyes water!

A shaky self-image makes women lash out at one another. Females crave the approval of their peers and often back away from a road that's been paved with grief and deprivation. A strong self-image may be found through one's husband or one's baby, but rarely in the eyes of one's female peers in the work world.

At present, there are only a few women at the top of the heap in corporate America. Women, sure that they deserve the best, are hard at work trying to do better. Many are ruthless toward those who have clawed, or married, their way up the social and professional ladder ahead of them. They often are somewhat ashamed by their own behavior, and the poor self-image is recycled.

Today's working women are anxious about the disparity between reality and their fairy tale expectations. There is a tough rivalry of Women vs. Women, with few women at the executive top—and plenty of room at the Bag Lady bottom. Neither self-image is very realistic, but images aren't expected to have much substance.

It may be that the mirror is heavily steamed from the nervous breathing of frightened females peering myopically at images they fear are not good enough. Self-acceptance, extended to all little girls within, can offer a promise of change. By breathing easier, they may view a less distorted image in the mirror.

3

You've Come
a Short Way, Baby

Women vs. Women didn't start yesterday. Business office warfare
has its roots in ancient struggles, and the history of fighting women
and their attitudes toward one another prove how little things
change.

Joan of Arc serves as an appropriate symbol for today's working woman. She took on an extremely difficult mission, and
brought to life her belief that the victory could be achieved by
merging her femininity with some ostensibly masculine traits.

According to a male contemporary, Joan, despite her soldier's
close-cropped haircut, was "rather elegant; she bears herself vig-
orously, speaks little, shows an admirable prudence in her words.
She has a light, feminine voice, eats little, drinks little wine; she
enjoys fine horses and arms, likes the company of noble knights,
hates large gatherings and meetings, weeps readily, wears a cheerful countenance, and is incredibly strong in the wearing of armor
and bearing of arms, sometimes remaining armed for as much as
six days and nights.*"

Looking like a typical woman of her time would not have

*This description is taken from a seventeenth-century account quoted in *Joan of
Arc: The Legend and The Reality* by Frances Gies.

sufficed. Joan's male garb of tunic and hose signaled her identity as a soldier. Elevating her status even further was the religious mantle she wrapped around her authority. This served to define her as a special person who took her direction from above.

As noted earlier, in the pursuit of her dream, Joan came to have little use for women; they had no place in her nearly all-male world. That isn't so different from the attitude many modern women display at the upper corporate levels. The lone female in a group of males has a better chance of commanding attention and respect. If more than one woman is included, the aura of "unique achievement" is diminished.

Was it a sin for Joan to isolate herself from other women? She might have benefited by having women of equally elevated status speak for her. They could have explained her threatening garb, her religious conviction, and her mixture of strength and tears, but there was no woman who cared enough—or had enough power to help her.

A contemporary of Joan's, Catherine of La Rochelle (a less-celebrated visionary), wanted to meet Joan as an equal. Joan put her off, but finally heard her out, put her to stringent tests—including the demand of a heavenly sign—and ultimately labeled Catherine's visions "pretensions."

Joan bluntly dismissed this rival visionary, and told her to go home to her husband and look after her house and children. She then reported to her king that Catherine was "a fool and a liar" in claiming she had spoken with God, and later quarreled with those who argued that Catherine could be useful. Joan barred Catherine from the inner circle.

When the ecclesiastical court of Paris questioned Catherine as a part of Joan's preliminary court inquiry, her damaging testimony was strong. It included information about "two counselors" who would help Joan escape from prison "with the aid of the devil, unless they watched her well." Catherine then went her merry way.

Seldom are actions repaid in kind. Not all women have the opportunity for direct retaliation that Catherine of La Rochelle did. But the Catherines and the Joans of the world still do their utmost to reign alone.

Ambitious women are likely to forsake women as business

equals even if they give vague assurances to the contrary. In the corporate crunch, most upwardly mobile managers feel the road is safer gone alone. Must their lesson be a hard one? Must they inevitably die on the business vine—alone—for Joan of Arc's sins?

Joan's backstabbing was not an isolated personality clash. There were always women at the periphery of Joan's world, and these she generally treated with contempt. In fact, her first battle was against the women who followed the army camps. Joan saw the camp followers as mere leeches who distracted the soldiers from more serious business.

Joan drove the prostitutes from the camps physically, brandishing the flat of her sword, shouting them down as whores. She obviously hadn't considered that others would put her in the same class as her "sisters"; each nightfall she, too, put up her tent alongside the troops' camp. When the English saw Joan come down to fight them, they called her a "whore and a tart." So it goes for all manner of enterprising women.

Most women today don't toss disparaging words quite so directly, perhaps owing more to slander laws than enlightenment. Although more subtle nowadays, the messages that women send male coworkers on the subject of the career goals of their sisters often carry similar subliminal meaning.

When Joan was eventually captured and imprisoned, she brought a masculine derring-do to her jail cell. She defied authority, and even attempted escape by leaping from a high tower. Her trial, extremely well documented, highlights her dry sense of humor as she continued a show of bravado. She even corrected the prosecutor in his recollection of testimony.

Her accusers hated every minute of her performance. Her claims to have heard voices and seen visions were less offensive than her refusal to answer to anyone but the highest patriarchal authority about even her garb. She said she would not change her armor "without God's leave." She was also charged with "rejecting the company and service of women and wishing to be served by men in the private offices of her room and her secret matters." This practice seems to have a modern counterpart: Consider the female executive who hires the most qualified person, who happens to be a man, as her secretary. It provides instant status.

As Joan's prosecutors returned again and again to such points, it seemed that she was judged guilty as much for her defiant, unfeminine behavior as for her heresy.

The life and death of Joan was extraordinary. Few heroines since have achieved such lasting notoriety. Joan was a young, religious farm girl who was convinced she belonged on the battlefield with men.

She left her comfortable home with hardly a glance backward, took on the mantle of the mystic, and entered the field as a soldier.

Living and dying during the era of the Hundred Years War, Joan was the first and greatest female leader of the emerging West. She takes her place in history above queens—because she was a self-made leader of men who stayed with her self-designated mission to its lonely and violent end.

Joan's career, as distinguished from her cause (to drive the English from French soil and reunite her country under her king), certainly gave her a firm place in history. But earning it required the ultimate sacrifice. To achieve her goals, Joan fought a solitary skirmish, and lost the battle and her life. The men won the war.

Joan was a soldier, true, but she was also a female public figure, a prominent woman in a man's world, a world at war. She rose to fame and power despite having no qualifications whatsoever as a soldier or leader of men. Her rationale for demanding leadership was that she had been told by two dead women to go and make a man a king. The prospective king liked the idea.

Joan wholeheartedly plunged into the male business of war, with a sincere belief that her motives were pure and this would shield her from harm. Businesswomen today also claim that they're doing things a better way to explain why they ignore existing corporate policies and protocol.

Today's midlevel working women share Joan's sense of dismay when they find that doing the right thing and following their own agendas seldom lead to success. Joan certainly ended up with little approval and appreciation.

For many modern women with unrealized great expectations, Joan of Arc serves as a symbol—the bold female fighter entirely consumed in the smoke and fire of a civil war. The mystical life and death of Joan of Arc provide the real precedent for the modern woman who, though she might not dream of changing the whole world, does aspire to influence her domain.

Women have to be careful when they break the mold. Joan was perceived as a greater threat to her enemies because she was a woman than because she was a warrior. A female soldier upset the rigid social order of the time. Her prosecutors first accused her of blasphemy, claiming that the bible had forbidden women and men ever to wear the garb of the opposite sex.

Disrupting the accepted social order can have harsh consequences; the dangers that destroyed Joan exist today. Modern working women who don't pay homage to the domestic sphere—marriage, home, and family—risk criticism, ostracism, or worse. Strong or not, they can end up isolated. By sticking strictly to business for a period in their lives, they run the risk of offending women at the sidelines. If they reject the efforts of those who would match them with potential spouses and who, by example, encourage a more "feminine" approach to work, they run the real risk of being cut off when the chips are down.

On some level women share an innate knowledge that this is true. Have things ever been any different? It seems not. Most women have long believed that their survival depends on self-centered recognition and protection of their own needs and the needs of those with whom they are close. This includes other women only when they accept these unwritten rules.

For the greater part of history, this sort of self-protection was essential to survival. By about 15,000 B.C., women had already made the greatest economic discovery of all—cultivation. No longer were they dependent on men to drag home food from the hunt. This was a precarious business, and their fortunes were uneven. Historians place women at the center of civilization. Men in the first human tribes were carrion scavengers; women were gatherers and growers. They stabilized life and made civilization possible.

While women scrounged berries and grains leftover on the ground in times of plenty (especially at old campsites), they noticed that forgotten scattered grain grew again at the beginning of a new season. Their observation was the source of their newfound economic strength.

Women were the center of the most deep-rooted of all historic institutions—the family. And although their discovery did not mean that they did less menial labor, it did enable them to protect their families by providing a permanent home.

In keeping with the literal translation of the word *economy*, the women managed the household. (The etymology is from the combination of the Greek words *oikos*, house, and *nemein*, to manage.)

In *The Story of Civilization* philosopher Will Durant explains, "Since it was the mother who fulfilled most of the parental functions, the family was at first organized on the assumption that the position of the man in the family was superficial and incidental, while that of the woman was fundamental and supreme."

The advent of agriculture, however, meant the start of civilization. This led to the notion of private property, which required a reliable source for organized labor—slavery. This slavery became part of the path by which man prepared for industry.

Gone was the comparative equality of the primitive life. Labor was divided on the basis of one's position in society: The strong were pitted against the weak. The inequalities of wealth and poverty led to divisions. The class wars began.

Did women's establishment of the home—with lessened needs to continue roving in search of sustenance—help all women? On the contrary. Men, for the first time, could own property, hold it during their lifetimes, and then pass it on to heirs. This created yet another role for women. Marriage began as a law of property. Gone were the years when the contribution of the seed to start life was noted but given little recognition; gone were the times when women controlled the property of the cave and soil.

The concept of real estate gave men strong motivation to demand fidelity from their women. They wanted to pass on their accumulations to children they could presume were their own. Cleaving to a woman for life was the answer. She'd provide the heirs and he'd just plain provide. He would take care of her needs so she wouldn't have the burden of those concerns.

All in all, women in early societies were subjugated. Through marriage, property was passed on to men. A woman's property, often her dowry, legally became a part of the husband's estate before the echo of the wedding vows faded. She belonged to her husband lock, stock, and barrel.

No matter who died first, the wife's goods remained a part of the husband's estate, to be distributed along his male family line. The widow was at the mercy of her in-laws to provide for her needs, from daily support to the possibility of another dowry. A woman's status diminished rapidly when her male protector vanished. She became financially worthless.

For much of history, antifemale bias has started at birth. In her book *The Weaker Vessel*, Antonia Fraser identifies a contributing factor to female suppression. "Women have generally disliked giving birth to their own (female) kind and as most were undereducated they passed on ignorance as a birthright."

By the seventeenth century A.D., marriage under English law provided the most financial security for women of the lower classes. Since they brought little or no wealth to their marriages, it was assumed that they would work alongside their husbands in his trade. If he died before she did, the law allowed her to go on working in the family trade—which she had probably mastered as she worked alongside her husband. This kept widows from relying on public charity.

If the copyhold (that is, the legal transcript) was in both names, she kept her share in her name. A woman married to a guild member (a printer, weaver, carpenter, baker, or brewer) could keep the valuable title.

Often widows petitioned—and were granted—the right to retain these valuable memberships even if they remarried. This guaranteed a woman an independent income unavailable to her upper-class sisters. It also served to make these skilled women attractive candidates to practical suitors. (These stipulations were written into a prototype of today's prenuptial agreements.)

Women with less money always need to be pragmatic. Closer to the poorhouse, or the street, they are more practical than their wealthier sisters, who have been lulled into relying on relationships, rather than themselves, to provide a lifetime of security.

However, women throughout history have willingly given up the greatest of personal powers. They once exclusively possessed the three key domains coveted by any would-be ruler: nature, economic control, and religion.

> Nature—women could bring forth life from casually scattered seed.
> Economic control—women discovered ways to wrest sustenance from the soil.
> Religion—primitive beliefs included the notion that female gods granted favor to female supplicants.

Religion has always been vested with the power to control. Matriarchies on the basis of female goddesses preceded patriarchies and male gods. In the second century B.C., the cults of Great Mother and the Egyptian goddess Isis reigned, and women of all classes were active—scholastically, socially, politically, and legally.

Later, men replaced goddesses with patriarchal deities. Male gods better favored the goals of men. The patriarchal religions of Judaism, led by Abraham, and Christianity, through the teachings of St. Paul, embraced the idea of relieving women of the burden of direct worship because it would interfere with their time-consuming duties at home.

Perhaps the disaster and death that plagued early societies motivated men to protect women, and women accepted the protection. Perhaps it was just easier to step aside and let men run things. In any case, women bought into the historic changes that have diminished their independence. These historical patterns don't provide precedents to encourage modern women to support one another in their careers and in achieving financial independence. Independence was, at best, secondary.

There is stronger precedent for personal competition among women. From the earliest times, women put their total faith in relationships with those who held power, thus making male dominance a self-fulfilling prophecy. Goddesses were given short shrift when gods commanded. This could not have happened without female acceptance and consent. Perhaps women were jealous of their own goddesses and stripped them of religious powers to the benefit of the gods.

The pattern of handing over power again survives today. Reigning at home, the woman was assigned housecleaning and child-rearing tasks, and placed on a pedestal as mom. Bedecked in frills and bows, she was the little woman. In a crisis, she was unceremoniously expelled into the work world. If uneducated, she was togged out in a pink or blue collar. Crisis over, she was pulled back to the home.

In the early 1960s, Americans began to consider equality for women. A series of landmark events led to this significant turn.

The election of John F. Kennedy and his picture-perfect wife—a former professional reporter and photographer—may have played a part in changing people's thinking about the New Woman.

The era's emphasis on social conscience may have been sparked by the women's movement, which had its beginnings in the suffragette movement early in the century and grew to maturity in the 60s. Common causes—frivolous and meaningful—helped women work together.

The Pill provided a medical means to control pregnancy that helped women to control their destinies.

Many other forces also helped women strive for independence and free themselves from family training and the expectations of men. Women began to move from the sphere of the home to the independence of the work world.

Women joined the American work force in a big way in the 1970s. Millions of these college-educated Baby Boomers born between 1946 and 1961 entered the work force at about the same time.

Proud to be working members of two-income couples, they wholeheartedly bought into the materialistic world they had disdained in their protest-peace-and-love college days. Everyone was growing up. Runaway inflation only made the digits on the paychecks more impressive.

Over half these intelligent young women viewed themselves as ready to practice in their chosen professions, although only 15 percent of all the jobs in the U.S. Department of Labor's job categories fall into the "professional" category. Clearly, a monumental problem of supply and demand was brewing.

The scramble started. There was an oversupply of teachers, social workers, librarians, and lawyers. Too many chiefs. Maybe even too many Indians.

The seeds of the conflict that would bring women to battle against one another were sown. Although their training might be equal to the men's, women watched as their "brothers" moved more quickly into available professional slots.

Women who could not find jobs to fit their training quickly filled the 20 million positions that were readily available—secretary, stenographer, typist, clerk, keypunch operator, and other low-end office jobs—hoping to prove themselves and be promoted. The remaining 25 to 30 million women started the long, hard fight for management positions not held by men.

Women were certainly free to try. Corporations welcomed female clerks with advanced degrees. As long as they did the work—their own and anyone else's they cared to take on—and collected their "half pay," they could try to fight their way into management. Some fancier titles, such as administrative assistant, made the crow easier to swallow and offered promise.

The law intervened. Affirmative action laws—which had their basis in the social legislation of the 60s—helped women enter the corporate doors. The number of women in the "professional, technical, and kindred" occupations rose 142 percent between 1960 and 1970, according to the Department of Commerce, Bureau of the Census. Women in the ranks of "managers, officials, and proprietor" swelled more than 56 percent. The total number of white-collar females in the work world during that period rose 117 percent.

This promised the dawn of a new era. Because the numbers were impressive, few considered the long-range import of the jobs to which they were assigned. Most were not savvy about the long-range differences between support and line assignments or the future of their entry-level token positions.

If anyone knew the ins and outs of paving the way to future promotions, they didn't formulate it for the masses. Media hype emphasized the glory. The new wage earners were courted and urged to spend their way to self-improvement.

The new superwoman would need many things to celebrate

her successful entry into the real world of her dreams. Her pay-check was her passport to advertisers' attention. She was urged to buy new wardrobes, labor-saving appliances, time-saving prod-ucts, gym memberships, and leisure toys. She was dazzled by new restaurants for nights out, new fast foods for nights in—and vaca-tions and new luggage to get away from it all. With or without designer babies, she was encouraged to buy on impulse.

Euphoria reigned until the early 80s. Then women began to notice they were running on a treadmill. Locked into payments on anything and everything, they began to check out one another's progress. They found that many had not advanced.

Working women wore themselves out reading the right books, going to any school or seminar with "management" in the title, following any guru and every rule. Still, not much room at the inn.

Women fortunate enough to be in middle management were loathe to rock the boat. Any boat. They tried to dress and act their role, and not complain. If they were dissatisfied or if their personal goals were in conflict with the corporation's, no one said much.

There was conflict between those who were dedicated to climbing the work ladder—and willing to forfeit their personal lives—and those who wanted to rise with them—without giving up their personal lives. Women were being drawn to opposing camps. All working women were not created—nor were they progressing—as equals. The following case history illustrates this point:

10 A.M.: Jill the temp strides into the computer company office, two hours late for the day's assignment, to catch up on clerical tasks for Miriam and Bill, two marketing managers, and Peter, department direc-tor.

Jill has temped at the company before and knows the ropes, Peter assures his staff.

A "9-to-5" Dolly Parton type, Jill flashes breezy smiles to one and all and refers to a mysterious good reason for her tardiness, having to do with hubby's breakfast requirements. She begins her work day by riffling through the secretary's In basket.

Miriam points to a stack of work in labeled folders. "These are in order of importance," she tells the temp. Jill ignores Miriam and grabs Bill's file from the middle of the stack.

10:30 A.M.: Jill stops work for her first coffee break. Moments later, Miriam looks up from her desk and sees Jill return, carrying armloads of summery gauze dresses, which she spreads around the department library.

"I'm helping my sister sell sample size-seven dresses," Jill cheerfully tells Miriam as she grabs the phone and office directory. Within five minutes the floor's entire female secretarial staff beings to congregate in the library, claiming "break time." They giggle, hold up the dresses, and open and shut the door to the new dressing room.

As her impromptu boutique business ebbs and flows throughout the morning, Jill periodically returns to her typing station to work on Bill's file. But that doesn't last for long.

She asks Bill to help make change for her buyers, which he does cheerfully, lifting his eyebrows in mock dismay. His friendship with Jill goes way back to the time he had hired her as a model to help at a computer show.

Miriam, trying to overlook the diversion, becomes ever more tense. She finally decides to confront Jill. Her voice is obviously under tight control. "Do you know that this dress gig is interfering with work, and you haven't touched my number-one priority project?" Miriam finally asks Jill. Jill smiles benignly, replying that she understands.

2 P.M.: Jill calls for a full staff emergency meeting in Peter's office. "The girls in the department should all take turns taking phone messages because I'm just swamped," she complains to the assembled group.

Miriam interrupts with more than a hint of chill. "This department's professionals are very busy and have a lot of work to do that does not include answering one another's telephones."

Jill bursts out in a hostile voice, "*You* haven't answered Bill's phone all day! I can't believe you won't even help me. You haven't even looked at my dresses—and I know you're a size seven."

2:45 P.M.: Jill disappears. Miriam's project is untouched. Only Bill's work has been completed. Peter tells Miriam that Jill had an appointment for extensive dental surgery and will be back the following morning.

"Besides, I think you hurt her feelings, Miriam," Peter confides. "It would be nice if you girls could get along."

True story, except for the names. In the 80s, it is tough to be both a woman in management and one of the girls. What's going on? Many things are happening at different levels.

From a purely business standpoint, the inept temp should have been sent back, with a stern follow-up note to the agency requesting that they send more professional secretaries in the future or lose the business. Handled as a gender-free business matter, the incident would not have become an issue about the girls not getting along.

But when women interact, the plot thickens. The men were willing to condescend to the secretary by not demanding competence. The female manager didn't have enough confidence to be assertive and take the real risk of being tagged bitchy by her male coworkers. Even the personal manners of the two women came into play. Jill used her sexuality to get by; Miriam continued to rely on the high road of cool professionalism that was expected of men.

Of course, the men can better afford to distance themselves; they had no real problem. The secretary had done their work. Their needs were met, and Jill provided an amusing diversion from the office routine.

Stories much like this deceptively simple case history are played and replayed daily throughout the corporate community. They have been a part of office life since women arrived in great numbers in the business offices in the 60s and 70s. Since the beginning, women have had a problem, not with the men they work with, but with the office work ethic.

Instances frustrating as the one above—so easy to solve and yet so unlikely to be resolved in a businesslike manner—haunt all working women. They reached a flashpoint in the early 80s, when more and more women seemed to get in the way of their sisters' career goals.

These goals had less to do with making a living than with fulfillment and supporting their life-style. The workplace became a powder keg.

A silent, but full-scale war had erupted over the few career opportunities available. The clues had been scattered all around, but no one seemed to notice. Fuses were short. Sparks were beginning to fly.

Consider the slogan "You've come a long way, baby!" The slick four-color ad of a slinky, young, full-grown "baby" who had come a "long way" to smoke a cigarette told the story. But the real message wasn't in the ad copy; it could be found in the warning on the side of the pack. The caution that "Smoking may be dangerous to your health" might have been paraphrased, "Thinking you can do it better, or differently from other women, can also be dangerous to your health."

The ad, designed to appeal to women's hopes, fantasies, and buying power, offered a feminine macho without substance.

Inhaling a sense of the struggle endured by Joan of Arc so long ago reminds us of women's wars that rage daily. A vision told Joan to lead. To fight.

She saw herself as bold and capable, and battled as a lone and superior woman in a bloody civil war. Her extraordinary expectations, like those of so many women today, could also bring crushing disillusionment.

How would it have altered history if Joan had experienced influences such as modern magazines geared to teen taste—and encountered advertising copy that addressed her as "baby"? Would her determination have been damaged even a bit if she knew that society preferred females who were smiling, seductive, pretty, everlasting babies?

In Joan's day, most women accepted society's expectations of home and hearth. Is the rare exception more admired today than in earlier times?

Santayana's warning is often repeated: Those who do not learn from history are condemned to repeat it. *You've come a short way, baby!*—and—*You're not a baby, anymore!*

4

Women's Dilemma—
Brass Ring or
Bottom Rung?

In the corporate work world, the Brass Ring is a symbol of all the rewards that success brings: promotions, corner offices, and company cars. It's taken from childhood days at the fair when even the most protected kids were allowed to ride the merry-go-round. Each had a chance to reach out and grab the Brass Ring to win a free ride.

But there's another business world metaphor used with as much frequency. The Bottom Rung is the bottom of the white-collar ladder, the lowest level of the corporate hierarchy. It symbolizes new hires and dead ends, inexperience and obsolescence, the one level above no job at all. It's where those on their way out meet those coming in. It's where most of the working women of the Western world spend eight hours a day, five days a week.

Given a choice, it would seem that all who qualify would strive for the top prize. This isn't necessarily so. Few are inspired to follow in the footsteps of Joan of Arc, whose stretch for her particular Brass Ring required that she lay down her life for her struggle.

A Joan of Arc level of leadership, daring, and achievement is

41

the Brass Ring of Brass Rings. It's the epitome of excellence. The challenge for most women falls far short of that ideal. Many modern working women are not all that repelled by the thought of spending their earning years clustered on, or near, the Bottom Rung.

Why? Because they're well compensated. Benefits include a less demanding work schedule than would be demanded for top success. Near the bottom, there is more room to integrate personal concerns within the workweek. This trade-off is mentioned by many working women at middle and low organization-chart rungs as a serious point in favor of staying where they are. Less dedication is expected at the lowest levels, and less is given by women who have little desire to move upward.

But even for Bottom Rungers, there is one feature of the Brass Ring that they reserve their right to try for. Many women would like to attach themselves to a genuine Brass Ringer and share in his ride. That way, there's no penalty for being a Bottom Runger.

Typically, such a Brass Ringer is a desirable male colleague. The Runger gets automatic equal status with the Ringer if she marries him. The wife shares the husband's status ride.

So, millions of women have incorporated this method of redeeming the Brass Ring for a bonus ride into their work world survival strategy to keep their merry-go-round whirl going as long as possible. Only divorce, or sometimes the death of an uninsured spouse, can unseat them.

Devotees of each camp—those who shoot for the top and those who prefer to languish at the bottom—could theoretically "do their own time" and make their contribution at their chosen level. It doesn't generally go that way. Women, especially those in low to midlevel, are often made uncomfortable by the very existence of women who strive beyond them, and the top achievers distance themselves from the average worker bees.

There's a clash between women who hold these varying work ethics, especially when there's a similarity in their middle-class backgrounds and education. It's an "elbows out" reflex developed during girlhood to not let the other girls push ahead.

"To commit to a career, or work at a job?" This is the question that working women ask themselves, consciously or unaware.

Once they've made their choice, the road taken becomes the right way. The next step is to discriminate against others because those who think differently must be wrong.

In the male work world, men decide what they want and how far they'll go to get it. They compete with whoever comes between them and their goals. Some go for the top, others level off and even fall back. Men and women alike expect men to go for the top. But when a woman goes for the top, it's an affront to all the women who have decided to stay at a low level seemingly more appropriate for women. To them, the success-oriented female must be confused. Her choice reflects negatively on the wisdom of their decision.

California's most notable female Brass Ringer, former State Supreme Court Chief Justice Rose Bird, is an example. Barbara Allen Babcock, professor at Stanford Law School, discussed Bird in reference to a 1986 recall vote. "The voting public seems hell-bent on ousting her." Although it's been confirmed that she is qualified and performed her job with integrity, she was singled out for her opposition to the death penalty in ways that Babcock, who specializes in criminal and civil procedure, says would not have happened if she were male.

"I believe this has occurred because she is a woman in a po-sition of power. Her opponents play on the submerged and inar-ticulate belief that is not quite right for a woman to be chief justice of one of the nation's greatest courts."

People discussed Bird's work habits, social life, and hairstyle. Babcock says that if Bird were male, there would have been no stigma attached to "a reserved demeanor, an ascetic life-style, or an improved appearance. And to mask the sexism, they say, in effect, 'see what an odd and peculiar woman she is.' "

Even a letter to the editor in The Los Angeles Times before election day from a self-designated "personal friend" had a critical word to throw in. The letter was from a female colleague.

Bird's opponents used another woman in their campaign to unseat her: Marianne Frazier, the mother of a murdered twelve-year-old, was featured in television ads seated beside her daughter's picture asking voters to defeat the three justices who overturned the murderer's death sentence. Frazier also challenged the two male associate judges, who tried—to no avail—to disengage their fate from Bird's. But the male justices focused their strategy on keeping to the larger issues. Their claim was that if they were unseated, their replacements would be handpicked by the state's conservative governor, George Deukmejian.

The outcome was capsulized in an L.A. *Times* headline following the election: "Chief Justice First to Be Rejected in Modern Era." The article began: "Losing overwhelmingly . . ." The male jurists were unseated also, with no public comment about Bird's campaign decision to do it "her way."

If there is a clear-cut moral to this tale, it might be that women who lead—with heads above the crowd—can ill afford to act as independent individuals with little regard to the way their feelings, opinions, and actions affect the lives of others.

In the real world, the reaction of other women must be taken into account in considering one's position in the big picture. Should a Brass Ringer consider it imperative that she fit in to keep the door open for other women to join her?

Will justice be better served in California without a liberal woman judge? Will another liberal woman be chosen in Bird's stead? Will male justices be eager to work behind the political scenes to help make this happen? Are female Bottom Rungers likely to encourage their husbands in this direction? There are more nuances here than in most television miniseries' deep intrigues. People don't always make known their deepest convictions—even in smoky back rooms, while sharing pillow talk, or when they are alone in the voting booth.

For women, career clashes are commonplace because they often devote much energy to keeping one another in place. Although everyone wants job security, most disagree on how to achieve it. For the Brass Ring advocate, security is latching onto a top-level management position. For the Bottom Rung contingent, who have less distance to fall to unemployment, refraining from "rocking the boat" seems the safer route. When Brass Ringers rock, Bottom Rungers get seasick.

An element of risk avoidance is present at both the high and low levels. Is it safe to stand up on the merry-go-round for a moment to try for the Brass Ring, and to try again and again as you whiz by? Or is it safer to stay seated and not risk being labeled a grabby failure time and time again? Those who prefer to ride un-noticed feel they have a better chance at getting by if their female peers stay in their places.

The office becomes a battleground. Women with similar educations, attributes, life-styles, and expectations fight one another over who is entitled to the Brass Ring. Most remain on the Bottom Rung, a station they grow accustomed to, and decide that it's a more comfortable place to be. To a large extent, the comfort in this lower rung is measured by the quality of the women who keep them company there.

All factional disputes revolve around the relative merits and demerits of work world positions. The majority of middle class women are at midlevel positions. On either side are the less affluent hourlies and the upscale professionals. Much of the thunder and the fury is generated by the movement among the camps.

The career goals of this largest group of women, whose jobs and ambitions fall somewhere between top and bottom, are apt to change through their years in the workplace. Passages in a woman's personal life—mating, mothering, and nurturing—determine how she handles her professional focus.

Those in midlevel positions who can manage financially sometimes decide to work part-time. Those who can't afford it remain—physically—at work full-time, but have a part-time devotion to the job. Content to just get by at work, they redirect their primary focus from the office to the home, often using frequent telephone contact as a long umbilical cord between the two worlds.

Friction ensues when the behavior of any one group reflects on the work ethic of the other. The way women react to their conscious or subconscious decisions to reach up or step down, the way their female coworkers react, and the way their respective male and female bosses respond produce the conflict and the fierce battles between the factions.

The increasing number of female dropouts—both Brass Ring contenders and Bottom Rung jobholders—strikes fear in the hearts of those who assume they will be the only ones left behind when the lights of working women dim. If bottom and top women go, who are they to want to stay?

Today, nice euphemisms help Brass Ringers back down the

ladder a step or two. If a woman has found that she doesn't care for all of the aspects of managing people, she can say that her job in management doesn't match her "preferred skills." The new language is meant to present analytical reasons to make her decision more acceptable to herself and to the world.

Jane Ballback, of Coil Ballback & Slater Associates, a career consulting firm based in Orange, California, reassures women who are in over their head, or have a personality conflict with their boss or have discovered that a new management position is less satisfying than expected.

Ballback's theory is, "Up isn't the only way to advance." This idea offers a less negative alternative to describe failure. The old-fashioned "downward movement" becomes "career realignment." A feeling of being lost and hopeless is "a state of moratorium." As some working women battle downward mobility, others explore the "positive aspects of demotion."

Brass Ringers and Bottom Rungers alike want equal consideration for advancement and equal pay, even though they're not giving it an equal try. From one point of view they are all entitled to be judged on their individual merits. Another faction of women insists that women will not be welcomed to positions of authority as long as some flaunt their ambivalence about their determination to reach the top. They must make it clear that they are going for the Brass Ring and are not on the painted pony just for the ride.

There's more than one way to view the carousel. The nicest way to see it is as carefree and colorful—all fun. It's a myriad of pastel tints, grinning painted ponies, laughter, waving to the one you love as you whirl around—an eternal symbol of summertime.

As the calliope plays, it's pure joy to stand on your tiptoes and try to catch the Brass Ring. It's an exciting possibility, but rarely does it happen. And as you sit back down, the movement stops and the Brass Ring disappears. It was a fleeting chance, but it made the brief ride more exciting.

In another vision, the merry-go-round has a nightmare quality. You're on for the ride, but it goes nowhere. Your smile becomes a grimace as artificial as the one painted on your garish pony. You turn to wave to a friend, but everyone else has wandered off to find a more exciting amusement.

The ride goes on. Your stomach feels queasy, but there's no graceful way to get off before the ride's over. Others are also impatient, prepared to jump off with you as soon as the movement slows. The music sounds distorted and tinny as you stand and self-consciously make a timid grab at the Brass Ring.

You sit down quickly, feeling silly. And you hope no one noticed that you even tried. You wouldn't want anyone to think you seriously thought you could get it. No girls you know ever did. What would you want it for, anyway?

While men are in the work force over the long haul, they often choose career paths that will ensure a steady rise. They're not apt to be consoled by their loved ones for their lack of achievement. Their strokes come from continuous business successes in giant steps toward the Brass Ring.

Women, who often focus on activities outside work, are usually let off the hook when they settle in at a Bottom Rung. As one college-educated woman at work at a lower-level job explained, "My husband will always be the principal wage earner in our home. I move when he's transferred—which has been three times in five years—so I just get whatever job I can in whatever city we're in. So I'll never work my way up. Or earn as much. I support him emotionally; he supports me financially. I usually take a few months to unwind and look around after every move. That's our trade-off."

Women are familiar with that line of reasoning. Even though the wife often has no nest egg of her own to protect her from the vagaries of the relationship, she redoubles her faith with a staunch refusal to focus on her own career. Most women condone and even applaud this Bottom Rung reasoning. The Bottom Rung is an acceptable place to start, stagnate, and stop.

Being on the Bottom Rung has its compensations (none of which are the bottom line on the paycheck). Some people even regard it as a place of special privileges, such as fewer work hours and less responsibility. Many find that better than money. Some young women, as well as more seasoned workers, prefer placing the better part of their time and energy on advanced schooling and leisure activities—and family matters—through their work years.

Meanwhile, a near crisis is brewing on the Bottom Rung. Although it has been an honorable place for women to begin and end a career, times are changing. The problem is that so many women are parked on the Bottom Rung that it has become too crowded to accommodate newcomers. No room at the bottom? Then what?

Consider the millions of women at entry-level positions. Most believe that if they finish school, work hard, play fair, smile, and act nice and not pushy, life will fall into place. The Brass Ring might be handed to them by some stroke of good fortune and result in a welcome, top-level, glamorous career. If not, if the men in power keep women out, then the Bottom Rung will have to do. The stigma of failure is lessened if most other women—friends and enemies—also remain on lower perches.

Then, rather than a problem to be solved, the shared situation is more likely to become the Lament of the Girls . . . Together in safe and cozy jobs they placidly bemoan their fate at the hands of others, and during the coffee break talk about the fun of a fulfilling weekend at home.

At the other end of the spectrum, women in top management hint that their elite niche is not very enjoyable because of the stress and the demands on their personal lives. Once superwoman types looked down on the drones who lacked their drive and savvy. Now, in Brass Ring position, they begin to wonder. And to hate.

And as the years toward middle age tick by, the Brass Ringer grows fearful. Has she inadvertently misstepped by heading up— instead of down and out? Said one, with a hint of panic in her voice, "Those women who didn't get to management may have been smarter. They goofed around, sure. They also snagged mates and had babies. I don't have anything of real value. Just cold nights in my own condo."

In disdaining the Bottom Rung and reaching for the Brass Ring, women know the hazards. Those at lower management levels, some in token positions, step carefully for balance.

But, in reality, each Brass Ring is only another Bottom Rung on an endless series of ladders that stretch past each individual working life into infinity. And meanwhile there's a war going on. The chances of getting burned increase with one's proximity to the fire.

The Brass Ring that Joan of Arc seized was her cause. Such

idealism is extraordinary. Today, as in other times, women like Joan are rare indeed. More hover at the lower levels, where there's less danger in a fall.

For those nearer the top rungs, there's also danger in competition of too many women soaring in search of the glittering Brass Ring. One's own luster fades in comparison. If there is only one female executive, she's held in awe. If two are trying for what still only amount to token numbers of senior management positions, there is competition that is not strictly business.

Many striving for the solitary Brass Ring retain more than a few of the personality traits and values they acquired on the steps left behind. If there is only one, it can be excused as an idiosyncrasy. If there are many, it becomes a problem.

One senior executive woman may decorate her office with a stuffed animal collection; another may enjoy including others in her afternoon ritual of "high tea" served on china. Consider the executive who keeps Alice-in-Wonderland curls and frills, the earth mother who brings her backpack and baby to work on Tuesdays and Thursdays. Soon the executive wing resembles a circus. Women who prize individuality, even in the office, prefer to remain loners. Their survival rate is higher.

Baby Boomers expected good careers to be professional, glamorous, and fulfilling. The dream was supposed to come alive for any women qualified enough to graduate college and enter the corporate fray.

That wasn't exactly the way it happened.

There are two ways to go—the glorious and the mundane—as the following case history illustrates.

Kathy B., 22, an administrative assistant, confides to a friend in a nearby cubicle. "No counselor ever told me that I could maintain a 3.8 college index and not get a job in management. I expected a chance to show what I could do with my education.

"This 'clerk work' is so boring, each day goes on forever. Mrs. Grendle is a dried-up old crone who's never going to leave. But I can't quit now. My boyfriend counts on my share of the rent. So I have to stay put—or watch for some kind of chance to transfer out of here."

Gloria C., 23, filing papers in the cubicle next to Kathy, overhears the conversation and laughs. She nudges a friend and whispers, "She's welcome to the club. But I don't mind as much as Kathy does. I get the pay I need and look outside for fulfillment. I don't take this job home with me. My education was meant to enrich the quality of my life. And it does."

But Kathy has other ideas. She has gone to a seminar on assertiveness for women. She's also heard an author on a TV talk show speak about "going for it." Deciding to act first thing Monday morning before she loses her nerve, Kathy throws her shoulders back and strides purposely into the office of Mr. Murphy, her department supervisor.

She taps on the partially closed door as she opens it. "Mr. Murphy, I have to talk to you."

Pressing an index finger under the nose bar of his eyeglasses, the man looks up from his newspaper.

"Good morning . . . Kathy," he sighs.

Kathy blushes at her abruptness, but remembers that a *Cosmo* article said that women apologize much too much and shouldn't keep saying they're sorry for everything. So she doesn't.

Instead, Kathy clears her suddenly dry throat. Mr. Murphy's face has the not-now-go-play expression of an annoyed parent. Despite this, she plunges ahead.

"Mr. Murphy, sir, Mrs. Grendle has me doing nothing but clerk-typist work. When I was hired, personnel told me I could be an administrative assistant. I hoped to prepare for management. I didn't plan to just sit here. My professor explained how we should leap into profit and loss and learn what makes it all happen. I have some great ideas that could really help the company—and I've been here half of an entire year already." The words come in a rush, and when Kathy finishes she gulps.

Mr. Murphy stares at her silently. Then he says deliberately, "We have a lot of work to get out no matter what it's called. But I'll talk to Mrs. Grendle about it." He stands in a gesture of dismissal. "I assume you've discussed this with her already."

"I think she knows how I feel." Kathy backs out the door, murmuring a quick "Thank you."

Mr. Murphy sits back down at his desk, muttering under his breath as picks up his newspaper. "Eight in the morning and she's complaining. And she's only been on board six months. If she was a guy, I'd pat her on the back and verbally kick her butt. Tell her she's on the wrong track. Ready to get into P and L. But, with a gal, it's not worth the hassle. I won't say anything . . . might get sued for harassment. I'll tell Grendle to keep her out of my way." He laughs. "P and L. Geez. Who the hell does she think she is?"

When Mr. Murphy talks to Mrs. Grendle, he finds out that Kathy has not discussed her complaints with her. Mrs. Grendle tells Mr. Murphy that she will talk to Kathy.

"I'll probably just chalk her up as a lost cause," Mrs. Grendle says to her husband at home that night. "She has no sense of corporate protocol—going over her boss's head with a complaint. Whatever her fancy school taught her, it left out common sense. The young men who come through are out for my job, but they play by the rules. She'll learn the hard way. Who the hell does she think she is?"

The next day, Gloria, Bottom Runger but not nailed to it, overhears the talk about Kathy's assault on the organization chart. She's annoyed. This signals a change in her career outlook.

"So," Gloria fumes, "she'd like to move on and leave me with all the scut work, even though I'm as qualified as she is any day. As long as I'm here, I wouldn't mind doing higher level work that would be more interesting. If she can do it, I can do it. And I've been here a whole year. Who the hell does she think she is?"

Meanwhile, Kathy receives a lecture from Mrs. Grendle on the general subject of working like a family and doing what it takes to get the job done.

Mrs. Grendle's tone is icy. "I will consider your request for additional responsibilities when they're available."

Kathy, humiliated at being scolded within earshot of Gloria, realizes that Mrs. Grendle is now an enemy and her chances for promotion are remote.

"Damn! The books says 'go for it' and now it's going against me. I wish someone would tell me what's wrong. It's like a silent conspiracy. She doesn't even want to understand that I have skills to offer that aren't being used. And anyone can do stupid filing. Just because she got to be a boss after a thousand years here, she thinks she knows it all. Who the hell does she think she is?"

Kathy's a Brass Ringer. Gloria is a Bottom Runger. Mrs. Grendle has been both, and at the moment is precariously perched midway between the two states of being. At lest at the start, each of the two younger women has a different job agenda. One yearns to advance and the other is content to nest on the Bottom Rung, and wouldn't be heartbroken to slide right off. Making their way through these distinct, separate, and fundamentally opposed processes involves some interesting turns. Inevitably, they find themselves face-to-face, locked in combat, screaming the battle cry: "Who the hell does she think she is?"

Associates become antagonists. The results of these collisions are unpredictable. Gloria may be angry enough to put the story of Kathy's faux pas on the office grapevine.

Gloria may benefit from the downturn in Kathy's fortune. With her less-threatening demeanor, Gloria has the potential to be promoted up. Just by doing the opposite of whatever Kathy does, she may taste success and develop a yen for more. Even the Brass Ring.

Or Kathy may be jolted into realizing that the academic world where she got so many of her ideas is quite different from the work world she was ready to conquer. Pegged as a troublemaker with no friends on high, what can she do? How can she respond?

She may quit and go to work somewhere else. Or she may quit and go back to school for her MBA. Or she may get married and look for something part-time. Or she may conclude that the hierarchy is against women and, ambition subdued, decide to do as little as possible to get by. Much less pain on the Bottom Rung.

Or Kathy and Gloria both might stay in the security of clerk-typist land, and make a habit of lashing out against one another as the years go by. New graduates will be hired at the bottom of the pay scale. Some will leave, some will stay, and some will get promoted. Eventually, Kathy and Gloria, long content with fatter paychecks reflecting minimum cost-of-living raises, will wonder how secure they really are.

For most women, the Brass Ring seems better than the Bottom Rung. However, the Brass Ring is usually an illusion. Almost every corporation in the United States probably has only a single, solitary spot for a woman on the traditionally all-male team. And things are not getting better.

The refrain in interviews with executives indicates frustration from women once poised for the Brass Ring.

Says a female bank manager: "Lack of grooming for top-level positions ten years ago makes me ready to accept the fact that I have topped out."

Another stalled executive confides: "It's a subtle feeling. High echelon officers lack a comfort zone with more than one woman aboard."

There is an untested myth that women are united by gender in their business ambitions. Author Liz Gallese in *Women Like Us*, makes the point that the women who achieve are

> . . . not part of the women's movement. The ones who get that kind of power think and act like men on the job. It is highly unlikely that (when they get in powerful positions) they will pull a switch and (want to humanize) a corporation.
>
> There is a temperamental type who fits into the corporation very well—the impersonal type . . . they are not going forward for women colleagues on the job, nor are they going to somehow "feminize" American business.

Tokenism hit its heyday in the 1970s. The ceiling became noticeable further into the decade. Women, experienced, qualified, and sporting advanced degrees, headed for coveted money and power positions. A quota of women had blazed the trail, and some were spotlighted in conspicuous positions. Some are still in there swinging, holding onto their midlevel seats for dear life, and hoping against hope, as one manager said, "for something to happen that will help me take another step up."

The action, however, is moving in the opposite direction. A director of an executive search firm identifies the fall-from-the-reach-for-the-brass-ring contingent. "After eight or 10 years, they hit a barrier. The trouble begins at about the $75,000 to $100,000 salary level and seems to get worse the higher one looks."

Although far from the Bottom Rung, these achievers can hardly be content anywhere below the top. Reason says they must be talented women. Most were tokens whose ride came to an inglorious end.

Whatever the total effect of Women vs. Women in the workplace is, the Uncivil Business War has not been a force for change. Although the Brass Ring and the Bottom Rung may seem worlds apart, they may be one and the same for most working women in the corporate world for the long haul.

5

Men's Reserved Seating—Ringside at the Office Catfight

What are men really doing—and thinking—as they observe the tactics and battles of the unacknowledged warfare of women fighting women? Are they aware, on some level, of what's going on? Do men care? Should they? How does it affect men in their own business struggles?

Don't men fight women as hard as men fight each other? The answer has to be a qualified yes. Businessmen certainly fight when they must, to protect their superior titles and wages. In the male world of commerce, these fights have had little to do with women. When women occasionally appear at a high level of competition, men need only stand back and bide their time. Women relieve men of the burden of doing anything much about them: Because of their unique approaches to "success," women consistently function as their own worst enemies. Men serve primarily as the catalyst—or the prize—of women's battles among themselves.

Men fight differently, for different reasons, and with different measurable results. Most men fight in keeping with the laws of the land and the rules of the corporation to advance their own careers.

Within these boundaries they can be selfish, unethical, and spiteful, or supportive, fair, and friendly.

For a man, losing in the world of business is a disgrace and the fight with his competitors is a fight to the death.

Men have a strenuous corporate fight on their hands, but at this time, it has little to do with women. Men are concentrating on their own problems in the competitive chase for raises, promotions, and perks. They're caught up in the often lunatic frenzies of male business culture with its battle for market share, hostile takeovers, unfriendly raids, and unrestrained greed. In their own daily survival struggle, they are pretty much detached from the lower level punch-out among working women.

In the office, the men are getting on with whatever it takes for them to succeed. But while they're at it, men have been known to set aside a few recreational moments of sport. They check out the score in a favorite workplace diversion. From ringside corporate seats, they observe women battling one another in inelegant catfighting.

Catfighting is an unflattering label for a vicious civil war that keeps many of the contestants for upper corporate management positions out of the running.

If women are cats, men have no need to fight them off as though they were tigers—equals invading the white-collar turf. Few women have led male soldiers into major battle since Joan of Arc's try.

It's difficult to accuse men of being troubled about women threatening their bread and butter. In fact, they meet more kittens than cats. Since men hold most of the titles above the level of director, they haven't had to prove their loyalty to female leaders on that score, either.

What kind of a man would stand aside and not interfere while qualified women battle one another? Does he believe in male supremacy and female suppression? Or is he merely taking working women at their word when they say they're as good as he is—and assume they're falling by the wayside because of individual shortcomings? Or, that it's another instance of Ladies' Choice.

Exactly what kind of men are breezing past women on their way to the upper echelons of the corporate hierarchy? All kinds.

Two ages: younger and older. Two intellectual types: smart and dumb. Two looks: handsome and unattractive. Two temperaments: outgoing and introverted. In a word, men. Beyond middle management, American business remains an almost all-male preserve.

Why are men outdistancing women? Is it because men are more concerned with going forward than they are with holding other men back? While women are rivals in a way that bypasses business considerations, the opposite sex is afforded the ultimate opportunity. They run the crowded field on a track largely clear of female competitors. And for amusement they watch the girls get it on.

Despite the evidence to the contrary, some people will continue to blame men for women's career stagnation. Yet, a close look at the men who occupy the cubicles and offices of corporate America won't support that belief.

Who are the key male players in the white-collar crew? First come the younger "great white hopes" so sought after by women today. As one woman enthusiastically explains, "They're 'keepers.' The men I work with are basically stable, steady, and have their act together. They've got college degrees and they're committed to something here at work. Most have a lot of talent. And they have well-rounded outside interests. Like small boats or playing a musical instrument."

Born between the late 40s and the mid-to-late 50s, the prototype for this chap was once the college buddy of many of the women who started out alongside him at their first job after college. He shared with her the rockin'-smokin'-blue-jeaned-love-in late 60s and early 70s.

Both graduated into Nixon's impeachment, the oil embargo, and the Saigon crash. They entered the work force along with millions of other intelligent young men and women. It was hard going that never got easier.

All the Baby Boomers who went to work in the 70s had illusions, but the women's proved particularly unreal. They touted equality, but also expected to be taken care of. They reprimanded men who extended courtesies they regarded as condescending, but they clung to the naivete that men should automatically be deferred to at moments of physical stress.

Social expectations led to business confusion and discomfort about how college equals should interact in the workplace. Life in the dorms had been lived with few constraints, but the corporate structure redefined them as young men and women.

By the 80s that young man had cleaned up his act from here to yuppiedom. He joined a company that offered him a fast track to the top and the halo of being a professional. Today, he's in marketing and listens to Mozart on a compact disc. He is married (probably not to his college girlfriend) and his wife works, but she earns less than he does. This is acceptable, although they need more money than they have to pay for the condo and the car. They'd also like to put something aside for starting a family.

How does he feel about working women? Well, he's married to one, isn't he? And he does his share at home. He's accustomed to the New Woman. He works with her the same way he went to school with her. In his book, women are equal.

Equality means the same on the job as it meant in the classroom. He wouldn't be caught dead in the role of knight in shining armor. He feels no call to do anything for her. She's welcome to do whatever it is she is able to do.

Ralph H., 36, marketing manager, says, "Some women managers are competent, capable, determined to succeed on their own merits. Others whine, take too much sick time, and do substandard work. It is just like school, with a few good ones near the top and the rest content to just coast—down the middle."

But there is also a backlash among some younger men toward working women in their own age group. Says Bill, age 27, marketing supervisor, "Equal is a joke. There are a lot of woman out there. They take good jobs and hold on to them by being cute. I sure can't compete by being sweet and smiling if my work's behind schedule."

Then there's the other man in every working girl's life: the old-timer. This boss is close to her father's age—and temperament. The younger man understands that there is a clean-cut image he must project to this boss to show that he's ready to settle down, nose to the grindstone. The younger woman, blind to the need for change, behaves as she always has toward these daddy types.

The middle-aged boss may be a World War II vet or a Korean War-era college graduate. He's happy to guide the young man with a future—now that the young man's long-haired past is safely tucked away in a family photo album. But what about this dad's attitude toward women?

This older man didn't attend a college with a coed dorm. He views all women much as he does his wife and daughters, as special creatures occasionally to be adored and pampered, rarely to be completely understood, but certainly not to be regarded as peers and equal partners during the long, hard work day.

In fact, he was reared to measure his success by whether the women in his life had to work. On the job, he doesn't take working women all that seriously. The 70s superwoman proved no more of a threat to his job security than Rosie the Riveter had been in her 40s heyday.

The older boss has seen working women change, just like his women at home. He's seen it all before. He doesn't feel the need to promote women if he has a budget that provides for qualified men. But he doesn't break the law and discriminate. If a woman is ready and serious and just right for the job, he'll take on the extra responsibility. But if there are problems, he prefers the rapport he has with men.

He believes that he doesn't need to tread as carefully with men. He feels that he knows how to motivate men for the upward climb, the stretch of years of working together toward a goal.

In many an older boss's eyes, all things being equal, women are not. But he wouldn't really hurt "the girls" for all the world. Not if he can help it.

John B., 59, marketing support director, says, "Sweet young things, I love 'em. They remind me of my daughter, quick and eager to prove themselves. But it's almost inevitable that some companies are going to stick a 23-year-old 'skirt' fresh out of college into the marketing communications position. She doesn't know a thing about the products or the market, and she doesn't care. But her price is right."

As for the older working woman, the senior male boss has seen many as capable as any man. "But," says John B., "I've known few who would sacrifice their personal lives for the company to the extent that many men do."

There is no conspiracy. The simple truth is: Getting to the top of the corporate ladder is beyond the reach of most people, women and men. In fact, of the millions of trained, qualified professionals working in business today, only a handful will achieve noteworthy success. Many will do well, but many, many more will just get by.

Quite simply, there are not enough top-level jobs to go around. And those available are like Ivory Soap, almost 99 and $^{44}/_{100}$ percent pure—in this case, pure white male.

A study released by AT&T in 1985 reveals the percentage of that company's women in management-level positions. The pyramid shape shows from the base: Level 1, managers 38.7 percent; Level 2, managers 22 percent; district managers, 15 percent; division managers, 8.3 percent; directors 2.8 percent; executives, 2.5 percent. Fewer than 3 percent of the top 800 executives are female. And this company is typical.

Far from resenting this situation, many women revel in it. They cozy up to the idea of strong, male leaders in control of their corporate destiny. But other women are outraged. There is constant tension between the two camps. But not enough power is generated to rattle the cages of senior management.

The tragic aspect of the situation is that the upwardly mobile woman's cries of protest, balanced by the cheerleader encouragement for male dominance, results in but another chorus of a hissing and screeching catfight. It's politic for the hierarchy to ignore both factions. In fact, it seems polite for men to abstain from taking sides.

Do women behave differently when men are on the work scene? Women admit that other women do just that. Many women say others flirt, wait on men hand and foot, cry if they're in trouble, and use feminine wiles if they want something from men.

Old habits are hard to break. Most Baby Boomer women are comfortable with the idea of powerful men at the helm. Born and reared alongside the TV set in the suburbs of middle America, they learned that Father Knows Best. Such "girls" are often oblivious to the results of their coquetry.

Although most females profess to see no link between how they behave and how their work is perceived, the result often is that men don't take them seriously as professionals. Women who do feel that there is a connection between the two are angry that this behavior seems to confirm people's prejudices about all working women.

Says Laurie C., age 26, administrative assistant, "Older bosses are troubled by assertive, ambitious women. They have wives who helped their careers by being the homemakers. My boss's wife doesn't drive a car, so he drives her to the grocery. He assumes I, too, need to be protected—and restricted. I have to lead him gently to giving me outside assignments, to 'put me on the road' in any way. It's often frustrating."

But others feel that encouraging daddy instincts is a positive thing. Sandy H., 27, media buyer, says, "The best bosses I've had have been men who have daughters my age. They seem to try to treat me like they'd like their daughters to be treated. They're proud of their daughters, like they are of their sons, and they get mad when they get held back. So, it helps when your boss can appreciate that you're a hard worker."

Confusion and contradiction abound. In the middle are the men caught between their early conditioning to defer to women and their recent education that women are peers who require only fair, not special, treatment.

Jeff H., age 36, sales manager:

First they want to be equal. Now we're back to square one. Take this "manners revival," for example. It's a small issue, but . . . c'mon. What's going on? Formal manners, like in elementary school, on things women can manage physically as well as I can—like opening their own car doors—were hooted out of existence as a put-down when we were in college. Now they're back. I can't believe women want to go through all that rigamarole again.

My company passed around an article on Return to Corporate Good Manners. Not only is it for which fork to use and what wine to order, but a section is about How to Treat the Female Coworker, carrying things for them and holding out chairs. It doesn't seem like equality; what it seems like is bullshit.

Women admit to having a double standard, to wanting equality in employment and pay along with privilege in social status. They underestimate the effect this has on their peers.

A lunch group of women was asked how they felt about male coworkers joining them at lunch or dinner—and paying the tab. One jokes, "We should be so lucky." Another says, "I don't think it's appropriate if it's not an expensed-paid company thing." A third says with a laugh, "Men usually make at least a half-hearted grab for the check. I really don't think they mind. Especially if it's just with one woman. And she just has a salad and they have a regular meal." In general, women think men don't mind paying.

Guess again. When men were asked, they said they did mind. One spells it out. "If the guys are going out the door and the lone woman or two hint strongly that they'd like to come along, I think it's ridiculous if they don't pull out their wallet and get ready to pay their share when the check comes. With the same assurance that it took to join a group when they really weren't specifically invited."

Another says, "It's not worth the hassle to insist they pay their few bucks and take an hour to figure their share of the tip and whatnot. But I think they should. Or make a sincere attempt." A third jokes, "They always seem to be 'short' or carry uncashed checks and no checkbook. Very convenient. How were they planning to eat if Joe Sucker hadn't come along?"

Other courtesies were discussed with both men and women, including holding open doors, pulling out chairs, and carrying bulky objects. Most women had a pet courtesy and were willing to bypass others. The majority felt that the traditional courtesies were appropriate at least some of the time. To a woman, they expressed confidence that "men don't mind."

But some did mind. They were confused about mixed signals. One was sincerely puzzled.

I'm five-foot-four and of slight build. I've learned to accept it. Here at work, I must look larger.

Invariably, women almost twice my size will call me from my office and disturb my work, to ask me to go to the reception desk to pick up large packages that have been delivered.

And then they put the chore out of their minds. When I strongly suggest they go get the stuff—I outrank them all— they just giggle as though I'm joking. And they never go.

Most of the time, I need to get a dolly and wheel it. Which they must notice would work as well for them. It's not exactly complex machinery. But I end up going every time. It's part of the price I pay for having good manners.

Informal interviews with the male sector indicate a backlash against equality when men are confronted with the double-standard in manners.

Cliff J., age 34, advertising manager, scoffs, "Women somehow think they get to make the rules as they go. They can do this, they can't do that. Here they're equal, there they're helpless. I don't buy it. If she can't manage to pull out her own seat and sit down, I'm not convinced she can do much else."

If male resentment of working women has a source, it has to be in simple expectations. And it started way back when. Traditional courtesies, in recent years considered a condescending throwback, are rooted in behavior learned in the home during the growing-up years. Since the telephone became a part of the American home, adolescent girls learned to wait for the boy's phone call. And every woman under 40 knows that on Dick Clark's "American Bandstand," girls tap their feet to the music and smile pretty to entice boys into asking them to dance.

Those girls grew up and went to work. Of course, the quintessential model for working women was perky Mary Tyler Moore, brought by TV during the 70s right into the home. Although she had a glamorous newsroom job and earned her own living, Mary always deferred to her boss, Mr. Grant. It couldn't be any other way. In the family structure, if there is a male head of household, he's the power figure. He is generally respected and deferred to.

Penelope Russianoff, PhD, in her book *Why Do I Think I'm*

Nothing Without a Man?, offers insights: "Women's needs tend to seep into all areas of their lives . . . for all their gains in the working world, they still tend to get their self-esteem and pride more from the home, the family, the man they landed."

So where does that leave work? Women aren't making progress in the business world, and career success doesn't even make third place among female priorities. So why are they blaming men? Back when men were boys they held importance and mystique in girls' lives. And there is no evidence of drastic change.

When did boys—these bearers of peer group status and prestige, these future desirables—become the enemy? When did men—these dinner dates and attention givers—become the squelchers? When did women stop viewing men as natural givers and begin to see them as obstacles to career success and fulfillment?

There was a brief time when men were labeled oppressors. If it was a serious accusation at the time, it didn't stay that way for long. It passed swiftly, leaving little or no damage to the basic pattern of male/female interaction.

Most women who entered the work force in the 60s qualified for entry-level jobs, so there was no immediate problem. Benevolent older men could be mentors in a paternal fashion; women could learn by mastering support tasks. This role was natural. Trouble started when it was time to move up.

According to Janis S., age 40, a supervisor in a data entry department:

> I started here 20 years ago and worked my way up for a time, then I heard 'Be patient!' Now I have girls working for me who have more education than I do. They'd love to have this job.
>
> I've been supervisor for five years, though, and if I don't go up, they don't go up. I hope. [She laughs.] The man who got me in here, a friend of my father's, is ready to retire. He's been like an uncle, but, we'll see. There are male supervisors who could handle the top job, too. And my girls like them. I'm the only woman at my level . . . in all these years.

After nearly two decades of well-educated women making their way into fewer and fewer upper-level positions, men are finally becoming aware of the fierce rivalries among women. They can feel the tension, see the infighting, and hear the personal attacks.

The handling of traditional courtesies can cause unexpressed tensions in business relationships between men and women. Office romance may be even more complicated. Sometimes it results in love and marriage, and a new dual-career couple joins the 27 million already on the scene. In that case, the problems, a possible department relocation, for example, are solvable. Other categories of office romance are more sticky.

Everyone in the office takes an interest in the illicit romance to the tune of countless nonproductive hours of chatter. These affairs can lead to marriages, lawsuits—or both.

John, age 44, vice president of sales, divorced his wife of one year. (She had been his secretary for three years. He had divorced his wife of 20 years, the mother of his three sons, to marry her.) He met Eva, the newest spouse-to-be, a 30-year-old divorcee, on the job. (She worked in administrative support.)

Their office romance fascinated the entire floor. His divorce came through and their gala wedding occupied the interest of all the participants. John, siderailed in his promising career by the first peccadillo, left for a better opportunity with the competition.

Everyone was invited to John and Eva's wedding. At honeymoon's end, Eva returned to find that the company had fired her; they feared pillow talk might threaten the business. Eva wasn't in a high enough position to know secrets and quite probably wouldn't listen if one were shouted in her ear. A multimillion dollar lawsuit is pending on the grounds that she was fired without due cause. Work undone is not at issue.

Who's at fault in office romances? At one time, women bore the blame. Now romances are so commonplace that often men and women remain unscathed. Nonetheless, romance on the job may exert a subtle influence on decisions made at promotion time. When male bosses are friendly and flirtatious, the women respond. Explained one, "It's not like harassment, it's just a way to make the day seem shorter. We kid around." Said another, "If I wear something new and pretty, I know the boss will comment. It makes it seem worth the trouble."

A widow added, "My boss is the only man in my life, in a work sense only, but still, when he flirts a little, I feel like I've still 'got it' or something." A divorcee says, "It usually doesn't mean anything. The old guys just want to stud around and make noise. Still, you never know."

One less-than-innocent bystander summed it up for many. "It's like someone threw fresh meat in shark-infested waters." When men act, women react. The game's on.

And the rest of the company is treated to the spectacle of grown women battling it out. This sort of catfighting allows men to pit women against one another for "fun." It encourages competition. But not for promotions. Women fight one another for the attention of men.

What's okay in the way of male attention on the job? When do work activities border on the social? And how do women feel about the subject?

Office behavior is central to the tension among women in the workplace. Some of the more common concerns result from social and business interactions built into the office routine.

Women at midlevel positions express their concerns. How do sharing meals, cocktails, and overnight trips affect business and family relationships? Says one, "I think most women know that nothing goes on over a meal." Counters another, "Except planning to get together later."

With women in midmanagement, the subject of overnight trips is more real than in the old days when sleepovers often meant shenanigans. A manager says, "Once in a while it's probably okay. Assuming one or both are married, it's a powder keg, though."

Another, says, "I think it's fine." Pause. "As long as it's not with my husband." Says a married female manager with a laugh, "I'm tempted to say it's okay if my husband goes on a business trip with an old, ugly woman. But that sounds terribly sexist."

All agree that it's much more a problem for women—whatever the circumstances—than for men. A female manager summed it up. "They [men] can just pack their bag and go. If they flirt, or more, it's the woman's problem to handle without jeopardizing her career. He may dislike her actions on the road and want to get

rid of her later. Then again, he may enjoy her company and not
want her to get promoted away.''

One happily married manager discussed the dangers:

> I came close to ruining my marriage with frequent overnight
> trips to my company's headquarters. My co-manager always
> went along. We left from work and shared a cab and took the
> same flight. I had traveled for the job I had before this one
> and I sometimes got real lonely in a strange town. I hesitated
> to go out on my own after dark. So it was great to have compa-
> ny.
>   A companion meant not having to always eat alone.
> That's all it meant. At first. We were equals and had a lot to
> talk about. I felt more certain of myself with this man than
> with my husband. He saw only the "macho" me. I began to
> look forward to overnight trips, and then tried to find flimsy
> reasons to initiate them. Work time took on the glamorous
> aspects of power meetings. Tired tongues are often loosened
> by a predinner drink in a shared hotel bar far from home.
> Marriages are pretty boring in comparison.

Throughout the ages, at home and at work, women have enjoyed the company of men. They may like women, too, but find
them better company at the mall than at the office. How do men
feel about women at work? Asked to talk about the problems they
perceive with the women who work with them and for them, men
responded:

Jim: Mary prefers back-up tasks, where she can help our
all-male group—which she refers to as family. She seems to want
to keep it as is. If we offer to get another women in to help with
support, she just stays and works longer hours—without pay. So
we try to do nice things for her, like send flowers after some major
effort.

She seems to want to be liked more than she wants to move
up. If we drag an opinion out of her, she sticks in a question at
the end.

Jack: Jennifer gets us crazy. One day she comes in like
Dragon Lady and we all rear back and get out of her way. An hour

later she may be at a meeting and suddenly turns cute. Like she needs all kinds of help and she giggles. We never know what triggers the changes. Sometimes, it's other women appearing on the scene.

Andrew: Marla is all women's lib when it suits her. It never suits her when it's to her disadvantage. Rather than own up to a mistake, she bats her eyes and pretends it's date time.

Cliff: I need to walk Karen through social work situations. She doesn't seem to feel comfortable in speaking up in a natural way, or holding her own end of a conversation with our male bosses. She waits for me to bring her in.

Mike: Betsy is a knockout. A looker. And I'll bet she's been spoiled on that score all her life. It's like she expects to be noticed and doesn't stop until everyone's attention is on her. She has a whole set of body-language tricks we see over and over. We know them by heart. She's great to look at, but the focus sure gets off the work.

Will: Our department has a girl jock who likes to play with the big boys. She's read somewhere that deals get made at sports events. But no deals get made at our racquetball or softball and beer busts. And a lone female changes the complexion. "Ve vant" to be alone. To be supergross. At least sometimes. Even if Candy's good at sports, she doesn't know when to butt out.

Burt: Lana's good. When she's with us. If her husband has a trip she can go on, she's not with us. If her mother has a cold, she's not with us. We're not the number one item on her agenda very often. We've not privy to her five-year plan.

Ray: I could call "our woman" superior. She blew in complete with MBA and a firm opinion that she can turn our corporation upside down and make it better. Today. Alone.

Thank you, gentlemen. Now the fights can begin. They've all described favorite losers. At their lofty level at work, it seems that there's at least one woman per department who causes puzzlement for at least part of the day. Will those gents contemplating adding more women to their staffs please step forward? If there are none, the battle for the lone position—or two—in each department is about to begin.

And what do these women want? To see women at every level rising up the promotion ladder in harmony? Perhaps not. An old Persian proverb wailed an answer: "Women want toasted ice."

Toasted ice explains the ambivalence of the modern businesswoman who wants equal standards but dreams of being the select female star in a world of powerful men. Women have not substantially helped, and have often subtly—if not blatantly—hindered other women trying to make their way in the business world. Publicly declaring "Men are out to get me," many women smiled at male cohorts and headed off other women too close in the field.

Says a male marketing vice president:

> I knew my phone would ring off the hook every time I promoted a woman.
>
> Other women would demand to know why someone 'no better' than they got promoted. Never mind who was more qualified. That didn't enter into it. It seemed to be all emotion with not much reason. Promoting other men brought fewer screams of indignation and backbiting. I didn't have to deal with innuendos and all kinds of personal overtones when a man was promoted. It seemed more natural to everyone and caused me a lot less grief.

Why do women work to defeat their own cause? Trained from infancy to view other women as rivals, they'd rather give up everything than take the chance of allowing other women to better them. At anything—prestige, friends, clothes, mates, or jobs. Men may watch and wonder why, but women do each other in—and die.

Consider that men may volunteer to fight for Joan of Arc, but they wouldn't want to date her. Women have a choice: to be the woman men want to date, or risk being the woman that men resent. Or, in the extreme, hate enough to kill.

Women have chosen to put their faith in catering to their professed enemy: men. And to fight, in every way possible, their professed friends: women. That may be the call of nature. It is certainly the nature of the current struggle of women fighting women.

6
Marching in Place—
The Charade Parade

Everyone loves a parade. It is stirring to listen to the martial music and see the movement and color of lines of musicians and floats marching through streets in a procession.

In the military, troops assemble in formation on a parade ground to march for review and display. During times of war, soldiers parade through the streets to bolster the illusion that they are marching off on an important mission. But the primary function of the wartime parade is to rally the troops and the people and distract them from the harsh truth of the danger and dreariness of war.

In Women vs. Women, the business office serves as both a parade ground and battlefield for female warriors. They march for display and review, and skirmish in carefully staged sneak attacks.

Most working women love and live a special kind of parade—their very own Charade Parade. They will admit that the office is a parade ground for showcasing their talents and desirability, but they refuse to acknowledge that they use the workplace for subterfuge. And as they march about, raising enough dust and commotion to blur the vision of the most clear-sighted, they deny other realities as well.

Generally, a march has a beginning and an end. It follows a

regular forward movement and makes progress. Although working women do not march in military formation, they do make a show of striding purposefully forward to their goals: in the case of most white-collar professionals, upper management. The most important truth covered up in their Charade Parade is that, for all the talk of careers and goals, most working women are marching around in circles.

The only honest women warriors are those who make no pretense about where they're marching: right out of the grind of the everyday work world. Others do the same but still keep up the Charade Parade. They march backward, away from the workplace, having convinced themselves that they are taken a step forward—toward personal progress.

Self-delusion is a key element in the Charade Parade. If they don't look forward, women can step briskly without noticing that they're not moving forward. A woman might want the title of supervisor and make all the appropriate noises expected of a job candidate. But if she fails to get the promotion, she can always stride about doing her regular tasks, grateful that she didn't have to add any more responsibilities to her workload.

Almost every female marching in the Charade Parade is a certified myth-maker. Those with credentials have a well-honed technique for ignoring any reality that threatens to cure their myopia. Before these women begin their trek, they work out a mind-trip, telling themselves that their fears of being a fraud have miraculously evaporated into feelings of competence and confidence.

From there, they convince themselves that they no longer dream of rescue by Prince Charming, but they are now emancipated and prefer to toil independently until retirement day. It's then a short hop to preen and admire themselves for having given up expectations of special treatment in return for equality.

Believing all this is true, they are primed to accept that there's been a change in social attitudes toward women, and that bias and discrimination have vanished from this earth. The myths may be as fleeting as the piped-in muzak that reverberates through the corporate hall, but that's better than no make-believe at all.

There aren't enough women moving up the promotion ladder

to tilt the statistics. Although they're consoled with high-rolling hopes for their futures, it seems that tomorrow never comes.

Many women make heroic efforts—long hours, children in daycare, and unrewarding low-level jobs in support positions. Disappointed, they are beginning to notice that their parade-drill jobs are leading them in every direction except up. But these women had been counting on steps forward.

It started long ago. All working women retain a soupçon of Joan of Arc, who acted out a charade from the beginning of her mission up to her death. Armed to the hilt, she rode into battle with a show of strength. Joan's battle drills became battles won. The parade is a glorious substitute for victory.

A root cause of the Uncivil Business War is the popular expectation that women march from entry-level jobs through middle-management positions on up to the corporate boardroom. There is scant evidence that this is taking place.

Educated, middle-class working women have been marching in place for decades. Statistics show that without question the majority of qualified working women are *not* advancing beyond mid-level. They aren't going anywhere in their careers, although major marketing and media themes tout their purported achievements.

Women have, for the most part, stalled out. Frustrated in their efforts to be promoted, many of the ambitious ones have turned from trying to open new positions to trying to displace other women who hold slightly better jobs. Others have directed their efforts at acquiring special privileges or perquisites. The infighting generates bad will as women battle one another.

Then there are millions of working women who have become indifferent, and have refocused their attention away from jobs toward their families and personal concerns. They seek to escape loneliness and achieve security by concentrating their efforts on their personal lives. In one manifestation of "parade rest," many career women have turned to passively filling the hours, as few as possible, at their professions. The Career, if not over, is definitely on hold. For the sake of appearances, however, most continue to go through the motions. The charade continues.

Another group, more honest but probably less helpful to those remaining in formation, are women in the new retreat battalions of the 80s. They smile as their professional careers are tagged downwardly mobile. They view their bailout as a success of a different sort. To their way of thinking, it is possible to be a successful woman without being a successful businesswoman. It takes all kinds of women to make a Charade Parade.

Fortune magazine (April 18, 1986) devoted the cover to a smiling Janie Witham, MBA (class of '76), who is "happier at home and working part-time." Attired in jeans and sneakers, seated with her youngster, she symbolizes yet another variation on the New Woman theme. At issue is "Why Women Are Bailing Out . . . Many of the best are quitting corporate management. And not just to have children." According to the author, Alex Taylor III, "One out of four of the best women MBAs, class of '76, have quit the managerial work force. They would rather start their own business, work part-time, or stay home. To keep them, and other promising women, companies need to show some give."

Janie Witham explains the ups and downs of her life after being recruited on campus by IBM. She left after eight years, when she became pregnant and preferred working part-time. It may be that corporate America prefers full-time executives.

Among holders of master's degrees, far more females than males drop out of work at some time during their earning years. Since the mid-1970s, men have garnered 25 percent more master's degrees in business than in previous decades; MBAs for women have gone up 344 percent. Current statistics vary in estimating the number of female dropouts after ten years. Figures hover between 21–34 percent as women go from full-time, to part-time, to no time. Men bail out at a rate of between 1–19 percent.

Corporations that hired women with advanced degrees assumed that they were in the work force for the long haul. At first aggressive and eager, these women paid approximately $25,000 for the MBA degrees that would enable them to run on the fast track. As they retreat, many say that the workplace failed, in a number of ways, to meet their expectations. Some cite organizational rigidity, some claim they felt stifled, but most say that the demands of rearing a family have changed their priorities.

These corporate AWOLs have caused some senior managers

to reevaluate the equal pay concept. Bosses cite the cost of training a high-level executive more likely to leave after short-term employment. In discussing part-time employment, job-sharing, work at home and flex-time, they claim that at the senior management level, executives have to manage, interact, and meet with their staff when those people are at work and need their guidance and input.

Women who remain loyal to their profession—or who have no high-income spouse willing to earn for two or more—are highly unlikely to support this rationale of paying executive women less than men. They're counting on their expensive educations to provide a sound financial return on the investment. This issue opens yet another battleground for women fighting women. Marching home endangers the credibility of all senior women at the front.

At the same time, political movements designed to fix women's problems are afoot. The U.S. Supreme Court has reaffirmed affirmative action; sex discrimination on the job is relentlessly hunted, litigated, and prosecuted.

And there's more legislation on the horizon to support parenting and subsidized child care and to fight age discrimination. Much of this, when made into law, is meant to help working women. Such social services represent a skeleton plan of mutual support and cooperation. This should encourage women, whether they benefit directly or not. But, at present, it's not quite that way. Each woman marches to her own drummer. Women are unaccustomed to working for the greater good.

Honesty can go a long way toward opening eyes to reality. Self-designated spinster, satirist Florence King, leads the way with her contrarian comments. She gave her own view of women's problems:

> I am sick of women's career vs. marriage complaints, and most of all I am sick of their damn kids . . . I refuse to be tarred any longer with their grubby, sticky brush. As soon as the fecund matrons of America found out what work, real work, was like, they started complaining like Victorian invalids . . . It is time Americans admitted that the old maid gives all women a good name . . . she does not spend all day on the telephone checking up on her little serpent's teeth.

King says, "I have no quarrel with the woman who works because she must. It's the overeducated, underlearned, bitching, whelping career woman who is giving all women a bad name. She is also taking refuge in an age-old female vice: jealousy. Women are always jealous of something; it used to be legs and bosoms, now its careers and life-styles . . ."

Young urban professional working women have been partaking in a charade of achievement. Rather than marching together toward their career goals, women are, more likely, keeping time with their individual interests. And, of course, it is possible to accidentally trip a colleague; it may even go unnoticed. Such things happen in real life every day, as, for example, in the following case history.

Ann and Betsy are in their late thirties. Both work in almost-management and as-good-as-management land where so many women dwell. Once roommates at a small midwestern college, they now live in similar midsize cities and keep in touch through Ma Bell. Their conversations illuminate their work struggles. They discuss their work philosophies.

Ann: I get just so far and no further in my job. I move insurance papers around all day until I could scream. I'm not giving you another chance of telling me I'm a pessimist. No one's doing good. All of us girls have been here for years, just doing the same work, day after day. We lunch together, we get our hair cut at the same place, we know each other's personal problems. Like cookies from a cutter. We've been together so long we're starting to look alike.

Betsy: I can just see the whole row of cubicles with a bunch of sad, little Annie faces in them. C'mon. Women are moving up. Just the other day . . .

Ann: Can it. I paid for the call and I want to complain. I personally am not getting anywhere. So, listen. We had two men in the office. But one got promoted and one left. That tells you this is a dead end.

Betsy: Okay, I won't interrupt again. Except you're really wrong. If you'd get out of your shell and look around, you'd see progress.

Ann: Haarummph. So you say. What you believe is a sham. The superficial facade. Get real. Neither of us is really better off than we were five years ago. Now that my kids are in school, I asked for extra responsibility. My supervisor won't promote me. Or any one of us. She'll promote the next man to walk in the door, instead. She likes to have handsome young men toadying at her feet.

Betsy: You're wrong, Ann. She'll promote you. My last two jobs I've been promoted by women. Fairy tales can come true . . .

Ann and Betsy's call ends with the familiar, "We'll talk again soon . . . love ya." Two days later, Betsy calls Ann.

Betsy: Hi, we don't talk for months, then twice in a week. I have to tell you, though, that I've thought about our chat about the land of working women and promotions. I've been thinking about how women don't really help women. They just make it look that way sometimes. Or they believe for a while that they care. The last two women who hired and even promoted me—fired me later, too. It wasn't my work, either. Au contraire. In the first job, I took on a couple of projects that let me interact with the president of the company about a reward gift for sales and an incentive slide show. When she saw me getting noticed on high, she took me off both and she finished them. Then she put me on filing papers, like every day I filed. It was me and the clerk. A real put-down. Eventually I got bored and stuck the papers anywhere and the job along with it. I gave her good reason to fire me.

Ann: [Laughing.] You probably got the clerk fired, too. I know you when you resent someone. Misery time.

Betsy: You know it. I had the other job when I was married, and Bob had a chance to take me with him on trips a couple of times. I didn't really have vacation time coming, but I did all of my work ahead. And was honest about what I was doing. I could have called in sick. Then she wouldn't have been jealous. She pitted me against a temp she brought in to make a point of the work not being done. [Betsy pauses.]

Ann: And . . . ?

Betsy: . . . she hired the temp for my job. A mealymouth who'd stay put. [Both women sigh.]

Betsy: So what's our solution?

Ann: Eat some ice cream. And if I ever do make manager, I'll never hire a woman. Do unto others as they did unto me. Gotta go.

Ann's female bosses also have personal axes to grind. Who hired them? How secure did they feel with an aggressive woman in their age bracket doing her own thing? Are women putting a good face on their roles in the Charade Parade by not owning up to their place in the formation?

White-collar female soldiers tend to fight a solitary, fearful battle. Most successful women say that an element of luck was involved. In their own minds, they minimize their competence and question their achievements. So they fear exposure. For them, it may seem safest to fight alone—so no one will learn of the fraud.

As evidence mounts that many women are falling from the race for the top, millions of also-rans are exhibiting signs of panic. Much fear is based on a domino theory of a downward spiral that will dump women from their middle-class world. Marching in place—and trying to believe the momentum is forward—has become a survival mechanism.

Nan, 18, decided she wasn't interested in full-time college and so took a teller position in a bank. A bright young woman, she had read that banking and finance opened up opportunities for people like herself.

Nan recounted her experience:

> Personnel told me that I'd be trained for my future. And they would support, although not subsidize for a while, my plan to take night college courses. And that they promoted from within.
>
> At my branch, every single teller was a girl. Above us was a middle-age female manager. It reminded me of my Girl Scout troop. She was nice and motherly. She talked to us about our lives and all.
>
> After a couple of months, when I got used to moving around in and out of the office upstairs, I noticed that all of the executives up there were men. I can't figure out how if it's all girls downstairs, and they promote from within, it's all men upstairs.

Maude G., age 46, bank branch manager, explains her point of view.

> It's true. All our branch managers are women. Then it stops. I'd like to show the district managers that I'm capable of producing management trainees from my floor.
>
> I took one of my girls to train on a new, advanced computer program. She gave up on it in a week. Said the rest of the girls turned cold and snubbed her. It's true. They came to me individually and complained that she got to learn something extra. I can't take them all at once. It's easier to not

bother. They're a happier social group if they're all at the same level.

Helen B., age 47, also a bank branch manager, agrees. "It's true that when young men come in as tellers they move up more quickly. They stand out. They're often single, and catered to by most of the girls. They're not resented and don't hold back, so if they're bright and work hard, they do advance."

A similar situation presents itself when women enter a predominantly male occupation with hopes for advancement. If too many get the same idea, the opportunity vanishes. A Stanford University economics professor, Myra Strober, did research ("The Glass Ceiling" was published in a *Wall Street Journal* supplement, March 24, 1986) on bank tellers, teachers, and secretaries. She found that men and women alike slipped in pay and status when women entered the fields in great numbers. There were few female bank tellers in 1935, but by 1980 they held down 91 percent of the available positions.

Strober reported that men left the field in World War II and never returned. When women came in as tellers, it became a dead-end job. Although women now hold one-third to one-half of the manager titles in financial services, insurance, and retailing, promotions after that are at a near halt. A midwestern banker says, "Tellers are treated like buses, another one every five minutes. Sometimes I think the gals take the job because they meet young fellas with paychecks in their hands."

Another national study (in *Computer World* magazine, June 3, 1985) by Strober and assistant Carolyn L. Arnold addresses the role of women in computer-related occupations. In a report for Stanford's Institute for Research on Educational Finance and Governance, they dispel "the myth that high technology is automatically a great equalizer of occupational disparities between men and women."

Arnold called the results "surprising, because they are now so many women getting degrees in math and science." She felt that one factor might be the engineering culture and the other that "work pressures in that area . . . may still be a barrier for women who are trying to balance home and work lives."

The census data used for the study compared 1970 (women were 2 percent of all engineers in the computer industry) and 1980 (women had risen to only 5 percent of all engineers in the computer industry). They concluded that most women continued to hold "low end" jobs at salaries significantly lower than those of their male counterparts. The study concluded that "women are still optimistic about high technology opening doors for them."

In some fields there has been a backlash against women. As women go through the charade of upward mobility without financial advancement, they are perceived as "holding back" all practitioners in that field. "The Impact of the Increasing Percentage of Women in Public Relations and Business Communications," a study by the International Association of Business Communicators (IABC) was subtitled "The Velvet Ghetto" (and published in IABC's *pr reporter* on April 7, 1986). Stating that 70 percent of those in public relations are now female, "The Velvet Ghetto" notes that this affects everyone in this field. The report documents that women have difficulty moving into management. Instead, they fill the role of communication "technician," and are paid less. This endangers everyone in the profession. All practitioners can be stereotyped, and thus prevented from reaching management via business communications.

A former female president of the Public Relations Society of America (PRSA) worries that this feminization may be seen by men "as an opportunity to put public relations down a notch in the corporate hierarchy." The report concluded: "There is not a conscious bias or discrimination against women, but rather a complex socializing process."

In the article dealing with the IABC study in the *pr reporter*, one faction of women were labeled "queen bees." Their personal success convinced them that there was no problem and they were willing to spread that belief along to others.

Their advice is not to "waste any time or energy thinking about what's different about women in this field . . . The women's issue just has no role in professional success."

Journalism is also becoming resegregated. A University of Maryland assistant journalism professor, Maurine Beasley, released a study claiming that pay, status, and watchdog power could

erode if the profession becomes dominated by women. The opposite point of view was given voice by Judy Clabes, editor of the
Kentucky Post, who labeled the report "the worst kind of sexism."

The female Careerists already established in these fields may
face these problems, or stand by idly as they watch naive recruits
join the glitter ghettos.

In talking with females about these problems, an odd conclusion emerges. It appears that many place their faith in "something" bringing about automatic recognition of their true worth.

Most women feel that the key to moving to the head of the
parade is in doing the job well. Yet, they fight one another for the
few glittery management positions in the hopes of escaping the
downward wage pattern. For both men and women, marching in
place can be dangerous to their financial health. The cost-of-living
index controls the drill.

While men face the problem aggressively—racing to senior
executive positions above the female crowd or revamping their resumes so they can move to other fields—women are often lulled
with increased responsibility and honorific titles. More often, they
place their faith in the system to do right by them.

"Equal wages for equal jobs"—the only feminist issue that most
women approved of—has its downside: All jobs requiring the same
amount of responsibility and training are not deemed equal. Almost
always, predominantly male jobs, at any level, pay better. Figuring
out the true meaning of equality could take a century or so.

The concept of comparable worth addresses the ambiguity of
the word "equal." This approach could help overcome wage discrimination. Would all women get behind it? A newspaper article
aired opposing views. The General Federation of Women's Clubs
is against it. Says a spokeswoman, "We feel it would force many
small businesses out of business." A spokeswoman for the National Committee on Pay Equity, a coalition of labor, civil rights,
and women's groups, objected to the federation's stand. They protest, "It's unfortunate when women stand in the way of all women
fighting for fair wages . . . It's sad to see other women (in the
federation) who may have other means of support fight this."

Some laws to protect women which are favored by many and
ridiculed by some also serve to pit women against one another.

One faction favors the illusion of financial protection by a higher, caring group. Another faction prefers to take its chances on being offered equal opportunity in the marketplace.

Sometimes the issue becomes confused. A congressional drive, launched in 1986, highlights the ambivalence. It's an action to guarantee both mothers and fathers up to 26 weeks of unpaid leave and job security after the birth or adoption of a child. A leading backer of the bill, Representative Pat Schroeder (Democrat from Colorado) noted that the United States is one of the few industrial countries that doesn't have a national policy of leave for at least one parent.

Representative Marge Roukema (Republican of New Jersey) warns that such a costly benefit could make employers reluctant to hire women, since they are more likely than men to ask for extended parental leave. She said that this may result in an unintended backlash.

Even in the military, longstanding laws "protect" female soldiers. The direct spiritual descendants of Joan of Arc—female soldiers—are kept far from any potential danger by the Combat Exclusion Law. The Charade Parade steps smartly here, separating women from their highest career ambitions.

With the exception of the Coast Guard, this law keeps women from battle situations. It also keeps women from reaching the highest command positions. The military provides a clear example of why women oppose each other instead of sharing common ground. One side wants to rise as high as it can, and the other would rather enjoy the protection of a supposedly benevolent system.

"Keeping women safe in an unsafe world" is the grandest charade of all. Not allowing women to participate fully inevitably puts them in a role of merely acting out the charade that they are as useful in the military as the male soldiers.

After the Vietnam War, when the draft was ended, a new look was taken at recruiting women. The feminist movement took the stand that there is no need to restrict women from the armed forces in a technological era; armies are run on brainpower rather than brawn. The male military establishment responded with anger: War is still fought by foot soldiers.

Many career military women who chose the armed forces for

secure jobs in support positions agree with the combat restrictions. Moreover, many wives of service men strongly prefer that their husbands not serve with women, for reasons ranging from fear that the close proximity might lead to romance, or the thought that their husbands would be endangered because they would have to protect the women instead of being able to rely on a strong fellow soldier during combat.

A *Wall Street Journal* article ("Women Move Up in the Military, But Many Jobs Remain Off Limits," March 14, 1985) explained the predicament of military women headed for naval top command posts. "The Navy's 6,606 women officers and 42,258 enlisted women are prohibited by law from holding any of the permanent posts on most of the Navy's 527 ships. This effectively keeps them out of jobs that aspiring male officers typically master on their way to the top." The situation still prevails.

According to a naval authority: "There are more women trained for command than there are places to assign them. Those above the rank of lieutenant are a glut right now, because they cannot command ships. Since they're not allowed to fight, they can't achieve top command.

"What would we do in case of emergency? Leave untrained people in charge and ferry the top command to shore?"

A female lieutenant commander in the U.S. Navy shared her frustration as she explained that she had capably flown prototype attack jets and was relegated to training male pilots to fly the missions she was not allowed to fly.

She says: "It's true I've been promoted to senior officer, but I'm shut out of the kind of commands that lead to the top. Few want to kill, but it's the bottom line of why the military exists. Not to participate is like playing poker for matchsticks."

Many others, though, have learned to live with the double standard. It's a matter of priorities. In an interview, women marines in the Joint Public Affairs Office at the Marine Corps Air Station, El Toro, California, discussed their careers in a positive light. A captain, whose husband holds a position similar to hers, is in charge of a group of communicators.

She explained: "As with many military couples, my husband and I met in the service and are both career service people. The military promotes us from a central location, at set schedules, according to our qualifications, so we're competing on paper with others across the geographical board. In the past, women competed for promotions with other women."

Since 1981, when Congress passed the Defense Officer's Personnel Management Act (DOPMA), women have competed for advancement with men. The men showed some initial resentment. A woman officer discussed its effect on her career:

> I did have a recent career disappointment. I was scheduled to rotate to a foreign public affairs base, but some hostility broke out in the general area, so I couldn't go.
>
> I knew I was qualified for the work that needed to be done, but I ran into "combat exclusion" geography. It was a number of miles from the flurry of hostility that only lasted for a few days during that month. But a few miles too close for women.
>
> It was the CBE law. I know I couldn't pass the male soldiers combat training, anyway. Even if I was allowed to take it. Not as it now stands. Part of the training for combat is carrying a pack of up to 80 pounds. I carried 50 pounds on my back on a recent hike, and it shed a lot of light on how far I could go. At least with a heavy backpack.

A first lieutenant in the same office, who recently returned from maternity leave to the El Toro base, said that her basic training was equal to the men's. It allowed her to test her physical limits, but she, too, felt that some of the requirements would have to be adjusted to accommodate female limitations. "I enjoy the structure of the military and intend to go as far as I now can. I'm signed up for four years, then I'll reconsider. Law school is a possibility."

Discussing career advancement, both women officers in leadership commands felt they were qualified to rise through the ranks. But every discussion of specifics stopped at the same point—combat exclusion. Both officers agreed that the law will not change their lifetimes. Marching in place "for the good of the company" in the military is a way to survive.

Marine Corps Brigadier General Gail Reals, quoted in a newspaper article, said that women are now an integral part of the Marine Corps: ". . . In today's world, we don't know where the front lines are . . . [men and women] undergo the same marksmanship and combat instruction."

Reals says, "Some women tend to think that only men think the corps has gone too far, too fast in the changes it has made. That's not correct. There is a segment of women who think that the changes in the corps have not been . . . positive. These women do not agree that there should be a woman general and they don't believe that women should occupy many of the jobs they now have in the corps."

Even in the military, some women find the Charade Parade comfortable protection from reality. If women are to be kept safe in the military, this attitude is even stronger in the private sector. Here, too, some try to reach out beyond traditional protections and others apply pressure to keep them in parade drill patterns.

Donna B., 34, white-collar worker, says, "I'm in the human resources department, but my degree is in the financial area. There's now a job opening listed on the board and I'd like to go for it. Hey, maybe it's a path to CEO, which human resources isn't. But my friends here all teased about my wanting to 'go where the men are.' I'm chicken. It would be too hard to mess up and have to come back here. They'd never let me forget it."

So women make decisions to "stay put." Peer pressure is alive and well in the adult female world. How can ambitious women who dare to break out of the circle enter the rarified atmosphere of the boardroom? Is there a possibility that the troops will march off the well-worn parade paths?

Although women are nearly a majority of the employees in Fortune 1,000 companies, they hold only 3–4 percent of corporate boardroom seats. And only 25 percent of the companies that have female directors have more than one.

A 1985 survey by Heidrick Partners, Inc., found that 31 percent of women elected to corporation boards last year had a business background. Says one qualified woman, "I jumped ship from corporate to my own service niche. Now, I'm out of the loop of trying to move up through the ranks. I plan to be so successful I can jump over women between me and the boardroom. This way

I'll meet top men and get tapped to serve. And leave other women in the dust."

A board director who made it is cautious about interpreting her success to be a sign of change:

> Disguise my business. Disguise my location. I'm already ostracized as a "turncoat." My husband was my mentor—before that word was a cliche—and I made it. I accepted gladly, figuring that everyone had some kind of help.
>
> But the badmouthing started. From women I had worked with. That hurt. I feel I proved myself. My husband died years ago and I still have my appointment. With no help.
>
> Other women feel I should lift them. But my job isn't to mix into political issues I know nothing about. If they're so equal, let them go to it. I never was a libber and I'm not one now. They shouldn't expect me to take on their problems.

A vice president of a small chain of women's dress shops takes the opposite point of view. "My feelings are somewhat akin to those of token blacks years ago. Like it or not, I represent women I don't know or maybe even care about. But, if it's appropriate in my job—such as an issue of women's benefits—and no one is addressing it, I bone up on the subject and voice an opinion. Ask me in ten years how I really feel about some women in business who try to hold onto the coattail of the one in front!"

During the past decade, women who dashed toward a solitary success were seldom publicly reprimanded. They were rewarded with superficial smiles and hugs by the "sisters" left behind, still on field parade. The price they paid was reaping a harvest of distrust.

Women fighting other women is the norm in elevated corporate positions. The process is somewhat akin to the Quaker custom of shunning. When social rules are broken, a form of banishment is the punishment. The perpetrator is ignored as though she does not exist. A peaceful method of punishment, it is nevertheless an effective form of social control. This method of punishment effectively raises a smoke screen of false sisterhood that blocks out the shouts of battle.

The Charade Parade marches full force toward the 1990s. It raises a storm of activity: more advanced degrees, specialization, networking, mentoring. Women are also breaking into male domains, feminizing the workplace, and spending more years on the job. If "ladies in waiting" work to age 80, they may do all of these and still only circle the perimeters of power positions.

The alternative is the messy opposite of an orderly parade. It involves full-out commitment to unbridled competition with men—and women—for scarce jobs, and money, and personal opportunities.

Women seem to prefer to continue as expert players at the game of Charade—mouthing the comforting words of failure, while acting on their primary concern—seeing that no other women get beyond them. This is accomplished by fighting other women to a standstill.

The Charade Parade creates the illusion that it is a march toward progress. The constant movement of hordes of working women pretending to act in unison goes no deeper than any other facade. And has no more substance. It's all show. And no one's telling.

PART TWO

The Fight/Flight Dilemma

A taste of history through the perspective of the life of Joan of Arc offers a baseline for evaluating the mind-set of today's professional women. Joan's actions toward other women, although abusive, did not much affect female mores. Since Joan's time, large numbers of women have not followed her example of creating a self-made path to do-or-die excellence.

The decisions of today's working women have more impact on the futures of greater numbers of women than at other times in history. More women today have choices regarding how far is too far and how much is too much before careers crash headlong into personal lives. Between the poles of do-or-die independence and complete reliance on the good graces of others is a middle ground.

These options center around the dilemma of fight or flight—should a woman stay in the workplace and fight it out every day, or should she flee to the safety of home? The panic can interfere with a person's attempts to calmly plot a course of action. Exactly what are fight/flight symptoms? *You feel the adrenaline pumping. Your breathing becomes more rapid. Your eyesight becomes more acute. Your digestive system stops working.* Any woman who experiences one or more of these symptoms on most work days—and wonders whether it would be best to go or stay—knows the fight/flight syndrome.

Part Two explores the ramifications of the fight/flight dilemma in the workplace. These chapters examine the "fight" urge to stay in the office trenches as opposed to the "flight" urge to run and hide. There are portraits of the self-defeating practice of self-hatred (often projected outward at peers), a roll call of exactly who's doing the fighting in the corporate trenches, a look at the games women can't seem to help but play, and at the effect of work uniforms on the battle scene.

In Part Two, *Women vs. Women* identifies the ways in which personal issues interfere with professional behavior at work. Having many choices can lead to a profound and often negative impact on the collective progress of middle-class females in the workplace. Serious problems are revealed.

To serve the purposes of this section, working women are divided into convenient categories. Chapter 9 identifies Careerists, Balancers, and Homing Pigeons. These categories may seem arbitrary but they defined a pattern in the lives of middle-class, mid-level women. Some women veer from one group to another at various phases of their working lives.

Categorizing helps to organize thought, and categories—never wholly fair to persons assigned to them—are a necessary shorthand for identification purposes. At issue is: What is keeping women from business success? Identifying behavior patterns will clarify the way in which certain interactions among the categorized groups fuel the Uncivil Business War. It is important not to let ourselves off the hook by getting stuck on whether it's nice to assign labels. To work out the hard question of why women feel that they must "fight or flee," it's imperative to name the problem, classify the information, and confront the all-important aspects of "who's doing what to whom by doing what they're doing in their own lives."

This section identifies the basic themes fueling the battle of Women vs. Women. It rips the disguise away from today's belligerent office practices. The great thing about a book is the privacy it affords. If a woman has a confession to make about her part in this war, she can make it to herself. And her only penance is to feel contrite and promise herself to do better in the future. If she meets no one she knows in the text, she can count herself most fortunate.

Deciding whether to fight or flee the trenches of the Uncivil Business War is the focus of Part Two. In many life choices, women evaluate pain vs. gain. Should they take the tough road that leads to their ultimate goals or travel an easier, less demanding route to a compromise? First, women need to realistically open their eyes to the big picture.

Understanding the fight/flight dilemma of the modern working woman is a first step toward awareness of the overarching problem—women's bloody uncivil war. Before any change is possible, the victim must have a strong desire to do something about the problem. If women are to give up their insidious war, they first have to confront the facts. If one starts by examining the current work situation, it will be possible to determine realistic goals and specific actions.

Women can utilize their much-touted sixth sense to uncover harmful behavior and practices in the work world. Detecting the symptoms will allow women to see the daily office game in its clearest light.

Part Two should shine a revealing light on current social problems and suggest ways to transform unhappy interactions into positive business relationships. This section offers information to enable the reader to isolate self-defeating practices by lighting the dark corners of weakness in females' perceptions of one another's abilities and goals. It will illuminate the possibilities of visualizing strengths. Rather than paying polite lip service, it will consider hard and fair business dialogue geared toward developing a personal approach to the fight/flight issue. The first illumination of this serious conflict may startle many. After all, the comforting dimness of platitudes is hard to throw off.

Later on, *Women vs. Women* offers specific suggestions to help change battlefields to grassy acres. For now, whenever possible, a spoonful of sugar, in the form of a sense of humor, will help the medicine go down. Part Two identifies some flashpoints in the wartime of women at work.

The questions for working women to consider are: How will the decisions I make in my own life affect other women, now and later? How can I ensure that other women's decisions will not harm me? Will I fight, or is it in my long-term best interest to flee?

By the time you finish this section, many answers will be forthcoming. It's a fact of life that you can run, but you can't hide.

7

You Can Run, But You Can't Hide

A good number of women are committed to their personal goals first, their men second, and see work as a distant third. That is why so many are eager to flee the office struggle. Flee rather than fight. However, even if a few have the financial and emotional resources to run, those who need the paycheck must remain. Of these, many are certain that dedication to work is time wasted— the prize fight has no prize. Many try to hide in the ring, giving only a fragment of their attention to the job.

As any worthy contender knows, that's a mighty unlikely way to win a champion's belt. If you want to be in the ring competing for senior management slots, it's impossible to jab and run without being on hand for the knockout punch. What's really happening in the office "ring" is that women who are in for the long haul fight other women who are not. The dilettantes who take a timid poke or two at top jobs check for an easy glass jaw, and are ready to give up when that doesn't work. These actions leave true potential female champs with little credibility as serious contenders.

In the workplace, white-collar women fight men for equal opportunity in getting better jobs, and they fight other women for everything else. The most significant source of female contention is the right (or perhaps privilege) to divide their time between work and home. Another serious issue is their casual disregard for those left behind when they take leave.

For working women, unlike their male counterparts, the home and the office are fundamentally at odds. Women, reared to think that a home and family are of primary importance, consider their jobs more of an avocation than a vocation. Much as Moslems face Mecca, middle-class women are oriented toward home. It's where the heart is—and the heat is not. The heat is in the office, where the competition is getting more and more desperate. The arena is open to public view and has an unmerciful spotlight glare.

Both men and women often give in to the wish that they could quit at the outset and not endure the fight for top positions. For dedicated management contenders, it's a fleeting daydream. Most men—and far fewer women—who have made it midway, take the falls, get up, and dust themselves off. They are ready to come back punching. They're convinced that there is no other way to go but for the top title and no place to hide if they want to get there. The business arena is theirs. They've come to fight.

For many women in the white-collar contest, their jobs, or even careers, are not center stage, the place where their self-worth lives or dies. In the same tough fight as their more dedicated peers, they lack the single-minded attention needed to survive each bout. Reared to think that a home and family are of primary importance, that the domestic sphere takes precedence over the work sphere, many pampered middle-class women are ill-equipped to stay the workaday course.

These women rarely persist in the fight long enough to even remain contenders, let alone challenge the champs. Their full intention is to leave ASAP. They're headed over the ropes and toward the exit at the first bell.

But some women cannot quit the ring, leave the struggle for economic well-being, or avoid the fallout of the Uncivil Business War. If they leave or lose their jobs, they still have bills to pay. Few have enough earned savings to retire at will. Those who have no choice but to stay and fight are hurt by those who turn and walk away. Casual retreat by some women makes it tough for the others to be considered equal to men in big-time competition. If women generally disappear midmatch, who would seriously bet on them to emerge as corporate champs?

Women who decide to leave depend on those who stay to keep the doors of upper management open—in case their husbands leave or lose their jobs. They might want to return when their children grow up or if they change their minds again. And they rely on the women who stay to guarantee that they can move right back to the level where they were last seen. They assume the equal-pay world will wait.

It's not so much a matter of women coming and going. They do that in the millions all the time. The issue is *how* they leave and *how* they act when they must stay. The Uncivil Business War is the result of not acknowledging that all working women are interconnected.

Why do the ones who stay fight in the office? There seems to be no place in the corporate world that can protect women from themselves: no crowded room big enough and no secluded corner small enough to hide them from the financial fallout they fear will be the outcome of being judged on their own merits.

What about flight? Society smiles on this alternative. If a woman can muster the wherewithal, she can flee to her personal better way.

The problem? Those who decide to run from the white-collar melee are apt to crash into the brick wall of their financial futures. Support systems, as well as the economy, have been known to change and falter, forcing these women to once again depend on earning their own paychecks.

In Women vs. Women, females who leave do it in ways that make it highly unlikely that those who remain will be able to hang on to the toehold women have gained in lower-level management. The opportunities for females with careers are not accelerating rapidly enough to provide holding spaces for those who retreat and may need to reenter later.

Corners to hide in are few in today's economic arena. The spotlight shines on those running and backtracking around the office ring in an unrealistic attempt to get out of the line of fire.

You would think that a CEO title would be the top prize for

most professionals. For men perhaps. For many women, however, the prize is enough points to retire from the ring.

Decisions of fight or flight lead to major conflicts for women. These take place in the office among coworkers, and in the home among family members as well.

The turbulence generated at home is returned to the office when women bring their domestic tensions to work. They feel guilty and frustrated about the choices they've made, or because they feel they have no options. At issue: spend more time with kids, work to pay the bills, or do a little something to get out of the house. The conflict at work is: stay at a job or go all the way with a career. There are vast differences between the plans of women who work because they must and those who work because they're headed for the top.

Elitist flights include cutting back on goals and hours for a more meaningful . . . well-rounded . . . personal life, or going out on one's own and trying self-employment.

With all the self-serving rhetoric from educated women in the air, the distinctions between fight and flight actions are sometimes obscured. Deborah Fallows in *A Mother's Work* (1985) explains women in their late twenties and thirties: "You plan to be there when your children are little, but also to do something for yourself." Some women prefer to think they are not staying home but going home: an extended time out in their work plans.

Other subsidized options, such as going into one's own business or becoming a part-time, service-oriented consultant, are meant to help reduce stress and improve the quality of family life. Succeeding financially at such an enterprise is not really the goal. If it were to succeed, then the advantage of more time and flexibility would be lost. A successful business requires too much of her time and attention. The enterprising one would be right back where she started, looking for her next flight out. Some former working women take part-time jobs to retain some of the prestige associated with a professional position. They do it for the ego strokes.

"What do you do?" is a typical question asked of a new acquaintance. For some, it elicits an "ouchy" dilemma. Few well-educated, newly unemployed housewives are prepared for the patronizing "Oh, really" response to the true answer—"I'm a homemaker." A more satisfying answer uses the qualifier "part-time" or "consultant" along with the title of a former position. In this way, a woman can retain her identity as a professional while enjoying her flight out of the fight where she earned that title.

Failure at part-time self-employment types of flight, a husband's financial reverses, or the enterprise going bankrupt might mean another job. And so the need to fight would be required once more.

Today, women seek balance in fulfilling their lives without the emotional penalties of facing the fact that they're sloughing off on their jobs. Running away can be done many ways; few are finding comfortable places to hide. Women aren't always sure of what's expected of them by society or their own families. No one today has the final word on what women's major contribution is supposed to be.

Before the 30s, a woman's place was more clearly defined. America, the great democracy, has its class levels, too: the working class, the lower-middle class, middle class, upper-middle class, and the elite and privileged ruling class. Women generally lived under the halo of their father's or husband's status, and were thus relieved of the burden of fulfilling expectations of them as individuals. They could marry up or marry down—and that was about it for chances of skipping about in the class structure.

The Great Depression shook the class structure to its financial foundation and served as a frightening forerunner of the possibility of rapid downward mobility that currently terrorizes today's middle class.

Almost all Depression-Era families struggled for economic survival. The middle class was dealt a seemingly mortal blow, and millions fell into a vague, destitute underclass. Myriad levels of status and prestige collapsed into two distinct categories: the Haves and Have-Nots. There were few In-Betweens. Men and women, once well off and respected, mixed with the poorest of the poor as they scrounged for any kind of work they could get. A job was a cherished commodity.

Sometimes the women of the family were able to land servile outside jobs, while their more skilled mates remained unemployed.

Women who remained at home were counted on to contribute heavily to their families mental and physical well-being. The women's strength was counted on to get their families through the hard times.

World War II rescued the economy. Scraggly "housedressed" women—during the Depression years they helped their families by eking out yet another meal of potato stew and watery soup—were happy to dress up and emerge into the sunlight by participation in the War Effort. It was an opportunity to flee the long shadows of poverty. There was somewhere for these women to go.

"Women Welcome" was the sign of the times. They pitched in wherever openings beckoned.

Women were involved in new activities, from highly paid manual labor in munitions factories to women's auxilary military units. Some danced the night away in the U.S.O. to cheer up the soldiers.

Women were lauded for their contribution to the nation's defense. Their hard work was openly recognized and rewarded with everything from medals to media attention. "Sweethearts of. . . ." every imaginable category adorned the front pages to encourage everyone within the beam of their smiles to try harder to match their unflagging patriotism.

At the long-awaited end of the war, women were again welcome; welcome to leave the workplace. Flight back home became a patriotic necessity. Heroic war vets returned and wanted their jobs back.

But there was new work designated for women. The postwar era was boom-time. Tract homes, available to the masses—with the help of GI loans—went up quickly. All that was needed to turn these houses into homes was a woman's touch.

Women were to be rewarded for work above and beyond the call of duty, by being banished to the creature comforts of a life in the suburbs. They had it made in the shade. War plants retooled to manufacture newly affordable peacetime goods. To keep the economy healthy, women were encouraged to go home. Their important contribution would be to make use of the new appliances so more could be manufactured. They were to lead the charge in the greatest display of mass consumption the world had ever known.

A fully grown woman in her own home, overseeing her own young—minus the time-consuming and backbreaking chores of previous generations—was considered a new and honorable occupation. There was no reason to fight and little desire to flee. Women settled in; nuclear families—dad, mom, and the kids—settled down.

If there were days when these women of the late 40s and 50s considered bolting, they could be lulled by family reminders of the bad old days. Mother's mother would moan, "What do you have to complain about?" at any sign of daughter's restlessness. A husband who was a good provider was prized above rubies. If rubies came along with the deal, that didn't hurt, either. Over and over, she was told, "You have it so good."

If more justification was required, homemakers had only to pick up a women's magazine of the day—*Ladies' Home Journal*, *McCall's*, or *Woman's Day*. Features regularly included the hourly wages that would be required to replace a homemaker's services with an outsider to do all the chores. A woman's work is never done. Patted on the head, she was soothed. "You work so hard."

Homemakers had little difficulty in believing what they heard in their secure, orderly world. The work world retreated. It was all so long ago and far away.

But all along, media testimony to the contrary, millions of women continued to work outside the home. By their free choice. And these weren't just the unmarried pink-collar waitresses of the working class. Many married middle-class women had jobs.

Usually they were nurses, teachers, or secretaries, and they risked their social standing if they didn't step smartly between their two worlds. It had to be clear that they didn't need to work. Most had help in the form of a day worker or maid to further attest to their financial and social status.

Financially secure, housebound women in this lethargic era found socially acceptable solace in daytime television, tranquilizing medication, alcohol, and equally compliant female friends. If they had to budget or do without, more the virtue. They were "able" to stay home. Being happy was their assignment.

Even in paradise, events began to forecast change. The outside world started, in a mild way, to intrude. While the dishwasher hummed and the baby went off to school, homemakers got severe cases of restlessness. Sated by too much of a good thing, they pondered their chances for a breakout. Their plans, after an incubation period of more than ten years, were propelled by not only personal desires, but by a global portent.

In 1957, the Soviet Union launched the first artificial satellite into space. Sputnik was the literal "cotraveler" that left America behind to play "catch-up" in the race—and eventually to enlist womanpower in yet another national fight. During the next four years, there were studies and commissions to examine the problems keeping the United States from the technological forefront. One conclusion was to more completely utilize all available brainpower. Harbored in either gender's brain cells.

Sputnik thus served as a catalyst to resolve the American middle-class woman's severe case of overpowering ennui. In 1961, the Presidential Commission on the Status of Women proclaimed that "we should be using our educated women. In Russia, women are doctors." The gauntlet was thrown. Women rose to take up the challenge. If the Commies could do it, Americans could do it. Careers outside the home held out the promise of glamour, independence, and equality with men. It proved to be a heady potion, brewed in patriotic fervor.

In the early 60s, most middle-class women were in a position to choose whether to stay home or get a job. In the late 80s, only a select few can afford that option. Women duke it out with other women to be among the fortunate few who have the financial resources to choose between fight and flight.

The political climate of the 60s also stirred women. During the Vietnam War, college campuses became hotbeds of activism. But young women took enough time from protests to graduate and enter the job market in large numbers.

These female college activists had also protested their second-class status in the male-dominated civil rights and campus antiwar movements. When they broke away to form consciousness-raising groups, the women's liberation movement was born. Thinking and speaking out were in.

By the 70s, they were ready to apply their progressive ideas to the workplace—and in the process, cut their ties to the discredited suburban values of their mothers. Or, so they thought.

They assumed their mothers to be self-satisfied dullards. Those mothers were still in the suburbs, true, and leading lives of comparative ease. But they were enjoying it less and less. With families off and doing, they pondered how to fill the ever-longer days.

Author and suburban housewife Betty Friedan anticipated these feelings of isolation in her landmark book, *The Feminine Mystique.* She attributed women's problems in the early years of the decade to their place in society, rather than to personal failure.

Friedan's message struck a chord. It was like a match hitting dry kindling, and women were ignited to action. When this powerhouse of healthy, energetic (and well-rested) women found that they weren't alone, floodgates opened. Fight (in the "real world") was in, flight (out of the suburbs) was in, work was the way to go.

Freidan became the first president of the National Organization of Women (NOW), founded in 1966. Angry women had found a voice.

On the fiftieth anniversary of suffrage, August 26, 1970, a record 50,000 women marched down Fifth Avenue in New York City and made their political statement of equality. A pop song served as an anthem. Helen Reddy's "I Am Woman" became a rousing exhortation. Women were on the run—toward fulfillment. It was a Camelot-like era.

Good-bye suburbs, hello offices. Women of the 70s had intelligence and determination, fueled by college educations and heightened by years of boredom. It was the time of "first women to . . ." Sex discrimination lawsuits against the largest of America's corporations gave notice that "no" was not an answer to ambition. Women staked their claim to a rightful share in the job market.

Mandatory for working women of the late 70s and early 80s was the Superwoman badge of high honor, summed up in the prize praise-phrase, "I don't know how you do it all." Superwoman cheerfully taking on career, family, and social activism. No challenge was unwelcome. Or shirked.

At last, having a job was no longer a stigma or a reminder of hard times for middle-class women. It was considered passage on a flight of personal independence.

Graphs showed working women on a dramatic upswing. Numbers continued upward. In 1979, when women made up half of the nation's work force, every age and economic bracket was represented in the ranks of working women. Times were definitely changing.

Eli Ginzberg, Columbia University professor and 1984 chairman of the National Commission for Manpower Policy, reports that the great number of women entering the workplace ever since 1979 posed as significant a change as any immigrant wave. He compares their impact to the Industrial Revolution. His opinion: "It's the single most outstanding phenomenon of this century."

By 1983, the Bureau of Labor Statistics showed that 50 percent of working wives were married to men earning at least $35,000 a year. A career became a status symbol. Having it all offered an independent income, a stage for stylish dressing, the opportunity for daily interaction with educated men and women, and the fun of taking lunch.

It was believed that showing what women could do would bring fulfillment. Many women felt that right makes might, and the fact that they had been hired meant that they could do the job. And they eagerly accepted every challenge. Working at their jobs was what they truly wanted. Being paid much less than their male counterparts was not considered a major problem. Equal pay for equal work was one of the issues that hard work would resolve naturally. Of course, it didn't happen quite that way.

Problems and dissatisfaction intruded into the Garden of Eden. The divorce rate rose; women wanted to be "free." A feminist response was, "Feminism doesn't cause divorce. Marriage causes divorce." There were also changes in stable marriages. The birthrate went down. Busy two-income couples had other aspects of their lives to focus on as they incurred two-income debts. Baby making was put off for a vague "later." At the moment, there was the prospect of owning a home, upscale adult toys, and European vacations.

"Buy now, pay later" is a slogan for easy credit, but it also was a sign of the times. Families with children found that the kids, largely unsupervised since both parents were away all day, were getting into trouble. And dad had his own problems. Unemployment rose. And even if older workers had jobs, young people were out of work, sometimes contentedly so. They became full-time consumers. Pay-up time was coming on more than one front.

Women's rights brought a full measure of new responsibilities, without much relief from the old ones. And the exercise of these rights brought guilt. The emerging women were blamed for many of the new ills. "Women's work" was being left undone.

In seesawing economic situations, women's fortunes in the workplace ebbed and flowed. Because of their lower pay, some women kept their jobs when mates lost theirs, making them primary breadwinners with far less income than before. Some divorced women with child custody came to depend on incomes originally intended as pin money. Their once proud, liberated role as "head of household" sometimes dropped them to the poverty level. Divorce laws supporting women's equality tended to eliminate alimony. Child support was often catch as catch can. Suddenly, the doors to a more protected life slammed shut. There was no place to run, few places to hide.

Just a few short years earlier, middle-class women had demanded exit from their homes and entry into offices. Now they were finding it as difficult to get out of the workplace as it once had been to get in. In only 20 years, an entire cycle had come to pass.

Many tough aspects of life for working women came to the fore by the early 80s. Fewer women were reaching levels of financial independence. Women reached midlevel management at best, and then plateaued. Qualified women poured into the economy faster than they could be absorbed, adding to the glut in the middle. Could everyone just stay put? Did they want to?

Trouble on such a large scale makes news, and the problems of working women were gaining media attention. There were solutions for every problem—in books, seminars, magazines, and on TV—and yet no solution was adequate to reverse the burgeoning problems or change the scene.

The pipeline to senior management was clogged to near closing. For many women, for many reasons, the discomfort level was rising. Some wanted to stay and fight it out. Others wanted to just plain get out. An opportunity to leave had presented itself before. Would working woman's history repeat itself?

Women vs. Women was bound to happen. Women were given jobs and left on their own to figure out how the corporation really worked. If there was a policy and procedures guide, no one knew where it was. If found, it hadn't been updated in years. At best, it wasn't written by those in the know. Beyond being trained for a specific job at entry level, no one was telling the real business of business.

The New Woman, promoted to first-tier management, was ill-equipped to handle the politics of work. She was bright enough to figure out how to seem savvy, without a glimmer of how to carry out the unwritten laws. She soon became lost on the highways and byways leading to upper management.

And still the hordes kept coming. From the outside, advanced-degree graduates presumed they would blast their way past middle management. A generation gap opened as older empty nesters and displaced homemakers joined the ranks of the newcomers. They arrived in tandem with the post-Baby Boomer young women born in the "birth dearth" 60s. The "no problem" attitude of the young working women added to the fiasco. The fact that their lives seemed easy created problems for the women who worked with them.

Monica C., age 35, management information services director:

> It's been a rough road up for me, even though I'm earning more than I ever hoped for. My life has been spent getting to this spot. I have 18 people working under me. But I must make my job look easy. Every young girl coming up wants it after six months, because I'm the only women in this department at this level. Which would be fine with me. Let these know-it-alls have it. I'm sick of it. I could go back to school. Or travel. Or freelance. There's only one problem with that. Money. What do they expect me to do? Disappear at their convenience?
>
> No one promotes me; no one marries me. I have a ten-

year-old son. You'd have to be off another planet to not have noticed how many like me are scrounging around for a better life. The sweet young thing can hand over her fiancee. Then, I'll hand over my job. Until that happens, she's on her own.

I came up from a clerk, college degree and all. Ms. MBA is too good to go that route. Where are all the fancy MBAs coming from? Harvard must be putting extra shifts on overtime.

Lini H., age 28, MBA:

I'm looking for a manager's position in finance as my way to senior management. The women I've met in what I consider entry management have been there for over ten years and haven't moved up. They started low with a BA and didn't go on. I consider an advanced degree a necessity. The older women have only worked up to where I'd like to begin.

And they seem kind of bitter about their lives. A lot are divorced. They don't do much but stay home nights with their kids. It's scary to talk to them. They paid a high personal price to go so short a distance. I'm glad they broke ground, but I sure think I can do better—without messing up my life. Happiness is a top priority. There should be a time for it.

Monica and Lini are fighters, but they also consider some form of flight an honorable option. They're on a collision course with one another and still others like them over a key issue: How to get what they want and who to take it from.

Both want careers and a well-rounded family life. Monica put her career first and paid the price; Lini seems willing to wage limited warfare in terms compatible with her overall life plan. She hints at full or partial retreat for times of personal fulfillment.

Korn/Ferry International, an executive search firm, found that more than half the current successful women managers over 53 years of age had clerical beginnings, compared with 23 percent of female managers under 37. This has enough ramifications to assure waves of friction between the two managerial groups. The older women, who started out worlds away from management, made conscious fight/flight decisions to climb step by step to make their painstaking way to management. The younger women may have made their way into management without fight/flight choices thrust upon them.

Since they have been in the work force longer, older women give evidence of a struggle balancing home and family problems, with 52 percent either divorced or unmarried, compared with 5 percent of men at the same level. A career without flight exacted its toll. They are committed until illness, death, or retirement do they part. Many are past the point of no return.

Younger women view the older ones more as misguided blunderers than as role models. To them, all history is ancient history. The consensus seems to be that older women made unwise personal and financial choices. The epithets "spinster" and "old maid" never had positive connotations. Divorcees no longer seem racy, and the merry widow faded with the last strains of the waltz.

Many older women have come to terms with being alone and have not given in to loneliness. Their choice is to find happiness in work and whatever social life doesn't interfere with the status quo.

Rena S., age 52, general manager, says:

> I've had marriage offers, but I'd be "marrying down." My first divorce had to do with me getting ahead faster and earning more, so there's no point in repeating that. It does make a difference. I want a man to pamper me and take me nice places. Vacations. And be able to pay. If the man can't ensure that I can leave the rat race if I want to—and still live as well— why would I need the legal huzza-guzza of marriage? I could end up worse off.

But her younger colleagues see things differently. Claire B., age 23, prospective manager, says:

> My first choice is CEO and also wife and mother. But my order of preference would have to be to sacrifice the title of executive for mother.
> If I meet older women who balance well, I ask for their

magic secrets. They just stare at me, like it's a ridiculous question. My thought is that it takes the support of a special kind of man to begin with. And maybe I could do my job from home for a time.

If Claire is planning to do work at home in her spare time and she is planning to work for Rena, sparks are likely to fill the office air. If she plans to learn, and make Rena her mentor, severe adjustments will be necessary. Claire will need to learn just how far apart past and present fight/flight choices are and how those differences can play havoc with corporate expectations.

Fight or flight is a dilemma of today's working women of all ages. Some have given up on male helpmates after a marriage or long-term relationship soured. Others remain ever hopeful of the dream of a Prince Charming emerging from a corner office on a rescue mission to the Land of Choices. The glass slipper, once maligned, has been restored.

Men know there is no way society will smile if they spend a year or more taking care of the kids at home. Others would think they were doing couch duty, watching the soaps with one eye on a toddler. Men give little serious consideration to choosing between fight in the workplace and flight to the home front. It's just not going to happen. They'll fight to maintain their workplace standing even through times of disillusionment. For them, the workplace at its worst is infinitely more comfortable than the humiliation and embarrassment of losing their breadwinner status.

Middle-class women still hope that it's possible to stop their comfortable world when they want to get off. Unlike their working-class sisters, modern middle-class women now approaching middle age are not accustomed to fighting the hard fight. Their mission is to defend the world as it is, even in its somewhat shaky state of being. Housewives with financially desirable husbands feel they are in personal competition with the women at work. Baby Boomers still sporting the cloak of Superwoman fear the day it will all fall apart and reveal them as mortal—and exhausted. On some difficult days, she would like to turn back the clock and reconsider her choices.

The female half of equality-minded couple works hard at maintaining the marriage that is also a partnership, and provides her expected share of the household income. Is flight allowed for her? Can she make a run for motherhood? Or is heeding her biological clock an old-fashioned cop out? What will her husband really think?

The only enemy women know well enough to take on in this melee is other women. And for good cause. The reason women in these camps fight one another is clear.

Fight and flight armies can be tagged, almost across the board as Working Women vs. Professional Mothers. Procreation is the only biological reason females can logically cite to separate themselves from the corporate patterns of males. Mothering can extend over any period of time that a woman designates.

Statistically, sides are divided almost equally. Elizabeth Crowe, editor of *Parents* magazine, reported that their 1986 survey found that ". . . about 50 percent of mothers who dropped out of the work force when they gave birth, announced they wouldn't go back for a substantial amount of time . . . until their children go to school."

An article in the L.A. *Times,* "New Breed of Young Homemakers" (November 29, 1986), reflected the effects of the conservative political mood on the attitudes of new homemakers. Many voiced approval of "taking off" about five years for each child and then reentering the office.

There is no mention of where these educated, midlevel stay-at-homes plan to resurrect their careers. A series of personal interviews brought forth these reactions: A female bank manager puzzles, "I had a heck of a time getting my job back after taking off for six weeks. The central office wanted to relocate me far away from my home. I fought. But I have little empathy for someone taking off until their kids are in school and coming back at the same level. They can go flip burgers at a fast-food joint until they get pregnant again."

Says a health care manager, "The work scene changes constantly. I wouldn't think I'd fit in if I left for an extended time." Says another, "We'll lose equal pay if we're known to leave after we're trained. Then we'd need to be retrained at company expense. If we expect that kind of special treatment we should think again. The job would be gone."

There are many ways to run and no new places to hide. "Going home" won't do it. Women are going to have to fight, and right now they're fighting each other.

8

The Office Misogynist: Who Holds the Title?

A misogynist is a hater of women. Many women in today's troubled workplace blame themselves—to the point of self-hatred—for the troubles in their personal and professional lives. Women vs. Women is fueled by self-hatred extended to all other women. From blaming oneself to blaming other women, self-hatred becomes misogyny.

For many, a scapegoat comes in handy. This state of mind provokes the Uncivil Business War. With few opportunities for flight, the fight rages along many battle lines, from self-hatred to misogyny.

What kind of woman is a misogynist? Linda likes to think Barbara is a friend, but she becomes increasingly enraged as Barbara changes her focus from career to home. Barbara tells everyone that her husband wants her to quit work and stay home and make her days what she wants to them be. Linda knows that Barbara's husband earns far less than Barbara does and thinks she's stupid to give up her good position and promising future to go home and just sit.

Linda also thinks Barbara is dumb to put all her eggs in an unproven matrimonial basket. She silently simmers as Barbara constantly claims how beloved she is in her new status. Linda also is annoyed as her coworkers begin to chide, "Guess you'll be next . . ."

Most of all, Linda hates herself for envying Barbara for her coveted seat near the exit sign. She's angry with Barbara, yet feels like a hypocrite. Linda loses her self-respect first, her friend next.

As working women battle for the fight/flight options that make everyday work tolerable, they internalize doubts about their ability to make changes in their lives and act on their available choices. When the going gets tough, many women loudly blame others— the boss, coworkers, politicians. But often, although they seldom say so, many cannot escape the nagging thought that they've brought it on themselves.

Stuck in the workforce, middle-class women who want the few choice upper-management slots compete not with men, but with other women vying for that one good job. That guarantees that most of the eligible women will fail. It's a bitter pill to swallow. It can damage the self-esteem of an ambitious, competent professional.

While a woman can still have female work friends, she comes to resent the others in the way of her ever-limited opportunities, and she resents herself for being powerless to do anything about the situation.

Many working women have no desire to climb the corporate ladder and are content to add to the midlevel bloat as they work to pay the bills. For these women, female coworkers can, in cheerful moments, make good confidants or, in angry ones, serve as the object of their wrath over the million-and-one workplace irritations that plague their days. They resent the women who get better jobs and more money, and vaguely dislike themselves because they sense that their ambivalence gives off mixed signals, to themselves as well as to others.

With frustration comes anger and bitterness, ill will, and hatred. Because women are socialized to deny these normal reactions, they may internalize their anger and worry: "I must be an awful person to feel this way."

Do women genuinely hate themselves? Perhaps, because of traditional conditioning, women are often less self-confident than men. Do women really hate each other? What about the war between the sexes? Is female misogyny worse than male misogyny? Of course, the battle between men and women remains alive and well. But in the world of commerce, men have no urgent necessity to hate the average run of women with whom they interact.

Men may dislike specific women and steer clear of them. But they also may encourage the friendship and love of those who bolster and adore them, for by and large, men get great satisfaction from pleasing and caring for women. Even nuisance females, tolerated in the office because they're attractive, stir up scant amounts of negative energy in the men—unless the women are so incompetent that business grinds to a near halt.

Although men also suffer bouts of self-doubt, they usually see women as comforters, not competitors. Rarely are feelings of inadequacy permitted to run amuck and take control of the daily life of an average healthy male.

Female feelings of inadequacy are something else again. Powerful self-doubt can stop the strongest, healthiest women in their tracks. And this carries over into women's regard for one another. Women will generally accept the male mandates, no matter how irrational, before they will believe the most logical argument of another woman.

Perhaps the harshest example of ingrained female self-hatred is best seen in a mother's reaction to her newborn. For background, it's common scientific knowledge that the sperm of the male determines the sex of the infant. Second, female babies generally survive better, live longer, and are smarter and stronger. Third, a woman suffers considerably more hardship to produce the baby than does a man. This should lead to a mother's superior pride in giving birth to a girl, a pride that should be unchallengeable.

Not so. Women the world over, as much in the Western world as in any other area of the globe, have convinced themselves and other women that they've erred when they produce a female baby. It's a "second-class" syndrome, usually unspoken, that is recycled with each female birth. Instead of viewing her accomplishment with pride, the mother is quick to ask daddy if he's sure he doesn't mind and assure him that they'll try again as soon as possible to produce the coveted man-child. It's the attitude of a loser coming up with a miniature loser.

Women voluntarily give up their innate superiority by denigrating their own gender. Why? Baby boys are no longer needed to work the farms, fight the wars, or bring home athletic trophies. Farms are mechanized, girls are the size of the men of a generation ago, and female athletes are competing on superior levels. The only reason for women to maintain these outmoded attitudes is to keep one another in subservient postures from day one.

This subject is something that everyone knows and no one admits to. Says Alice C., age 29, "When my mom's friends had a new baby, we'd go to visit and take a gift. We'd tiptoe to the nursery behind the new mother and peek in the crib. Even as a kid, I'd pick up on the heartier tone and full approval behind 'It's a boy' instead of the more forced joy in 'It's a girl.' I once asked if boys were better and my mom gave me the sweet 'Don't be silly.' But everyone knew."

Girls understand early that their own mothers often begrudged them their place on earth from the moment they emerged from the womb. Their relationship recycles misogyny. Although most American mothers say, "As long as it's healthy," further conversation brings, "Having a boy first would be nice, because . . ."

Success is giving birth to males. Sophisticated obstetrics for two-income couples who want small families could lead to a decision to have only one child—a son. Because of the fairly safe ultrasonic tests and amniocentesis, mothers can now know the gender of their unborn babies. This could lead to the ultimate choice in favor of baby boys.

This may seem farfetched, but in countries suffering from overpopulation, a preference for baby boys has already created problems. A newspaper article (*Los Angeles Times,* July 13, 1986) reported on the situation in Korea when leading obstetricians noticed boys significantly outnumbered girls on school playgrounds—though the opposite generally prevails—and checked birth ratios over a two-year period. Dr. Kim Seung Jo, secretary general of the Korean Association of Obstetricians and Gynecologists, said the medical profession ". . . could no longer afford to remain aloof in the face of overwhelming evidence that baby girls are being killed in the womb because of their sex." Abortion without cause is illegal in Korea, but a 1962 government program to reduce the birthrate has made enforcement lax. Officials say that the preference for males stems from a religious ethic emphasizing male family continuity and is reinforced by a family law allowing only sons to carry on the family name.

China has social and economic sanctions against families with more than one child. Cultural traditions have undergone dramatic changes, but male Chinese babies are still far more welcomed and prized. It is suspected that Chinese families are also acting on that preference.

In India, a woman interviewed after the birth of her twelfth said that even though her family was poor, and even though they believe in the government's program of birth control strongly, ". . . I had to keep trying for a boy. I had eleven girls. In some families, the husband would not have been so patient; he would have taken another wife. Now, our family is complete."

Giving birth to females generates self-doubt and self-hatred in women. Although the ways women exhibit hatred of their own gender are generally less lethal than willful abortion, more than a few American couples have kept trying until they produced the coveted male child.

Analyzing female misogyny in an old-fashioned brainstorming session in a women's gym elicited a fast and furious stream of ideas. A group of middle-class women of various shapes, sizes, ages, and beliefs were invited to shout out what they would hate about other women—if they did happen to hate other women. The women surveyed were members of an evening aerobics class, a mix of homemakers and office workers.

Most insisted they didn't really hate other women. But none had a problem in coming up with some hateful things other women did regularly. They offered these conclusions to the opening *I hate women who* . . .

　　. . . fink on women's secrets.
　　. . . get off in cliques at parties and turn it to girl-talk. It's

hard to get away and it's less boring to go join the guys, but it looks bad to be seen as the only female talking to men.

. . . sneak out of work with some lame excuse on Friday, right when I'm getting ready to.

. . . stick me with car pools just because they work outside. I don't like to penalize their kids, but these women seem to think their job makes them special and me their inferior.

. . . come on to my date.

. . . giggle when the check comes in a mixed group and pretend they don't see it. Or don't want to tip enough.

. . . say they don't have change or forget to get their check cashed. Or something else that's lame.

. . . act as if they like me, then talk about me behind my back. Just like grade school. But they still do it, and I always hear about it.

. . . stay home from work with PMS, like it's a catchy disease no one else has.

. . . act macho and want to join the guys at male-only after work sports. Just to be there, I think.

. . . show up at the gym to whore around.

. . . act different when men are around and go into a whole "girly" routine. Like flip their hair.

. . . suck up to the boss. Male, of course.

. . . brag about their affluence.

. . . know it all and don't mind keeping the floor to tell about it, over and over. Like, "he said, she said" stuff. Especially when it's at work and men are around to hear.

Although it may be superficial, it's still a breakthrough for women to confront their dissatisfaction with one another in an open forum. For most, it's a new approach to identifying the problem, if not to solve it.

Hating women's behavior isn't the same as hating women, at least in most female minds. And hatred seldom translates into physical actions. But the psychic damage caused by resentment, envy, and anger is real and tangible.

In rough competition, the soon-to-be-middle-aged white-collar working women challenge newcomers. Bogged down in the workplace, immersed in changing home lives that portend inadequacy if not doom, they struggle on many fronts. Myra C., age 38, office supervisor, sounds exhausted.

I shoulda stood in bed. The whole last twenty years. I'm in a no-win situation. My job is the pits. I almost got to management, but there was always a reason I didn't. Schooling, babies, you name it. I'm bored. And tired. Bone deep. I start dreading the day when I hit the shower in the morning.

My husband, Joe, and I are mortgaged to the hilt. I did my share to get us into this. Now, I'd really like to quit for a year or so. But there's no way. I hate to admit it, but I feel old and used up. I need to sit in the sun. Just sit.

I hate every women who jumps this trap. Or never got in it. I don't have more, I just work more. I don't want to be a manager. The only thing I want to manage is finding the door.

Joe isn't doing all that great, either. Too much competition where he works. That's another thing I have to face. Joe's limitations. That I didn't pick a winner. And frustrations, like that he didn't buy into the business long ago.

My husband's from an ethnic background that kept their women at home. Especially if the wife wants to be there. And he can't do that for me. He's a plumber in a small family business and he feels women in blue-collar fields like his are starting to get in the worker's way.

It's a new thing. The dad's bringing in a daughter who'll be over him. Mostly working in the office, but trained for the actual work. Boss and Daughter. Instead of a son.

Joe feels crowded by the new females. Yet, he wants our daughter to be able to do anything she's able to do. God, that's frustrating. I hate those young women pushing in, but I want my daughter to have the opportunity.

Who do you trust? My whole life sounds like a rotten TV show! I'm laughing, but it's not funny. Some days, lately, I hate everything.

Baby Boomers were teens in the era when love was supposed to be all. Although they didn't hate anyone, "Never trust anyone over 30" was an article of faith. Even adjusting the age upward to 40 didn't help for long. Today, many women are deciding to "Never trust anyone under 30" as they fight to hold the eager newcomers at bay, in the office and socially. Hating the new and young isn't difficult.

One of the trickiest love/hate relationships is manifested in the mother/grown daughter relationship. In a television interview, a successful news personality quoted her college-age daughter's feelings about following in her mother's footsteps. The young woman felt her mother's dream interfered with her dream. The mother responded: "She wanted me at home when she was younger. I was often working. But had I been at home, she may have wished I was elsewhere. Who knows? We all make choices we need to make at the time."

Daughters often express at least borderline misogyny by taking the opposite path from mother's as they mature. Sarah G., age 48, executive legal secretary, shares her story.

I thought I struggled so that my daughter, my only child, could go on beyond me. I didn't get as far as I hoped, but my daughter, Nancy, saw my struggle. Her dad died young. I had to work. I never took time to try to find another man.

Anyway. Nancy and I were talking about her grade school days recently. All these years later, she has really bad memories.

Nancy remembers the depressing feeling of coming home to a chilly, empty house every winter day in Pittsburgh. She was told to push up the thermostat when she got in. Even now, she said, the sound of a thermostat clicking on makes her feel lonely and sick to her stomach.

The way we got into the conversation was me telling her I was disappointed that she wasn't using her Seven Sisters college degree that I struggled to provide. I wondered why she didn't want to get a good job. She only wants a good husband. Nancy made a point of saying that she wants to stay home and be there to serve up warm cocoa when her kids get there.

That's a slap in the face to me. But we get along.

Maybe daughters can see deeper than we can see our-

selves. She knows I couldn't have upped and left my job. Just
as well. I was ambitious. I went to work right out of school
and might have wanted to keep on even if I didn't have to.
Then she'd really have it in for me. Actions speak louder than
words.

To women fighting the office battle daily, flight is a recurring
daydream—and to some a shameful nightmare. Even harboring the
thought is an admission of failure to the New Woman who once
believed in a career future. It's a bitter pill to accept that her
supreme effort has led to thoughts of getting out, instead of going
up.

Hating women who make "fight or flight" decisions that en-
danger her own credibility as a serious careerist, the ambitious
working woman also hates the side of herself that is tempted to
make any concessions. American-born Golda Meir, late Israeli
prime minister, once explained, "At work, you think of the child
you left at home. At home, you think of the work you've left
unfinished . . . Your heart is rent." This ambivalence was expressed by a female head of government who lead her country
through war and uneasy peace.

A backlash that allowed for second thoughts about total career
commitment started to emerge about the time of the defeat of the
Equal Rights Amendment in 1982. They began to think that it
may be unwise to give more or equal importance to work than to
home. Values were shaken.

The climate of the times has given credence to feelings of self-
doubt—if not self-hatred—among women who had fight/flight
choices and opted to stay with a career at the expense of family
life. Even the mythical Superwoman and Supermom short-changed
something, at sometime. Today she calls herself to account. Guilt,
servant of self-hatred, is a powerful tool for self-flagellation. Many
accept blame easily, making themselves fair game for misogyny.

Modern working women have taken it upon themselves to
prove that their ambition has not endangered nature, man, or government. They want to keep their lesser efforts from getting in the
way of the more global male movers and shakers. Viewing themselves as less valuable in economic terms, they have willingly re-

turned to embracing government protection instead of equal participation. Women defeated the Equal Rights Amendment.

The media—especially in magazines catering to the young, fashionable, and homebound—have recently placed greater emphasis on issues guaranteed to awaken the misogynist within. Self-doubt. Roads not taken, doors unopened. Secrets unshared.

Front-cover magazine teasers appeal to the unsure. Subjects such as "Why Mothers Should Stay Home" and "I'm Sick of Work! The Back-to-Home Movement" are on the rise.

These join the tried-and-true articles on indoor sports such as "Catching That Man" and weighty issues such as "New Faces: Throw Out That Stale Months-Old Makeup." Women constantly paint over the faces they hate to become the admired pacesetters they know they are not.

Women insist they see through such simple ploys—but have been known to fall for them anyway. Just in case the woman in the next office will split for home, wearing fresh makeup, hand-in-hand with a caring and wealthy mate.

A psychologist specializing in the attitudes of women says, "The more successful the woman, the more she believes in magic cures and knights in shining armor. The result is a self-hating female contingent buying the latest cure-all issue."

These feed the pangs of envy and jealousy suffered as women compete with themselves and all other women on issue after issue, at home and in the office. It hurts and it won't stop.

Nancy Friday, author of a book aptly titled *Jealousy*, says, "Envy involves two people. It's when you want something someone else has—a job, a car, a lover. We live in an envious society, the Age of Envy. Nobody's satisfied . . . The culture and the economy grind themselves on envy, keeping us constantly dissatisfied. Jealousy has envy flying in all directions."

Friday explains that she delves deeply into the subject to resolve her own troubling bouts with jealousy. She felt that, at one time, the emotion was in control of her life.

A lunchroom conversation at a cafeteria filled with upper-level white-collar administrative workers offers a hint of their mixed feelings about themselves and their beliefs. A dash of self-hatred is mixed into the friendly misogyny.

Elise G., 37, says:

Men approve of women who can't make it at work. And can't
get along. Deep down, they want us at home. They want to
take care of us. The dumber I act on issues, the better Chuck
and I get along. He favors the ditzball within.

When my friend Cindy comes over and flashes her baby
blues and does her entire Dumb Dora routine complete with
giggles, Chuck goes all out to take care of her every need.
Keeps her wine glass filled, rushes ahead to open doors she
might need to open. Even though she's as normal as anyone
when he's not in the room, there's always a minute when the
three of us are together that it's all I can do to not walk over
and slap her.

What gets to me is that her *shtick* works so well. It's the
only work she perfects in a long day in her backyard lawn
chair. I should go home. We'd manage. He'd do better at
work, I bet.

"True," chimes in her lunchmate, Callie, also 37.

The idea of barefoot and pregnant never really died. When
we're out, we may be committing adultery. Like they may be
doing.

I know they have plenty of chances, if where Tom works
is anything like here. I can't stand the way those slutettes strut
their stuff.

No one is out of bounds for them. I heard one who shall
remain nameless ask a guy on our floor if he was "seriously
married." Hey. If you go, I go. Don't leave for home without
me. Or you'll be on my personal most hated list.

Also at the table, Lynette, age 36, says, "They like us best
working part-time. Then we bring in some money, but we don't
have any real power. We stay lower. Beneath them. I'm not going
higher; it won't be much trouble to go lower. [She turns to Callie.]
But you better stick as long as I do. I hate all housewives. Especially those who once were work friends. You'd be like a turn-
coat—going to the enemy."

"Listen, this settles it." Elise sums it up. "Part-time may be the answer. It's like when you visit vendors or go to the satellite office. You can be shopping and everyone thinks you're working somewhere else. Except you, Lynette.''

They all hoot. "Yeah, Lynette. Going to the office supply warehouse for two hours and coming back with a new hairdo. Now we all get the fisheye when we leave." Lynette shrugs. "You all do it. I was just more upfront. Honesty obviously isn't the best work policy with you people.''

Mindi K., age 35, part-time temp, ignores the kidding:

> You're right about part-time. It's the best of both worlds. I couldn't make up my mind whether I wanted to try for the top or just stay home. I married a man who could afford for me to go either way.
>
> I kind of planned it that way from the days I got high at concerts with cool guys named Moonglow. I knew they were good for a party, but not for a marriage.
>
> I looked ahead enough to cultivate a nerd or two for the future. I married an accountant, not a guitarist. You guys don't seem to know what you're trying to prove. That you're good workers or good women. Or both.

The women stacked their dishes back on the trays and readied themselves for the afternoon's work—and ambivalence.

Today's college women are confronting the same dilemma of conflicting fight/flight goals. Nancy Friday's recent research included a survey of college women. They were asked: What message do you think you give to the men? Women want to:

Be treated as equals.
Be taken care of.
Both.

The "boths" won the vote. Friday's conclusion: Baffling.

It's baffling to white-collar women, too. Younger and older women give high marks to personal happiness. The only difference may be that many of the young think they can have it all, while those who tried now doubt that it's possible. Misogyny is bound to be part of the clash. Independent women, content in the company of other independent women, is an idea that has faded, like love beads and threadbare jeans.

It is an advanced case of "What goes around comes around." Locked in unacknowledged battle, torn by disappointment and hating their own failure, women are taking last-stand battle positions against one another.

Many working women hate themselves. That self-hatred is rooted in a sense of failure, frustration, futility, and fear. They are trapped, cornered in a sterile work world from which they cannot escape and in which they must continually struggle to survive. Flight is impossible.

Few working women will have a chance to marry a man who can afford a nonwage-earning wife. And fewer have the option of just leaving the work force to pursue personal interests without concern over finances.

Many women hate themselves for the failure of their dream. And hating themselves, they hate other women for the pain of the impossible quest for independence and the shakeup of the old world and its values. Misogyny has sentenced most middle-class women to work days of continuous fighting. It was supposed to be so different.

9

Roll Call for
the Hate Squadron

Three main groups divide white-collar offices into Hate Squadrons:

Careerists: put business concerns above personal ones.
Balancers: desire harmony at home and at the office.
Homing Pigeons: work because they must earn their way, but their primary energy is focused on leaving.

Within each group are myriad subcategories: Newcomers, Displaced Homemakers, Real Working Women, the Giving Class, and the huge, demotivating Taking Class. Women are in constant flux as they change roles in the work force, and take on the coloration that characterizes their lives at any given time.

Women generally develop antagonisms on the basis of these categories. Careerists are constantly at odds with Homing Pigeons, and both have trouble with Balancers, who cannot decide where their loyalties lie and, as a result, don't further the cause of the other two. Balancers who perform their act well (though sometimes their performances are short-lived) have little time or energy to deal with the long-term consequences of their crammed, self-centered schedules. Mutual animosity turns all three factions into Hate Squadrons.

Women fight to leave as often as they fight to stay. By not giving a full commitment to the workplace, they exhibit passivity and elicit a negative response. In the fight to stay with it, or in the euphoric decision to take flight and be done with it, women find themselves backed into inflexible positions. They're surrounded by enemies and forced to take sides.

Identifying warring factions amid the carnage helps to clarify the role of white-collar working women in the great hate struggle. No uniforms are needed to announce Hate-Squadron affiliations. On some level, all know where they stand and with whom they do battle. And exactly why.

They know their allies when the fight begins. The ties that bind are sometimes unlikely, but they do tie for a time, and they do bind all women.

How do working women identify their friends and enemies? Which women does a working woman hate? Rivals? Equals? Older women? Younger women? Inferiors? Superiors? Which women will she like? Only those who share her values?

Are work friends the ones who are easy to get along with on a personal level? Are enemies those who are difficult under all circumstances? How about women who are difficult at work but enjoyable on a social basis? Or the other way around?

Within a single office may be found:

Feminist vs. Traditionalist

Recent Grad vs. Displaced
    Homemaker

Predatory Bitch vs. Rule-
    bound Priss

Princess vs. Toiler

Prolife vs. Prochoice

Martyr to the Company vs.
    Title Hound

Ms. Luck vs. Ms. Skill

Ms. Dress-for-Success vs.
    Miss Dress-for-Attention

Fulfillment Generator vs.
    Provider

Wifey Dear vs. Mentored
    Single

and an unsupporting cast of
    many.

During the time of their collaboration, women align against a specific enemy, and, for a while, they hate their coconspirators less than all other women. This union eventually ends, either because they leave the work force, or because they drift apart to form other on-the-job allegiances—following the same guidelines.

Hatred is a harsh word to describe the motivation driving these bonds. Harsh but true. The damage rendered by one squadron establishes a standard of behavior that makes it acceptable for others to use the same tactics against their enemies. Unacknowledged Hate Squadrons are unrestrained.

United in hatred, the squadron members thrive on secret exchanges with fellow members as well as on clashes with outsiders. The roll call—who's in what group and why—is coded in euphemisms:

> "She's nice, but . . ." "I always defend her when other people say . . ." "Some people seem to think . . ." "It really shouldn't matter, but . . ." "She seems more interested in . . ." "If I'm reading the rules right, she . . ." "No one more than I wishes she were capable . . ."

Most squad members condone their actions on the premise that they are defending the right way to think and to behave. They hide under the banners of a loving sisterhood, even if their only purpose is to keep their enemies in line.

Men behave more directly. It's easier for them to spot their enemies. Enemies are other working men with enough experience and professional savvy to dog their tracks and try to unseat them. It's one-on-one business competition, and although it is tough, it's kept separate from their personal and home responsibilities. Hate Squadrons, formed largely over fight/flight distinctions, are uncommon among men.

Female Hate Squadrons, on the other hand, group and regroup on the basis of personal fight/flight concerns. This prevents even those who have dedicated their lives to their professions from being judged on individual merit—the way their male colleagues are.

These Careerists are in for the long professional haul. They are well educated, well qualified, and sincere in their ambition to climb to the top. If Careerists were judged on their individual merits, they'd have the best opportunities for success. They know their jobs, know the price of success, and are willing to pay it. Careerists have the most reason to hate the other squadrons of working women. And generally they do. Balancers and Homing Pigeons return the favor when they're made to feel uncomfortable by the relentless standards of Careerists.

Careerists are often undermined in their professional goals by women in the other groups, who undervalue their contributions. Driven to achieve top-flight success, these women are in condition for a do-or-die battle. If it's lonely at the top, they're willing to accept that. Careerists are motivated.

Gloria B., age 35, director of marketing services, says: "Every time this happens to me, I have trouble believing it could happen again. I was in direct line for a promotion. For the third time. Passed over for a man who was less qualified.

"I could see the V.P. backing off a little more every time we talked near the issue. No other women were even close to being tapped, so I thought I might get it just for the tokenism. I'd be happy to take it anyway I can.

"Being passed over may have nothing to do with the new wave of *mommie-uber-alles* factions making their maternal wishes known, but that's my guess. I place the blame at the doorstep of the latest personnel concession to the supermothers among us.

"Managerial mommies are much in vogue. Some women—two of them backpacking nursing babies and excusing themselves from meetings when nature calls—are bringing infants in to work at least two or three days a week. There are cribs in two offices and disposable diapers in the rest room. It smells like slightly soiled babies. It's Mommie Power—this year's corporate idea of caring about people—and none of the male directors are willing to come out against motherhood. I sure can't."

Herb S., age 56, vice president of national marketing, says: "There is an undeniable male discomfort level here that has been mentioned in the press. We're afraid to talk about it for fear of bringing a lawsuit on our company's heads.

"But if two women up here on the executive floor constantly gab about their babies and take off a lot of time for one family thing after another, you can bet it's unlikely we'll tap for more. It costs too damn much in time. We can't afford it."

Ellen C., age 40, director of regional marketing, says: "The mommies among us infuriate me. What they don't do because of their distractions falls on my plate because I didn't go that route. Some won't go to meetings that end later than four o'clock because they want to be home on time for their children. They avoid business appointments that don't conform to the mothering agenda. And I'm judged by their shenanigans. That they're hurting the careers of all women is certainly not among their concerns. They're completely self-centered. How could I not resent it?''

Professional mommies tend to wrap themselves in a protective mantle. One says, "I know there's some animosity because my priorities are temporarily reorganized. Over the years of my work life, it'll all be a wash. I'll put in more regular office hours other years. If those squeaky-clean women turn up their noses at my priorities, let 'em. They'd do the same if they had the chance. They're green-eyed. Jealous.''

Another mother in her late thirties says: "I'm doing two full-time jobs with little sleep or rest. My eyes are red. I drink too much coffee. I'm jumpy. A milk stain on the front of my good silk blouse is an aggravation I never figured in my equation. I know I'm getting on the nerves of most of my coworkers. I'm getting on my own nerves, too. Maybe I'll quit when our bills are paid. They can all take up a collection.''

Careerists feel that other working women may be dissipating their talent, but having made that choice, they should stay away from the office without complaint. To their mind, in a well-run world, or corporation, their decision to focus on a career would also determine their promotability. But in the real world, it doesn't always work that way. Exceptions tend to make the rule. In the corporate world, women are still considered a minority group. Discrimination is silent, but equal. As a result, low achievers may walk away with occasional token positions even though they haven't really tried. It may be a result of timing, favoritism, or winning ways. This does the most harm to the Careerist and is of most benefit to the Balancer. Once in a while, it even works in favor of the Homing Pigeon.

The Balancers outnumber the other groups combined. As they pull off their tightwire-walking routine, they alienate jealous homemakers, annoy Careerists, and frustrate unsuccessful Homing Pigeons.

Balancers, often as educated and qualified as Careerists, sometimes pass as fully committed strivers for a number of years. Poised for the top, they stop short at some point on the ladder to substitute a well-rounded life in place of senior management. Often they refuse to admit they made the trade. The Balancers' goals are to have happy personal lives and good jobs, and be able to enter and leave the workplace for due cause. This can stretch to any amount of time they deem appropriate. They strive to have it all. Without much malicious forethought, they do in anyone who gets in their way, almost always other women.

Balancers may admire Careerists for their personal sacrifices and dedicated performances, but are unconvinced that they really understand what life is about.

Balancers also harbor the thought—and sometimes they are right—that they can get as far up the ladder as the Careerist at less personal cost.

The Balancer also understands the Homing Pigeon—all too well—and is more apt than the Careerist to adopt a patronizing let's-be-friends-and-get-this-work-done attitude to enlist her support. Superficially allies, they often work together on office activities, like planning social events or department meetings. They share personal problems more often with one another than with mixes of the other groups. They socialize.

When they do come into conflict, Balancers exercise their options beyond the reach of the less affluent Homing Pigeons. And flaunt it.

Valerie V., age 32, magazine editor, boasts:

My family is proud to own the most unused vacation home, the most untilled garden, the most band-box new VCR in our entire town. Gil, my husband, has as many floating deadlines rising to haunt him on the weekends as I do. Our recreation toys could be thought of as our hope chest. For now, they're conversation pieces.

My plan is to go full-on with my career for the next year. Except for our annual two-week vacation to Europe, which is our reward time together. It's important to fill our memory book as we move along together. Everyone admires our closeness.

Our daughter is two, and I find that day-care is fine for her now. She's learning to be comfortable with other children. But, I'd like to enjoy her on a one-to-one before she's in school full-time. It's my number one priority.

So I'm going to opt out of the magazine for two years. To enjoy. I hope my job will wait, but if not, it won't. There'll be another out there waiting. I'm good at what I do.

It would probably come as a shock to this Balancer that her in-and-out-for-personal-convenience routine undermines the credibility of other working women. To do as one wishes when one wishes is the almost exclusive preserve of the wealthy and the middle-class, married Balancer. Balancers are also the most envied work group. Even those who hate them may secretly wish they were in their shoes.

Perhaps the Balancers would benefit by taking a leaf from the way men separate their outside lives from the office. If balancing is an honorable solution, it would be less harmful to other women if some of its more flamboyant characteristics were banished from the office. Covering the cage doesn't harm the canary.

Homing Pigeons wish the hardest that they could be magically whisked away to a better place. Many Careerists and Balancers laugh away their contained—but real—hatred for the Homing Pigeons. These women would seem to be unfair game, perhaps beneath contempt, because they are there, purely and simply, to earn their daily bread. For as short a time as possible.

In their hit-and-run dash to return to the sitcom suburbs of yesteryear, they're likely to carelessly run off with their more serious sisters' job positions—or men. Homing Pigeons know that it's dangerous to antagonize Careerists and Balancers, but they're rarely aware that these others try to maintain their distance from the Pigeons without losing surveillance. Homing Pigeons are the one group most often guilty of underestimating their enemies.

Homing Pigeons may be every bit as talented and bright as the first two categories of working females. But perhaps because they are more realistic, they express far fewer illusions that hard work is the way to the top.

Homing Pigeons exhibit the most feminine ploys at the office.

They enjoy creating a soft atmosphere, using old-fashioned wiles. Playfully twisting men around their little fingers, they seize the moment in ways that drive their more equality-minded female co-workers to distraction. They also enjoy that.

Homing Pigeons smile, but their real work is deadly earnest. They're fighting hard for the first opportunity to flee. Working primarily for their paycheck, their personal rewards are outside the job.

Homing Pigeons are the true disrupters of the office. Working for income, they seldom comprehend the devotion to work goals evidenced by women who don't work just for money. But, not seeing women as equal to men, they don't apply this standard to male wage earners. They see the usefulness of male ambition. It could buy an eager and adoring Homing Pigeon, for one thing.

Young Homing Pigeons prefer short-term job goals. Many are in the office to find desirable mates. Seldom do these women think they can make it on their own to the kind of life they want to lead. Their chief annoyance is to be forced to work with female colleagues who allow work to get in the way of the Homing Pigeon's more serious concerns.

Even though most Careerists and Balancers have long accepted the Homing Pigeon's cavalier attitude to work, they find it more difficult to forgive her comfort with girlish trappings. Through a reverse halo effect, her unthreatening and supportive personal interactions with men—such as offering to run errands or sew on their loose suit-jacket buttons—often create unwelcome expectations of all women.

Young Homing Pigeons generally show a casual disregard for professionalism and the success or failure of the company. If it fails, and goes bust, the Homing Pigeon feels it's not her fault and she can get another job.

Working until "something better comes along," means until something more pleasing presents itself. It may mean part-time or no time work, or leaping to a management position that suddenly opens before her.

Older Homing Pigeons, like the younger ones, view jobs in a short-sighted way. They are contributing to the family, making life more comfortable, or funding a child's braces or college tuition. They have long ago made their decision on the fight/flight issue.

In essence, they needed to work and went out and got a job. Older Homing Pigeons tolerate the vagaries of the more dedicated Careerists and Balancers and regard them with the same degree of mild amusement they would give to neighborhood youngsters who make the backyard into a play battlefield.

Older and younger Homing Pigeons care the most about their personal lives and the least about the women who precede or follow them in their jobs.

For these women, the office is a convenience store of sorts. It exists to fill their immediate needs. The quicker the better.

Jolie H., age 55, legal secretary, says: "This has been a good field. I came in after college and earned good money. On my own, I can do most of the forms that the lawyers need.

"I left for eight years to raise my kids and came back and fit right in. When my husband and I want to travel, we do. I quit for two years a while back, just to catch up on things and redecorate our home. It was a rewarding experience. Now, I'm back. I may go to part-time. I've always been able to get good jobs in law firms. They're glad to have a steady worker."

Linell B., age 21, also a legal secretary, says: "I'm learning on the job. I may go back to school and become a lawyer. I'm developing a taste for it. Or, maybe better still, I wouldn't mind marrying a lawyer. I'm meeting some nice ones here.

"I always had this dream about reading and relaxing in a bright home, painted yellow, with crisp curtains blowing in the breeze. I want a house with a kitty door in the kitchen for my two cats. I can see myself sipping coffee on a summer morning and watching the kittens go in and out. Soon, I hope, while I'm young enough to enjoy it."

It's difficult to count the Homing Pigeons. They fly fast. Some evolve into fighters in spite of themselves and find themselves as deeply engrossed in their careers as Careerists. Often they evolve into Balancers, keeping their personal goals at the forefront. Many remain Homing Pigeons in their heart of hearts.

Ambitions, desires, dreams—and the way women try to forge them into reality—give rationalizations to female soldiers at war.

That is how Hate Squadrons achieve their formations. Claudine B., age 36, personnel manager:

> The primary sources of conflict that I hear in women's complaints to me are between professionals and clerks. Whatever category either woman falls in, they fight all the time. I started in clerical and moved up, so I can identify with each.
>
> There's a lot of jealousy as to who deserves to be where and who should be doing what and when. Both groups monitor the activities of the other. It's not a clear-cut job description issue. It becomes more personal.

Working women know their enemies. Enemies are women fighting for goals similar to their own—but in ways deemed unacceptable. Among middle-class women of similar qualifications and backgrounds, hate is expressed when one is granted more privileges than the rest. A small issue serves to show how far apart seemingly compatible women can be on a daily basis.

Karen B., age 33, secretary: "In all confidence, the word hatred is right on. It burns my buns when a manager my age, with the same BA, flits out of here for a double lunch hour, and I have to punch a timeclock."

Melinda C., age 33, account manager:

> It's more than annoying. My secretary goes over my head, bats her eyes at my boss, and is granted the favor of leaving an hour early on Fridays to see her son play in Little League. So I have to type my own week's-end activity report. And answer my own phone. Which I did before I made it to management.
>
> Now I'm stuck doing clerical again. I'm being penalized for not having a son playing ball. It's been established that leaving early is okay, so it happens consistently. I'm sure she enjoys her afternoon more knowing I'm stuck with clerical. She galivants in her show of power. If I say anything, I'm a bitch.

Candy D., age 25, secretary: "The women in our group take everything personally. And so seriously. If I misplace a phone message, they act like they were expecting a call from God. If I ignore their command, for the moment, no matter how unimportant it is, I'm out to get them. Everything's a big issue."

Zennia M., age 36, training support manager: "Some managers have their own secretaries and hold on to every minute of their time for dear life. They don't easily share. There's a status thing in everything some women managers do. A power struggle."

Lena B., age 43, sales communication manager: "When women defy protocol, just for the sake of taking the easy way, they hurt us all. This isn't a family, it's a sales structure, designed to sell. It works better when boundaries are respected. Every function should be run like a business."

Conflict grows in all of these areas, as women attempt to define and obtain their piece of the pie on as many fronts as possible. Hate Squadrons are formed when business becomes visibly intertwined with life-styles. Consider them in another formation: rows of soldiers with a pair of unmatched bookends gracing each end. These bookends have little in common but gender. And mutual dislike, if not outright hatred. The irony is that they're so alike, but come to their sameness from different directions. Their motivation provides enough distance to make them totally incompatible.

One bookend is the Newcomer. She's open and eager to begin her adult life in the white-collar office. She's breaking loose from the value system of parents, particularly her mother's. Yet emotionally she is not straying too far from the protection and guidance of her home.

The other bookend is the Displaced Homemaker, who falls somewhere between a jaded woman and a realistic type who learned her lesson the hard way.

The Newcomer is a slim and graceful figure. Young, college educated, and self-assured, this woman talks a good game of Careerist.

But a hint of the Balancer creeps in when she speaks of longterm goals. Her mother didn't raise a fool. Many in this group also drift to Homing Pigeon roles. The Newcomer may live at home and soon decide to use her wages to pursue other interests—such as advanced schooling, a bit of travel, or marriage to a divorced man who has custody of the kids.

The figure of the Displaced Homemaker can often show signs of physical deterioration, bending slightly toward a bowed, defeatist position. Older, undertrained, and perhaps showing bitter traces of divorce or widowhood, this woman also talks a good game of Careerist. Her sense of identity may have suffered along with a loss of long-term alimony. She'd like to find a secure niche in the work world and show them all.

Her personal life is somewhat like the Balancer's. Participating in the lives of her grown children brightens her day. She has a lot of the stuff of the Homing Pigeon in her, and may take flight at the right opportunity. She holds out hope that someone may need her more than her job does.

In the middle are the Real Working Women. In unprecedented numbers, the most ferocious combatants have entered the scene to get what they came for. With the highest body count in the corporate world, these formidable fighters came for rewards. Educated, qualified, assured, and prepared, they assume success will be theirs.

Reared to expect fame and fortune, they stormed out of an affluent middle-class youth onto the work fields, ready to claim top level careers. Titles. Money. Glory.

These Real Working Women are a part of every major squadron. Some are single, some are homemakers, businesswomen, mothers, often everything-all-at-once.

Displaying the arrogance of the generation that had the leisure to find themselves, they are willing to do battle for the luxuries they believe are their due.

Real Working Women past the age of 35 are very serious. They're Careerists, Balancers, and Homing Pigeons—out for the kill.

What can get in the way of all these female soldiers in Hate-Squadron formation? Perhaps, only the supersquadron that takes them all on with no problem. Enter the superhuman bounty hunters. The Taking Class. They exist to make dogmeat of the others.

They are nervy; they grab what they want as though they owned the place. In full force, they are capable of immobilizing other women, men, and any other form of life. Their power is fearsome.

Who are these women? From what planet might they have fallen? The shocker is that everyone knows who they are. They live in our homes and offices. How is this possible? Every woman belongs to the Taking Class. Not all the time, but everyone at some time. It's a female state of being.

The Taking Class aspect functions within each of the three major groups. The Taking Class Careerist works long hours and makes personal sacrifices to get what she wants. Almost never will she return anything by being a mentor to other women, or hiring and promoting other women. The personal qualities that enable her to make it generally rule out any spirit of generosity. She distances herself from all other working women as much as humanly possible. Her witty comments in the company of men may well undercut and undermine other women. Sharp and true with verbal rapier, her motive is to keep other women at bay. Her weapons are drawn from the full female artillery and used against all women she hopes to confine to corporate reaches beneath her own.

The Taking Class Balancer works the hours and makes the sacrifices, but only to a point. She puts personal priorities first, and so jeopardizes the performance of coworkers who count on her output. Professional deadlines, and those who depend on them, are apt to fall by the wayside. Colleagues are at the mercy of whatever family duties take precedence—and most do. Home priorities are first. Her home. Her priorities.

She not only will dump a vital work project on the other members of her team in midstream, but will always manage to come out the martyr. Her abdication is geared toward unselfish attention to a relative's surgery, an insecure child's theater debut, a charity she must help along, a husband's needs.

She has a knack for bailing on an ill-fated work mission after she has piloted it toward failure. Turning over dead-end projects to others, she snatches more prestigious ones from subordinates.

If a female subordinate earns accolades, she will downgrade

the importance of the accomplishment or even the reward itself. She may magnanimously decide that the honor should be shared with the entire team.

When she disappears on Friday, she is sure to refer on Monday to toiling alone at the office all weekend. She moves in all directions to grab and redirect all perks to herself. Her good deeds are accomplished at the expense of others.

The Taking Class Homing Pigeon is the epitome of success at doing the bare minimum to survive the next layoff. She performs spurts of hard work in a crunch, usually in a grandstanding gesture in full view of the gallery. This is effective enough at the time to keep things quiet, but it makes more conscientious women feel like fools.

While merely putting in her time, the Taking Class Homing Pigeon often gets more credit than worker bees. Keeping abreast of the most interesting work, she can smilingly ignore the mundane. Although she has no staff to burden, her work often remains in sliding coffee-stained stacks until it disappers into the round file. Later, any hapless victim of her slipshod work must begin at square one to recover lost paperwork. Should this victim retaliate, she will pay for it. Having no say in management, the Taking Class Homing Pigeon allows herself to roam in and out of senior offices working on nonthreatening chores, like bringing in flowers from her garden. Tossing conversational asides as if they were innocent petals, she can exact her revenge. She can drop hints about lucky loos who leave early, and lucky loos who ignore the rules.

She hears of all job openings, office politics, and personal goings-on. She hears all, knows all, and spills all—when it will do her the most good. Feared by the wise, she may be disarming, but she knows what she wants.

All human beings with even a modicum of the survival instinct do their utmost to stay out of the range of the Taking Class. Few manage to escape being burned by them. The Taking Class also has a flip side. Members of the Taking Class can be transformed into the Giving Class after the corporate or home work day is over. After hours, the Taking Class is in the business of pursuing what is best for all women, but they often force their values on other women in the name of a greater good.

The transformation of "Takers" into "Givers" can best be understood in its application to an issue such as abortion. Most women have a clear-cut point of view: Some are for it, and some are willing to allow others to practice it. And there are those who are willing to fight about others' opinions of it. A discussion of abortion brings out the best and worst on both sides of the issue. Members of the Giving Class want to fight the good fight, but they are also willing to use Taking Class tactics to impose their judgments on other women. Those who are against abortion are ready to press their views on women who are not in a strong enough position to resist them. Of course, there are pro-choice advocates who are willing to use strong-arm tactics as well. Both exhibit little tolerance for the opposing view.

According to sociologist Kristen Luker, the factions are battling about issues larger than abortion. Their feelings on abortion are part of a larger world view, so for them to question their beliefs about abortion would be to challenge their values about the roles of motherhood, the sexes, or morality, of religion, and of human rights. These evoke passion.

Luker's research on the subject shows: In the 80s pro-life people spent as much as 40 hours a week on the issue. Pro-choice put in less than five hours. Her profile of each camp shows the differences in life-styles that influence their value systems.

Luker portrays the typical anti-abortionist: A 44-year-old woman married at age 17, with three or more children. She attended college, and now stays at home. She attends church at least once a week. She is most likely a Catholic. Her family income is less than $30,000 annually, earned by the husband in a small business or lower-level, white-collar job.

In the opposing corner is another married woman 44 years old. She married at 22 or older, and now has one or two children. She's a college grad, employed, and married to a professional man. Their combined family income is $50,000 or more annually. They are not regular churchgoers.

Giving Class women fight on many issues—the life of a fetus is only one of them. Women in Hate Squadrons have difficulty believing that others are caring or capable of balance in considering opposing points of view.

Their fight/flight choices define their life and challenge how they have chosen to spend the days of their lives. For women, the business of life is always first, and the business of business is a remote second. And women are ready, willing, and able to form Hate Squadrons and march to battle.

10

Women's War Games Defy Logic

As part of the Uncivil Business War, women play office war games against one another to keep their competitive skills sharp. These war games are played according to an exclusive set of personalized fight/flight rules that have little to do with corporate mandates— or men's office war games.

Although men and women may play at one another's games occasionally, and both often battle for businessworld prizes, there is a key difference in their intentions. Men fight to win more power and higher salaries; women fight for the option to quit the game and go home. They may not actually exercise that option, but having the choice is vital to their sense of well-being.

Not only do the results of business war games mean different things to men and women, but, even though they don't realize it, they're not even playing by the same rules. Their objectives are as different as the board game Monopoly is from the card game Old Maid.

In Monopoly, the winner ends up owning all or most of the real estate. It's the men's business world in microcosm. In Old Maid, players draw cards from one another to match pairs. The loser is stuck with the single card—and is the old maid. A simple game, it warns children who play it that a lonely spinsterhood awaits the unpaired. One is a war game of all-out competition for capitalistic gain; the other is an undemanding way to pass the time. Girls play Monopoly some of the time, but boys play Old Maid only when their mothers insist they entertain a little sister in bed with the measles.

Girls grow up to play office war games according to a feminized version of the Business Rules. Women's Rules are derived from Mother's Rules.

Mother's basic and easy-to-remember rules were:

Cater to the males in one's life and engage in personal infighting with rival females.

Hide competitive instincts behind a smile.

Reserve a fight/flight option as soon as possible.

Mother formulated two commandments to lead daughter to perfect happiness. "Thou shalt do only what's best for you at all times" and the vital "Thou shalt never let other girls get ahead of you."

Arriving in the white-collar world after the men were already in play, women started their own game. They had been taught that business was economic warfare and that one learned how to fight by first playing war games. They studied men's business games and learned men's Business Rules: how to buy and sell, how to develop skills and refine their knowledge of customers, commodities, and services.

Men base their relationships with one another on the team concept they had learned as youngsters in sports. Men who were part of the military learned about bureaucracies and hierarchies. But instead of taking this boring approach, women played another kind of war game. They found out what the guys were doing, but didn't get much beyond the jargon. For their real war games, they revert to the tried-and-true rules mother taught them. Playing by their own rules, they puzzle those who don't know the name of the game.

The most confused souls are females who play by male rules and win: They can be winners at Monopoly, but if they're losers at Old Maid, they're losers in the eyes of women. Most women accept mother's notion that their professional triumphs really constitute time wasted.

Psychotherapist Diana Adile Kirschner, codirector of the Institute for Comprehensive Family Therapy in Spring House, Pennsylvania, explained her single female clients. She was quoted in an interview in the *Los Angeles Times* (November 30, 1986):

> They are highly motivated, coming for treatment from as far as Boston and New York. These are women who have master's degrees and PhDs. They are lawyers, they are women who are into management-level stuff in corporations, and they are doing quite well. At this point in their lives, they could care less about career. They don't want to hear about advancing.
>
> Many have opted for a career, then turn around and find themselves devoid of eligible men . . . We are returning to a traditional value system . . .

Men's Business Rules, explained clearly in the policies and procedures manual and MBA marketing texts, are easily understood, adapted, or ignored. But men have unspoken rules also, the who-you-know insider stuff that makes for vicious front-line games played by teams with savvy players. Women seldom, if ever, get even a whiff of such action. When they want to play the man's game, they try to do it by the official Men's Business Rule book. Which is but half of it.

Men's Rules seem to allow women the chance to move comfortably along the path to their next promotion. They don't always win, but neither do all the midlevel men who play this game.

For example, Monday morning's casual chat with the boss about the weekend can set men and women worlds apart. If women talk of baby-teething keeping them awake and men talk about sports, it is unlikely to create a bond between a working woman and her male boss. Talk of late nights at the office gives the impression that she might prefer to be sleeping in. It sounds like a poor-me complaint. It's not an enjoyable topic the boss would like to hear more about in the near—or distant—future. Male conversation offers a give and take that is pleasurable to both speakers.

Women either are not aware of the unspoken rules of the business war games or choose to ignore them. Working women naturally need some kind of performance rules. With few respected role models to provide clues, they regress to the only effective discipline they remember. Mother's Rules, neglected during periods of rebellion, are revived. Women of every age know them. The only difference between younger and older women is how far back in the mind's closet they have to dig to resurrect them.

Today's middle-class women do acknowledge the necessity of warfare, and many feel they have little choice but to attack all women who stand between them and their goals.

Men and women extend themselves for different reasons. Napoleon Bonaparte credited his success to discovering that men would fight and die for scraps of cloth and ribbon.

Women scoff at that notion. More practical by far, women fight only for home, hearth, and personal posessions. Possibly they would defend their families if, as one woman put it, ". . . the enemy was at the corner house and my husband wasn't due home for an hour."

This is proper form in keeping with mother's rule that you shouldn't do anything for yourself that you can get someone else to do for you. Women fight when they must. And for the things they believe in.

Women's Rules govern female games. Defying all logic, female business procedures are adult versions of permissive Mother's Rules. On-the-job guidelines come together from a potpourri of Mother's Rules. When the educated, middle-class woman enters the business office, the rules of home and family meld into her version of the rules of business. These are her weapons as she charges into the fray. The ensuing war games are not pretty.

Fears and insecurities prevent many women from accepting traditional corporate challenges. At each business success, women stop to assess the impact on their "real" lives. One danger for some mid-management women is to swim too fast and too well. Those who have inadvertently succeeded in using their business talents to race ahead must deal with the fact that they have left many potential life partners far behind.

According to Mother's Rules, this business win could certainly score as a loss. It can tilt the game toward spinsterhood or divorce—and an existence of self-support and social isolation. When women reach this shoal, many abruptly turn tail and swim furiously downstream. Upwardly mobile men are amazed at the sight of women scurrying away. To them, women's office games are imcomprehensible. The few women who decide to continue swimming against the female tide must buck a highly arcane male power structure.

Many working women make a great deal of noise about going as far as they can up the corporate ladder. Their posture gives the appearance that all women are of like minds. It makes it impossible for senior management to know which women intend to attain the highest levels of business success and which women will break loose to head in another direction.

Puzzled male bosses, and some confused women, are primed for one kind of warfare, and experience another. Ordinary business war is transformed by Mother's Rules.

Women enter war games with a fairly flexible set of rules. These rules allow women to move in and out of the work force at will. Business Rules have nothing to do with it.

Women happily "shower" one another when they leave the office for weddings, babies, and any and all reasons. Women do not associate these leave takings with the fact that they're not being promoted to levels which demand continuity and dedication.

Leaving to prepare for a wedding with a working man—how odd the phrase sounds—with whom a woman has been living for five years is viewed as a normal career decision by her female co-workers. Stretching a maternity leave to several years or infinity despite the fact that the position has been held for them is met with no dismay by other women. They understand all this. These are victories in war games according to Women's Rules.

This fact supports the idea that women, on some level, consider that exercising the fight/flight option is supportable under Women's Rules. This notion doesn't appear in the general business rules nor is it known to men. If men left for the reasons women leave, they would depart more quietly. Very few men would comfortably indulge in celebratory leave taking. Men would not be feted for leaving. For men, it would be more like being benched.

Men consider paying obeisance to the corporate attitude to be a Business Rule. Women evidently discount it as of little or no importance. Giving the appearance of being businesslike during the time workers are in the office didn't even make the "give a shower for every occasion" rule book.

Unwritten and largely unacknowledged, Women's Rules include the acceptance of friendly rivalry and infighting among females over popularity, position, and privilege. These are a major aspect of Mother's Rules.

Women's Rules constantly evaluate who looks better as a measure of personal worth. "What works" is a statement about wardrobe, not corporate strategy. Women's Rules allow for fierce competition on this point.

Female soldiers fight to maintain their individual positions, rather than joining together to support mutual goals. The motto is, Every woman for herself.

One problem with Mother's Rules is that what works at home may fail in the office. For many women, the office is an elaborate stage for "real life."

The backdrop of midlevel management spotlights the working woman's special qualities, not as a functioning member of the office structure, but in a starring role. The idea here is to discourage any and all female competitors who might think themselves equal to invading the territory of the star.

Even though women often ignore the business rules they already know, they like to learn as much as possible about them. They want to understand the rules of Monopoly because they want to win any prizes they can. Trade secrets and assorted shortcuts are what they seek. They've already heard about hard work. It has nothing to with the game of Old Maid they are playing.

Professional classes and women-only seminars are a favorite refuge of the unemployed or underemployed female with hours to fill as she considers entry into or movement within the wild and wonderful world of work. She feels comfortable in the mall halfway station. This is a fight/flight approach in familiar territory.

Maud B., age 43, sales support manager, says, "I really enjoyed these during my 'housewife' era. It's kind of funny now, to see ads with programs almost as silly as *Managers R-Us*, makeovers, and the whole bit. Now I don't have time to even think about going to those. [She laughs.] Well, maybe. If I see one that's *Vice Presidents R-Us.* It's worth a try!''

The annual Conference on Women had it beginnings in the early 1980s in Anaheim, California. It began as an outgrowth of a statewide Business Development Conference begun in 1979 by California State Senator William Campbell—and was geared toward men and women in small businesses. Later, Campbell decided that since so many women attended, he'd hold a separate conference for them. (Few note the unstated acronym COW.) The conference has done a phenomenal business. In 1986 it offered the motivation and inspiration of 150 speakers to a crowd of more than 10,000. COW is also sponsored by Chrysler Corporation and the Small Business Administration. It is billed as ''comprehensive,'' combining political, business, and personal approaches.

In 1983, a group of feminists picketed the event, angry about Campbell's voting record on women's issues (which he defends as ''good'') and the seminar's agenda. An advisory board of 100 women, including a representative of the National Organization for Women, helped plan the conference. Some feminists evidently felt that the agenda was sound, while others felt it was sexist.

Attendees apparently enjoyed the eclectic subject matter, which featured a wide range of topics: political appointments, cosmetic surgery, physical fitness, religious ministries, comparable worth, infertility, car leasing, psychological help, and career counseling in real estate. Booths sold jewelry and lingerie. Women's Rules of what constituted a sound professional approach were evidently in play.

For a sponsor-subsidized $30 fee, there seemed to be something for everyone. About 20 women attended a debate about abortion. More than 80 percent found something more to their liking. They attended a meeting, held at the same time, with the talk show radio psychologist Irene Kassorla.

Kassorla explained that women are ''mostly interested in family and love.'' Women who seek her advice do so to relieve their ''terror of rejection and humiliation.''

A key Woman's Rule is to avoid what you fear most at all costs. Consequently, Women's Rules naturally affect career plan-

ning and inevitably come into play in office war games. Reaching
for the top of the corporate ladder involves risks and the possibility
of a humiliating failure.

Senator Campbell attributes his conference's success to the
fact that "we offer a good range" to the "ladies."

Other, more professional workshop conferences geared to
qualified, select audiences also serve to help women blend Wom-
en's Rules with Business Rules. Such conferences are often affili-
ated with local business management groups and universities.

A full-day lecture and discussion was held at a Conference for
Women premeeting sponsored by the Coastline Community College in California. Entitled "Women Managers in Male Environments: Trying Harder May Not Be Enough," it dealt with issues
affecting women who have been in the work force for a while and
who have achieved a certain level of business success.

Judith B. Rosener, assistant dean of the University of Califor-
nia-Irvine Graduate School of Management, seminar leader, explored whether the influence of women makes any difference in an
organization. She investigated the position of women who participate in management teams and outlined theories to explain why
women have such difficulty moving from middle to upper management. She suggested three possibilities:

The first, a psychological theory: Women tend to be more
emotional than men. A second theory was sociological: The
problem is cultural values and norms. "We socialize our children
. . . to be professional is to be a man." The third theory is struc-
tural: Men are at the top of the pyramid because that is the
natural order.

Says Rosener, "Women who make it to the top tend to be not
very attractive, which again says . . . that men are more comfortable [working] with women who don't arouse the sexual instinct.
. . . the three theories are not mutually exclusive. Women, who
are earning more MBAs today than ever, still have trouble climbing higher than the middle rungs on organizational ladders."

Many women prefer not to know the "good news" that unattractive and less sexy women are more in evidence at the top.

According to Women's Rules, being unattractive enough to
secure a senior management chair is not a victory in women's war

game. The only consolation is that women who don't make it are just "too pretty," which beats every other reason.

Other universities are also researching the lack of progress by female middle managers. Barry Leskin, department chairman, management and organization, University of Southern California, School of Business Administration, identifies problem areas. He says, "Although 90 percent of women of working age will be in paid jobs by the year 2,000, I just don't see that many women in key operating positions who are going to move to the top in Fortune 500 companies . . . women will never get into power positions from staff and middle management jobs where they are now clustered . . ." But in keeping with Women's Rules, these jobs offer more fight/flight options. That spells success for many women.

Leskin notes that "women are much harder on other women [than men are] . . . they have a tendency to set high standards . . . and don't want to be seen as being easy on other women." The corporate game played according to Women's Rules requires a personal competitiveness not expected in men's Business Rules.

Leskin explains another fact of business life that affects female aspirations: "With an increasingly global economy and deregulation at home, big business is looking for ways to cut costs and stay competitive. This causes them to be less willing to train and develop minorities and women."

Like minorities, women are also at a disadvantage in foreign countries, where other cultural norms rule. Countries in which women are regarded as unequal to men interfere with progress in American business.

According to foreign Business Rules (female managers are even less prevalent abroad than in this country), the female work force should not openly aspire to outflank males. Men rule, and as there is more formal concession to the status quo, that also means there is less reason for Women vs. Women.

The Japanese influence had reinforced the idea that women, who generally have less corporate power than men, are inferior. The result is that women enjoy less respect and are often not sent to conduct business in countries where their attendance would be considered an insult to the senior management staff.

The popular Theory Z (a concept that advocates a team approach to work tasks) and other Japanese management techniques have posed problems for women. In general (although of course there are exceptions), the Japanese culture does not encourage women to be part of management teams in other than support functions. In Japan, the role of women in business follows the traditional values of their culture. When Theory Z is applied in corporate America, women generally take a back seat.

Women's Rules admonish females to refrain from actions that may be judged pushy or aggressive. This makes it more difficult for them to counteract unwritten signs that "Women Need Not Apply."

Despite improvement in American women's rights, there is a minority within this country's management work force that suffers the problems of women's rights—and has a few added issues to deal with. Consider the situation of black women. For most American black women, racial discrimination adds another dimension to the problem of women fighting women. Perceived as strong women on the home front, blacks must stretch their own personal Women's Rules to accommodate work war games. Though they have the same fight/flight aspirations as other working women, they are even less likely to meet their economic aspirations.

Black women who have made it to midlevel have more individual staying power in the work force, because they know they must remain focused on creating their own security. Black women may be a step ahead of white women in realizing that their best chance of financial security is likely to be the result of their own efforts.

Black women are a minority within a group treated like a minority. Successful black women disagree about which prejudice takes precedence. A profile of black women highlights special factors in their fight/flight responsibilities. Two-thirds of black women age 15 and older are single, divorced, widowed, or separated, according the 1980 U.S. Census. A large number of these are single parents.

Shirley Chisholm, first black congresswoman (from New York) and now a professor at Mt. Holyoke College in Massachusetts, said (in a *Los Angeles Times* interview, April 15, 1986): "I view myself first as a black, then as a woman." She once found it difficult to interact with white males. She now says she has "a gentle critique of feminism" for being doctrinaire and not "lifting others as they climb."

Joyce Owens-Smith, one of the few women in the executive ranks of the 90 percent male-dominated National Urban League, says black men often do not treat her as an equal, treating her instead much as she had been when she was in a white male-dominated environment. "What I was experiencing had nothing to do with color; it was because I was female," she reported in a panel discussion at the University of California in Irvine.

Dorcas Eaves-Hill, an attending surgeon at the University of California (Irvine) Medical Center, says, "Women refuse to refer to women; they will refer to a man before they will go to a woman, even when women are as qualified, if not more so, than the men . . ." Rita Walters, president of the Los Angeles Board of Education, says, "Black women are still the most marginal group in the work force."

Small wonder that women of every race still have problems adapting subconscious Women's Rules into workable Business Rules.

Women making personal plans consistently break and bend Business Rule mandates. Careerists, Balancers, and Homing Pigeons use basic combinations of Mother's Rules as a constant measure for their priorities at work and at home.

Women generally follow their own private stars and inevitably find themselves in direct conflict with other women playing their own solitary war games. If the enemy had once been the man who kept her from career glory by acts of discrimination, a more mellow attitude now prevails. The professional woman who makes it to middle management has a good understanding of the workings of the forces of the universe. She has a healthy admiration for the male contingent who act out the right stuff of war games. This narrows the enemy list to women only. Women's Rules permit open guerrilla warfare with no Marquess of Queensbury to chart rules for winning the silent, deadly struggle.

Had women attended the Geneva Convention, they might have come away with some succinct articles of war to guide them. Since there are no formal rules in the Uncivil Business War, the battle rages uncontained.

Thou shalt not commandments were not handed out along with the key to the executive washroom. Men's Rules are respected without being understood; Women's Rules don't know business right from wrong.

Today women are adrift, cut off from paths leading to promotion. Those with booster attitudes coax others to struggle onward. Women are told they're in good position for the future. They're being misled by gurus urging them to outqualify their males bosses who will then promote them. This follows no logic or precedent.

Young women aged 23–28 have studied Business Rules that should help them elevate themselves to the top echelon of their profession. Single, educated, and cherished, they talk a good career game. Almost to a woman, however, they build in their own set of flight options. Women's Rules, still.

Older women aged 50–65 have achieved a fight/flight balance adapted to their individual work positions. They want and need their paychecks, and will fight hard enough to hang on. Flight is flexible, since they enjoy the social and supportive aspects of their lower-level boundaries. Women's Rules.

In the swollen center is the largest group, born between 1946 and 1960. At entry level nearly a quarter-century ago, they now swim in a stagnant pool.

Most women working today are part of this contingent. They are busy learning which rules will bend, and which can be broken without hurtling them down in the direction of the drowning pool of poverty.

Women's Rules in war games defy all sense of logic. No one admits they're playing. No one admits they've won or lost. No one is sure when they've scored. No one admits to declaring the action. So, there's no one to say knock it off.

11

Office Combat Uniforms Bare Female Flanks

Business dress is the uniform of the Uncivil Business War: It enables a woman to know her enemies, and it lets them know her.

Women bare their fight/flight intentions through their choice of clothes for office wear. The outfits women select announce their long-term plans in the business world. Fashion offers a variety of wardrobe choices. Each choice telegraphs civilian rank as clearly as uniforms distinguish officers in the military. Clothing is the most visual flashpoint in Women vs. Women.

Rather than accept business clothing as a nondescript equalizer, many women explain away their unwillingness to abandon the dress-up fun of work. Those who take the high road proclaim, "I'm making a statement of independence from a male-dominated tyranny." Those on the low road say, "Who wants to let men think we want to look as dull as they do?" Both belabor the point. The office is not the place for executives to indulge in fashion posturing. Clothes shouldn't distract from the business of business.

By her clothes shall ye know her. It's not that every woman

who comes to work in jeans has a kinship with other women who dress informally. But their thinking that this is proper attire means they share more with each other than with the woman in a three-piece gray suit. It's unlikely that Ms. Jeans and Ms. Suit will form a close business bond.

Combat uniforms are a surefire way for women to identify their enemies. It's:

Low-cut necklines vs. high collars.
Miniskirts vs. long skirts.
Filmy synthetics vs. natural fabrics.
Casual dresses vs. austere suits.
Toeless sling pumps vs. flats.

Women on both sides are dressed to kill. Clothes communicate whether a women is in business to shoot for the top, or to settle for less because she prefers a more diverse life-style.

Only the most serious contenders will adopt a female version of the male work uniform. Executive men seldom give in to the lure of the casual. They like to appear above it all even on Halloween, St. Patrick's Day, and the day before Christmas. A splash of color on a tie is about as far as male stalwarts go. If they fail to "dress for success," they've simply failed.

The woman "dressed for success" understands this. She is in suit for the fight. Her dressed-for-attention colleague in the frilly outfit might understand the concept of propriety, but she couldn't care less. Her attire reveals that she is open to all of life's options, including flight from the workplace.

Even maternity wear offers across-the-board options. Two pregnant women conversing in the elevator compared notes. One was in a dark business suit, longer jacket, and a soft-collared bowed blouse. She said with a laugh, "I told my employees they could only ask pregnancy questions on Friday at our four o'clock meeting. If they forget, I just smile, ignore it, and go back to a business issue."

The other woman, in a bright silk maternity dress festooned with floating balloons sighed. "I'm not that lucky," she said.

"Even people I hardly know at work come up and ask if they can feel my tummy. I usually say okay, but I hate it."

Work wear neatly separates the women from the girls. It allows a woman's colleagues to easily recognize her intentions, whether or not they are aware that they are making this judgment. A woman's choice of clothes exposes her to her enemies. Business attire provides a perfect target.

Women label themselves in ways that employers cannot—by force of law. They literally wear their intentions on their sleeves. Working women use clothes to show who they are and where they plan to be—next week and in five years. Clothes make the woman, too.

There is nothing in a girl's upbringing that teaches her to blend into the sartorially boring woodwork. She has been reared to never take leave of making the best of her looks. The drab working woman goes against the grain.

Female combatants who've drilled for years to look better than the other girls fight hard to meet fashion expectations, and clothing is another of their weapons. The power business suit could have been welcomed as a tool to present women as a serious and unified force, to announce: We are competent; judge us only by our skills. We don't mind putting our femininity on the back burner, even though some may mock us by saying that we are emulating men.

But the business suit is boring for many. As one female executive put it, "It's so much more fun to dress up. It puts sparkle in my day." Current workplace fashion trends promote individualism and call attention to appearance and personality instead of capability. Uniformed for combat, working women are putting their priorities where their hearts are.

Careerists in for the long corporate haul most often follow the unisex rule of dressing for their hoped-for next position. Of all working women, they are the most realistic about the role of clothing in promoting upward mobility. With the jaw-clenching firmness it takes for women to ignore fashion fads and dictates, this group's determination marks them as contenders. Women who face each day in bland suits that blend into the corporate scenery are fighters. Women in camouflage are serious about their careers. Even these women sometimes balk at facing another Friday in a suit, when all around them are in more casual attire. Occasionally, they pass up protocol and decide to be one of the girls for the day, showing up in silk jumpsuits or tailored cashmere sweaters and designer slacks. They go the girls even one better.

If Careerists do this even once, other women compliment their taste. They are happy to encourage any sign of flight tendencies. Sending out mixed signals makes the Careerists one of the sisterhood.

And they are often complimented by male coworkers, who consciously or unconsciously desire to neutralize female professional competition by encouraging even the most successful woman to express her femininity and have men find her physically attractive. Like the one bite of the forbidden apple, the fruit of positive peer strokes is tough to resist.

Balancers are the group who most often show their colors. Women who work some years and take off at other times dress accordingly.

They have a look for every occasion. They may wear regulation business suits for a meeting with upper-level bigwigs. On a day when plans are desk work and lunch with homemaker friends the Balancer greets the morning in an elegant silk dress with co-ordinated color accessories and high heels. When summer breezes dictate, she'll wear cool pastel jacket outfits. An occasional Friday or a weekend stint may bring out a fashion statement of fitted, designer pantsuits that look preppy. It all says "look here." Always in good taste, the Balancer is generally not bored or boring. She's intelligent, educated, and motivated to have it all.

However, upper-level male management may ultimately feel uncomfortable with this type—perhaps simply because she forces them to recognize her personal life and the priorities it has over business concerns.

Moreover, she stars in different roles daily: "Ms. Corporate" one day, "Mom" the next, "Mrs. Socialite" another. Because of this chameleonlike behavior, the Balancer may level off midway up the promotion scale. Often that is fine with her. This woman will continue to enter and leave the work force throughout her career, and she will always be properly dressed for the occasion.

The largest numbers of women are at midlevel, not being fired and not being promoted. They are Balancers in a holding pattern. They are the fashionably garbed workers of nearly middle age. Many are subsidized wage earners who can opt out of their careers. They can afford to present themselves their way.

Reserving the right to express themselves (a holdover notion from their formative years in the 60s and 70s), these women haven't decided to follow the leaders unless the rules make sense in balancing work and home on a daily basis. They flaunt their ambivalence by putting their paycheck where their eyes are—on the season's new look.

The feathery Homing Pigeons are, most often, the eternal girls. They are perpetually poised to flee the work world at any moment, and they are dressed for it. At work, they clothe themselves for a more comfortable world.

On a good day, these girls are dressed for attention, in colors and fabrics that flatter and catch the eye of the beholder. On days when their personal lives aren't going well, the disheveled look begs for mercy or warns off demands for work.

The lower level of clerical and support workers often wear business clothes that say "if I win the lottery or get married, I'm out of here." Some look that way because they think that way; others are in that position because they look that way.

In terms of their work wardrobe, these women might as well have been banned from the businesswear department of their favorite stores. Casual pants and tops, skirts and fashion blouses, bright-colored dresses in trendy styles, patterned hose and high heels, bare legs in open-toed sandals—and the obligatory white cardigan sweater to warm sleeveless arms in the corporate chill, temperate for three-piece suits—are indicative of the imminent deserter.

Women hunting mates in the corporate jungle spend a large portion of their paychecks on clothes. What they can't afford all at once, they pay off on time plans. The Homing Pigeon does anything she can to make her plumage do the job and show her off to advantage. Her clothing budget is expected to propel her into a fairy-tale dream world—onto a jet down to Acapulco. Or any honeymoon land.

Clothes accentuate the Homing Pigeons' strengths; their work futures are vague. They aim to prove that you can go home again. Some women fight them as rivals and others hate them for lowering the level of female credibility.

For the past decade, women have been well informed about the purported advantages of power dressing. When the dark skirts and jackets in conservative fabrics and cuts first appeared on the scene, they enjoyed a surge of popularity. Eventually, though, these styles were judged outdated and summarily abandoned by many working women.

The business power look for women was first formally advocated in John Molloy's *The Woman's Dress for Success Book*. He told women they needed a "power look."

"Power" was the intoxicating promise and the "look" would fulfill the image of a top executive. Conservative, it would reassure those at the top that women fit in.

Molloy, a New York business consultant, used standard marketing techniques to prove his premise. He says, "It worked. Most businesswomen—lawyers, accountants, editors, bankers, product managers—accept the fact that on important business occasions when they want to be authoritative and effective, the thing to wear is a conservative skirted suit in navy or gray."

Molloy explained that many women adopted his look, complete with subtle shirt colors and plain accessories. Scorning the cutesy poo looks advocated by the fashion industry, he says that his advice still holds.

The problem, he offers, ". . . is that [women] wear conservative clothing for ten promotions, then deny that they were tough as nails to get there, and start dressing like Madame Bovary. They fluff out."

For whatever reasons, women at midlevel hardly mirror the appearance of the male population in the corporate hierarchy.

There probably isn't an employer in the nation who would dare order women to dress in costumes that identify their rank, salary, and career intentions at a glance. Yet, conversations with women in the business world reveal the politics of wardrobe:

Lydia D., age 38, director, national marketing, laughs: "I tried the power suit and it was expensive to buy good quality and then keep wearing just three or four outfits. Even varied with different shirts and scarves, it just got monotonous.

"And the women I worked with teased me for looking like a short, skinny man. Then that's all I saw when I looked in the mirror in the morning. Somehow it seemed wrong."

Ellen B., age 32, advertising account executive, agrees: "When I power-dressed, men didn't compliment me at all. I wasn't used to dressing to be ignored. Looking back, maybe our male peers didn't care for us to look their equal.

"Maybe complimenting us on our prints and bright colors was a way men kept us in feminine roles. In our place. Eventually, I was the only woman in a suit every day. So I quit wearing one, too. Except for some major client presentations."

Hillary M., age 36, sales manager, muses: "The shoes that went with the suit, comfortable low heels, were so great. If only all women would have gone along with them. If only . . .

"But men's heads always turned at the gal in spiked heels, and I got tired of all the attention being paid to women with legs no better shaped than mine. I'd rather be miserable and totter around if the other gals do. I hope low heels come back."

Women dress to impress other women. With the discretionary funds they appear to be able to devote to a wardrobe. With their good taste and status. With the number and quality of men they can attract.

Valerie C., age 30, creative director, says: "I always thought gals dressed to please guys. But if we *all* wore blue suits and flat shoes, men would still date and marry us—and father our children. So, I guess we dress to please ourselves. And one way to do that is making other women turn green-eyed when they see us coming!"

Any look that equalizes is out. Women don't care to look equal; they care to look better. The huge fashion industry has a vested interest in enticing women to flaunt their personal best by wearing the newest. Fashion fosters rivalry.

As if women's business suits didn't have this to contend with, their good quality also provides a drawback. Those of good fabric, although costly, take years to wear out. Women do not need to shop until their suits need to be replaced. This is a serious flaw.

The problem is that many women regard shopping as a relaxing hobby. Indeed, shopping is a major American pastime.

Only the leisure-wear industry smiles when women confine their watch-me attire to after work. The plain business suit offends female shoppers and retailers alike.

Women stuck at midlevel positions devote much time and study to selecting their work wardrobe. It relieves job frustration and provides opportunities for conversation with other women in the office. *Whereja get it? You look fabulous. That style would look great on me.* Much of this peer chitchat leads to more attention-getting styles and fads that defy good sense in office wear.

Recently, major designers gave the middle-class American woman enough trendy fashion mandates to keep them competing for years. They urge:

> Turn the clock around, wear your nine-to-five clothes after
> five, your evening clothes for day. Diamonds for breakfast.
> Turtlenecks for dinner. Velvet and satin for the office.
> It's the last-minute way to tell fashion time . . .
> The gray flannel suit was given a decent funeral and every-
> body is glad.

Hair is also "creative." A top hairstylist explains: "New power cut? For men, it's medium short and effortless to maintain. For women, the idea is long and wild. Half permed, half unpermed and kind of crazy looking."

A hosiery designer: "Add a touch of romance to your every-day routing with new lace and textured hosiery to dress up your daytime wardrobe.

The *Wall Street Journal* reported: ". . . low-cut trend in women's shoes is exposing toes to new scrutiny. The shoe industry calls the cracks between toes 'cleavage.' "

Comments Doris D., age 39, financial analyst, "It's laughable, but we should cry. No wonder older men at the top feel uncomfortable—like they say they can't concentrate on making major decisions with women on board. Can you imagine how a woman trying even a small portion of that stuff would look around a boardroom table? And I've seen some of it. Why do we do this to ourselves?''

Men have no problems ignoring the fashion industry. Regardless of how often the fashion industry tries to suck males into new fashion cycles, work attire remains relatively stable. A fraction of an inch off a lapel, cuff, or tie is about as wild as it gets. Most men shop when they need to add an item to their business wardrobe, buy good quality in good quantity, and leave. Rarely will men seriously consider how colleagues will react to the buy. It's the boss who must be impressed. Middle-class, midlevel men wear well-tailored suits, shirts to blend, serious ties, dark socks, and black or brown shoes that fit well. Quiet accessories are added to suit the occasion.

The men above them are comfortable with that appearance; the men below them are also comfortable with the look. Men's work uniforms solve all problems of rank, offering subtle distinctions of upward mobility by fabric and fit, as they can afford it. Their clothes don't create jealousy or attract undue attention.

Confesses Alicia B., age 37, fashion consultant:

> I admire men for not wearing the old polyester leisure suit in the back of their closet to work on a rainy day. I'm glad they don't come to work in adaptations of unrestricted Miami Vice-type jackets and t-shirts. I'd hate to see short-sleeved shirts and bare wrists under summer suit jackets because it's hot out.
>
> I'm certain I'll never caution a male about wearing thongs to work on the muggiest of days, or shiny fashion boots on the coldest. But women are different in the work-clothes department. And the difference makes the cash register ring, so I'm not the one to put the knock on it.

Clothes provide ammunition to women on the prowl for one another's weaknesses. As they debate the merits of what's in and what's out, they also decide who's in and who's out.

Office wear—and its psychological impact—crosses all age boundaries. Most new contenders begin with a basic business wardrobe, although there are those who hold on, at least some of

the time, to the affordable and comfortable college clothes. Older
women who reenter the work world may empty their piggy banks
to go corporate with the mark of the fashion consultant embla-
zoned on sports jackets. A like number may decide to make do
with all the sinister polyester.

Strict three-piece-suit Careerists consider the frivolity of the
other groups a detriment to the gender. Melanie B., age 35, bank
branch manager, says, "I think women who refuse to trouble
themselves to dress 'right' on the job hurt all of us. Some banks
have gone to required uniforms for all employees—skirt, shirt, and
blazer for women and the same with slacks for men—because wom-
en were coming in such outlandish getups that it would make our
customers wonder if we had our heads on straight."

Female clerical workers—many of whom make up the ranks
of the Homing Pigeons—are more comfortable with Balancers, who
lean toward expensive dress. Unfortunately, although the Pigeons
always admire the Balancers' stylish outfits, they ignore the seriousness of their work demands. (Their friendly "between-us-girls"
attitude also derails the business concerns of the three-piece suits.
The battle rages.)

Secretaries unable to distinguish between Careerists and Balancers—between the serious and the semiserious—place less importance on the work demands of all female bosses.

Homing Pigeons seldom bother to differentiate among the
plumage and rank of the office flocks. To them, every woman is
one of the girls. They imagine that they're merely playing a different game of make-believe for the moment.

The fashion industry continues to tug at working women.
Clothing manufacturers, designers, and retailers encourage Balancers to reward their success by returning to femininity. This is as
counterproductive as rewarding successful dieters with sugar treats.

Although not every woman dressed like a brown sparrow will
make it to senior management, corporate women who do rise will,
most likely, not be sporting dangling deco earrings and rhinestone
Maltese crosses.

Current research confirms that the Fortune 1,000 corporate
hierarchies, generally composed of males between the ages of 50–
60, feel "uncomfortable with women at the round table." Women

may be inadvertently contributing to male discomfort by demanding visual recognition at every performance.

Men who are attracted to attention-provoking women generally don't have business on their minds. It may be a natural response, but many male executives do not welcome the distraction at work.

Statistically, women who have garnered top corporate positions are more plain than perky. This also helps men explain the woman's rise to the inner circle. Looks were not responsible.

Is the woman in a bright silk dress being provocative when she seats herself at a meeting and crosses her patterned-hosiery legs tipped in narrow high heels? Is she responsible for the attention directed to her as this gesture inadvertently flashes a bit of thigh at her audience? Are mixed signals a part of her career bag?

Is she behaving like a professional working woman? If so, is it likely that her female coworkers will respond with catty remarks? And are these female coworkers going to be drawn to support her career goals? Is her body language guaranteed to turn women off and entice men—probably to something besides a job promotion?

"Tight and slinky" fashions are touted to business women. One designer advertised a collection as "shaped for rape." Do most women—be they Careerists, Balancers, or even Homing Pigeons—really intend to bare their bodies along with their souls? Why do so many women feel the compulsion to provide visual treats along with their business expertise? Many women do not admit to using clothing to make a social statement. What helps a woman decide what to wear? Weather? Fashion? Pocketbook? Taste? Custom? Purpose?

Even those women who aren't that interested in clothes often admit that self-worth can be intertwined with a stiletto pair of high heels. (Women who wear low-heel shoes to work often change as soon as they arrive.)

The issue of clothes at work undoubtedly fuels many women's battles with one another. The military usage of the word *flank* provides some helpful insight. As a verb, it means to pass around, or attack, the side of an enemy unit. As a noun, it means one's side.

In today's world of mass merchandising, franchised store chains, and identical malls, females have access to clothes priced in a wide range in every possible style. This makes dress choices an issue of judgment and self-image. In earlier times, addresses and wardrobes were status labels. Today, the clothes of midlevel women at work also define their attitude and battle positions.

If women aren't dressed for business success, they are dressed to portray their own version of personal achievement. It's like a costume party invitation that says, "Come as the person you'd most like to be." Some will respond by dressing like housewives or born-again hippies. Few will risk ridicule by coming as the first female chairman of the board.

Dress states a woman's position on the management team. Is she there to pursue her company's goals and rise along with the profit statement? Or is she using office hallways as a fashion-show runway for an outbound flight?

Clothes telegraph the positions of combatants more obviously than the chess-like pieces of any war game. Most women signal that they're light years away from equality with men on the corporate battlefield. By their choice of business clothing they regress to the days when men went off to do battle in regional garb, and wore everything from flowing desert robes to heavy metal suits of armor. Eventually, most learned the hard way that great-looking outfits were often just not conducive to getting the job done.

PART THREE

Word from the Battlefront

War is harshest for soldiers in the trenches. Traditionally, women have borne the pains of war far from the heat of the front lines. However, in Women vs. Women, they are the foot soldiers face-to-face with the enemy. It's all the more painful when the enemy is recognizable—other women who have hopes and dreams similar to their own.

Women have tried to ignore this war, usually in the name of friendship. Best friends or no, the Uncivil Business War threatens to rage out of control and is resulting in more and more fatalities.

Part Three includes discussions among females in the trenches. They tackle issues that all women are aware (at least to some extent) exist in their lives. Those rare exceptions who have never suffered in this war may read and rejoice that they have escaped. The walking wounded can use this opportunity to take stock of their lives and consider their seesawing involvement in the war, in which they may have played both good guy and bad guy roles.

The point of these shared experiences is to clean the wounds and allow the bruises to heal. Early in the history of medicine, doctors were divided into two camps: homeopaths and allopaths. The former advocated more of the same (the sweat-it-out school of breaking a fever) to help nature with her work. The latter believed in halting the symptoms (cool cloths to bring down a fever) while hoping to cure the illness. Modern medicine combines both theories, and both will serve to help here.

In this section we hear the composite stories of many women as they tell their wartime experiences in their own words. They tackle major issues—work, politics, motherhood, sex, stress—and focus attention on the global ramifications of women at war. Voices from many areas of the United States merge into a chorus. Women discuss survival tactics in a rough business environment. They address a key issue: When women act in ways detrimental to all women, they also thwart their own personal ambitions.

The Uncivil Business War isn't likely to fade and die on its own. Undeclared wars are the worst, because they sneak up on an unaware populace. After this book, this war is no longer a secret. So ignorance is no longer an excuse.

The chapters in this section deal with large matters and everyday concerns, but they are crucial concerns. Women at war cannot be ignored. The issue filters directly into every working person's daily life and strongly influences the long-term quality of life. In this section, women share their own approaches to finance. Sometimes it's like the game of "Truth" once popular at girls' slumber parties. No one really wanted to hear negative comments about herself, but that was the only way to get in the game.

In Truth, players sat in a circle and offered each other "constructive" criticism. Fear and anger blended with relief at hearing it wasn't worse. Others had their flaws, too. And the good part, really, the best part, was in the suggestions for improvement. In girlhood days, the criticism might be, "You try too hard to be the teacher's pet." Or "You dump us if a boy walks with you." Adult criticism might include some of the same. And more. Now, women might say, "You downgrade and undermine us behind our backs, you won't delegate authority, you flatter the men, you want my job . . ."

The airing of these grievances may lead to peace. Consider this line from the Scottish poet Robert Burns: "Oh, what power the giftee gee us, to see ourselves as ithers see us."

12

Danger: Women's War Zone— Sex at Work

Romance against a business backdrop takes on its own fire. Sexual attraction can enliven the mundane work day, or become a factor in high corporate intrigue. Both men and women can be responsible for harassment, sex discrimination, office romance, and other work-disrupting clash and contact.

The women's war zone is in the work place. Its psycho-social borders are the sexual expectations honed by Mother's Rules of doing what's best for oneself and fending off rivals. Her rules include: "It's just as easy to fall in love with a rich man as with a poor man." Men at work may not all be rich, but they are gainfully employed, and that's a start. Mother's Rules encourage finding a good place to shop. She didn't suggest her daughter stop flirting, sit down, work hard, and stay there until she retires.

As individuals, women clearly see the hazards in mixing sex and work, but seldom consider the results of their own actions when there is romance in the air. Jane S., executive secretary, age 32, told her story:

I felt I was on the way up when I got this job seven years ago. Since my boss was promoted from director to vice president, my status, if not my pay and title, seemed an advancement, too.

Also, a big also, my boss and I drifted into a caring sexual relationship. Cliff and I were both married, so we understood the boundaries. We had long lunches and occasional business trips, but were careful to not hurt our spouses. Then came the thunderbolt.

A single, young secretary was added to help with my expanded duties. Alicia was 22 and ambitious. She intended to use both the position and our boss as a stepping-stone. She found it in her best interest not to acknowledge that Cliff and I had a personal relationship. She moved right in, inviting him to guest-lecture at her evening college seminar, thanking him with a small, cute gift. She'd always come up with bright ideas that involved participating along with him at office presentations. The next step was needing to confer with him about her career for just fifteen minutes over a happy-hour drink.

Once she got him in social situations outside the office, it escalated fast. A quick sandwich and coffee. Then came dinners. When it got to late nights, Cliff's wife was finally troubled. Which didn't seem to upset Alicia. Once the news was out, Cliff's wife made sure my husband knew about my involvement, which was largely past tense. Their marriage was over; I'm not sure mine will survive.

Alicia's on cloud nine. She and Cliff are openly dating. She's pushing for a promotion and hoping for marriage. I'm stuck with almost all of the office work and hoping I won't get fired. I know I make Cliff uncomfortable by being yesterday's mistress, and Alicia wishes I were gone. Yes, I'm bitter. I hope I can transfer within the company and survive until Alicia gets hers. Sex and work are like oil and water. They don't mix.

Experiences like Jane's are not unusual. Mother's Rules have become so ingrained in adult behavior that women have a problem restraining their natural responses in favor of the unnatural ones set forth in Business Rules. While regiments of female warriors fight for male attention—and those not involved watch and hate—the pattern repeats. Men use their power and position as surefire aphrodisiacs. More often than not, it is the women who fall when there is trouble. Although they are not always fired, they are unlikely to be promoted either. *Sex at Work* is a sign that could hang on the front door of every business office today. It would warn of high voltage in the Uncivil Business War. It would warn of danger.

Consider sexual harassment. Some women are harassed, and others have been known to harass the male prey. Those who are blatant in their "come hither" signals are resented by those who are certain that this tactic leads to grief for all and those for whom "come hither" doesn't work.

Consider sex discrimination. By now, most midlevel women have heard that senior level managers are uncomfortable with women. Some business women attribute this discrimination to the ploys of women who flaunt their looks. If those token numbers who are promoted are regarded as unattractive, they are unfairly labeled. Today, beauty is no longer dependent on classical physical features. Women can shape their looks to fit their business personas. The faction that flaunts is in one battalion, and those who play it straight fight in another.

Women who participate in office romances are hated, feared, and admired for the fire and the glory they bring to the workplace. Even romances that end in matrimony can be a source of contention.

Gilda B., group creative director of an art agency, says, "I married my boss ten years ago, and I feel he went overboard in not showing favoritism. Still, when I'd sit down in the lounge to join the other gals at a coffee break, it got suddenly quiet. I felt resented enough over a year's time that I quit the job I loved."

Why do sexual overtones transform the business environment on such a grand scale? Are equally qualified men and women really all that different? The answer must be yes. It may become more understandable by examining the etymological differences between the words sex and gender. They're not the same.

A number of otherwise meticulously careful linguists use the words *gender* and *sex* interchangeably, and incorrectly. The term *gender* as a distinction between male and female was borrowed from philology (the study of languages) by John Money, professor of medical psychology and pediatrics at Johns Hopkins University and Hospital in Baltimore. *Gender* signifies a person's personal, social, and legal status as male or female without reference to sex organs. For Money, "gender role" means the things a person says or does to reveal him- or herself as having the status of man or woman; it is one's public presentation as male or female. "Gender identity" is the private experience of gender.

Sex is the division of men and women according to their reproductive functions. (Those with variant sexual preferences aren't considered in this discussion since they generally apply discretion as a tactical office strategy.)

The sex drive, rather than gender roles, ignites the dangerous women's war zone. Those who believe that sex stays clear of the office door and that business neuters come to work are mistaken. The issue of the sex act—anticipated or consummated—catapults women from their midlevel perches faster than it helps a fortunate few become senior managers.

It's easier to understand the women if we consider the men's role. Men are ready, by nature and training, to respond to women in a personal way. From mom to teachers to dates, they know their masculinity is anticipated, welcome, and expected.

Some men are always lawfully, emotionally, or sexually available. Some men enjoy a little interaction because it brightens the day. Others truly resent the intrusion and are discomfited by women who presume all males are a part of their audience.

It's been estimated that as many as half the men and women in the workplace feel they have been sexually harassed. Expectations about how the other half ought to behave and what happens when they don't have proved to be an explosive factor in today's offices.

There are wide individual variances in the ways men and women choose to deal with sexuality at work. Sex isn't necessarily the act of intercourse. It's also expressed in the different ways men and women behave and in how they incorporate their responses into the workday. *Vive la difference* isn't always in the best long-term interests of working women. The losses outnumber the wins.

It's not difficult for women to admit to feelings of rivalry with other women in the office. Even though it's not usually discussed, everyone knows that's just the way it is. A group of lunchtime regulars took on the subject.

Mary C. (age 28): "As teens, we tried to be dumber than the boys, to not scare them away. But we wanted to be smarter than our girlfriends, which was okay. We acted dumber than we were, that's for sure. We all judged each other more by if we were getting dates than getting good grades."

Clara E. (age 32): "It was like that for us, too. No one discussed it, but it was something we knew. Don't be labeled a grind or hang out with girls who always carried a bunch of books home. I said my parents grounded me if I didn't study for tests, as an excuse for my better than average grades."

Melanie B. (age 29): "Yeah. In elementary school, it was cool to be smart. Then, suddenly, in junior high, we wanted to do worse than the guys. It seemed expected. And it became easier. And true. But we really didn't care. By high school, it was the least important thing to worry about."

Glenna B. (age 33): "We all spent more time worrying about the chemistry of our hair—split ends, style, shine—than high school chemistry. I only passed by sweet-talkin' the teacher. He told me to bake him a cake to prove I knew at least that much chemistry. I wasn't sure if he was serious, but I did it anyway. I got a C. Maybe for chocolate."

Carol M. (age 34): "Most of our rivalry was over who looked prettiest. I still size up every woman in the room when I walk in and mentally judge how many are better looking than I am."

The question was posed to women across the country: Have your female coworkers ever felt that some women tend to take advantage of their female attributes to gain business advantages?

Almost 96 percent responded yes. Some shared specific experiences:

Says a California-based armed-forces officer in her midthirties, "Basically, some female officers take advantage by just not being professional, expecting someone else to do the work." Later, she made a cryptic remark: "Fraternization is a consideration in the military."

From Colorado, an engineer in her midforties comments: "I often wish the secretaries could see themselves. The men do not respect their minds when they perform their cute act. They think the men are stupid and don't see what they're doing. But that's not true."

An Oregon computer support supervisor in her midthirties explained: "Two women in my company have wrapped their bosses around their fingers—both women have each received two promotions in the past year. They flattered their way up the ladder."

A personnel director in her late fifties from Nebraska says: "One woman here can be counted on to turn on the personality-plus when men appear in our office. She undergoes a metamorphosis."

Many women feel that sexy clothes play a significant role in the way co-workers strive for advantages over other women.

A nursing supervisor from Tennessee, who is in her early thirties, remarks: "Even though we wear uniforms, some try to take every chance they can think of to show off in sexy clothes. And they wait on the doctors hand and foot while they flirt like anything."

A California computer sales training manager in her late fifties says: "We usually have two or three women in each class who may rarely have traveled and they come out here for training and strut their stuff. They count on their clothes to say a lot after class hours. They compete to be the most noticed and it carries over to the next business day."

An Ohioan in her early forties, director of public relations for a Fortune 500 company known for guiding younger women, explains: "I have known, and I assume others have known, women who play helpless to avoid penalties or act sexy to get ahead—although both are short-term successful, and backfire."

Even in the late 1980s, it is still reported that women are trying to sleep their way up. Women who observe the office show say that it's almost impossible to hide office affairs. In response to a questionnaire, women across the country revealed their thoughts about sex at work:

The word from Pennsylvania: "Sex, sex, sex. However, they soon learn the gains are short-term. They fall soon after."

A Georgian: "There's a woman on my job now who had a personal association and this contributed to her promotion as manager of a department she didn't work in or have any knowledge about."

From New Jersey: "I know a few who do use sexual favors to gain, but it's been short-lived—unless sometimes the woman is also very competent and she's able to go on her own from that point."

A branch library manager from Michigan explained that her field is female-dominated. "Most of the branch managers are women and want to gain favor with the male directors. I've known of several sexual liaisons that have worked to the advantage of the women involved. They refuse to take a stand, even on issues they strongly believe in, if there's a personal reason to do otherwise. They bow to the male's opinion."

A ploy from childhood can be a part of the office day.

Crying was the "female" attribute cited as "a popular manipulative device" across the land. Women said that others cry to get what they want.

A management consultant concurs.

Sex and tears are good for a 15-minute discussion anywhere in this country. I hear about this concern over and over again from men. They really are afraid of handling women's emotions and becoming a part of sexually awkward encounters.

Yet women didn't seem to pick up on it. At the same places of business, the females would come in and ask me, "Do you think men see me as competent?" When I pursued the subject, many defended their right to tears if they were sincere. We didn't seem able to move beyond that point.

Many women feel that other women exhibit jealousy when good things happened to female co-workers. "I can understand feeling envy or jealousy or whatever. What hurts is when they carry it to the men and whine about what other women can't do or won't do," is the opinion of a supervisor of physical therapists in a Maine hospital. "In our field, a lot has to do with fawning over the doctors. A few in our hospital have married doctors and moved away. It's just as well. It's the green eyes of jealousy from then on."

Female colleagues seem to understand what they can and cannot get away with among themselves. Do the boundaries change when men enter the scene? Most women seem to think so.

A computer information manager from Oregon explains, "It's

amazing. One woman in particular alters her voice pitch, verbal style, and entire countenance when she's talking to a man. It's like she turns into someone else entirely. You'd have to see it to believe it. But every woman does it to some extent. It's like when company comes and you're on your best—or in the case of men—most provocative behavior."

A personnel manager from Georgia points out, "When certain men in our company arrive on the scene, the chemistry in the room undergoes a change. It crackles. The women almost preen and go into their transformation. They turn seductive."

A marketing manager at a Massachusetts computer firm notes, "We have just one woman who acts different, but she's a champ. She ignores the rest of the world when an attractive guy is around."

A Michigan high school principal says, "I see a certain phenomenon often. When men are a part of their work group, the women seem to weaken in their attitudes. They get fluttery and act unsure of what's going on. They wait for the men to take control. It's tough for female elementary school teachers to move up to management, and this may have a bit to do with it."

Women give every evidence of having real problems in exhibiting "proper" female behavior at work. In part, this is the direct result of the fact that women, far more than men, consider the workplace a social setting as well.

Careerists generally intend to rise strictly on professional merit, and so keep within the bounds of Business Rules. A Careerist in her late thirties, says:

> To a point, I'm in the office strictly to work. That's true. But I do want to find a mate and within this corporation I know who's at my level.
>
> I don't want to go to a singles bar and waste time with a guy who turns out to be a manager somewhere. That may sound harsh, but I put marriage off until I got to a directorship and now I'm hunting fair game. And they're few and far between.
>
> They're hard enough to catch when you know what you're looking for. So I have to let the business guard drop now and again and try to let the men know there's a woman

inside this suit. I go in for more obvious flirting than before and hope the word gets around that I'm desirable.

A Balancer, divorced mother of one, in her midthirties, and a manger, says, "I can't afford to hide my light under a bushel. I'm here to work, true, but I'm here to get some dates at least. You have to act sexy or the men are afraid to come on to you. They're afraid of being rebuffed by the barracudas. I'm a woman, not just a coworker, and I want the men to know it."

An unmarried Homing Pigeon who is an administrative assistant, shares this: "I had a choice of jobs and picked one with good-looking guys. I already quit two jobs in two years because there was no one there. So anyone who wants me to be a mousey workaholic has another thing coming. My message is that I'm respectable, but available. I can't come out and say it, so I have to let men know in other ways."

Many men and women feel that sexual games between available and willing players are honorable. If the players are not eligible, that's a problem for individuals to solve. For men, the rules have always been more clear-cut. They've been warned to not mix business with pleasure but were forgiven if they did.

For women, regarding romance as a natural outgrowth of a good working relationship is more risky. On-the-job romances are apt to have repercussions. When both participants are legally eligible, the concerns are: who works where, who may need to transfer, where promotions will take them, who gets them, and where loyalties lie.

When the mix is more complicated, the territory is rougher. Mary Cunningham (of Bendix Corporation fame), now mercifully faded from public view and married to her former boss William Agee, could serve as a shining example of how distressing the mix can be. As an MBA grad, a young woman full of the zeal of the new employee, she became embroiled in the toughest of top-level intrigues at the troubled company.

Her story was told in the press and she wrote a book to defend her position. The sex-at-work drama was acted out in board resignations, takeover attempts, romance, divorce, resignations, firings, and remarriage. That gambit earned her the titles of Bendix

Mary, the Queen of Bendix, and worse. This example has an element of soap-opera thoroughness that demonstrates the sturdy psyche needed by those who hope to travel unscathed through even more modest versions of the shoals of sex at work.

In addition to the players at the office, the war extends naturally to the home. Even the most work-oriented people have personal lives. In two-career couples, each spouse has an office life and a home life. It adds up to an involvement of a lot of people on the game boards. Participants and even innocent bystanders in the sexual battlefields are apt to be affected by the fallout.

At midlevel management, additional hours are expected, and are sometimes even necessary. These may involve food, drink, and overnight lodging away from home. One battle-weary woman says:

> How simple life would be if everyone slept in their own bed at night. Wars would cease, fights would end, the divorce rate would tumble.
> In real life, I often preserve the peace by white-lying my way through after-hours business/social functions. It's all strictly business when I tell my husband about it at home. The meetings stay on the subject, no one orders alcoholic drinks, no innuendos are spoken, and I never linger after the meeting gavel adjourns us. The men are old, the women are pals, and Alice is secure in Wonderland. It makes life easier and nothing serious happens anyway. So why beat myself up by initiating controversy that will keep us up at night arguing.

Another says, "Sure, one person is always more attractive and appealing in a semisocial setting. I may go so far as to ask a neat guy to walk me to my car in a deserted parking lot. Sometimes, I'm tempted to take one step more. Someday . . . ?"

A woman from North Carolina says:

> My mother wasn't a professional manager, although she did work in our home as a hairdresser. So her boundaries are different from mine. So are my temptations.
> My hubby was my high school sweetheart and is still blue collar all the way. Not like the men I meet at the office. I'm beginning to see more differences, his lack of polish—like the beer can in his hand all weekend. He likes the way he is.

And the way he thinks I am. High school forever. I guess I come on as a little bit of the belle at work, just to test myself and see if I can pass as the type of woman the men here would date.

A single woman, who takes business trips for her position as a sales manager, says:

It's lonely. Women have just started to take jobs that involve constant travel. This company used to require trucks instead of company cars, which kept most women away. Now, there's no requirement, so a few women joined. It's still mostly male. I don't think sleeping in a different bed every night is fun anymore. Neither is staying in my room after dinner.

Another single traveling woman agrees:

It's still considered a come-on if a woman goes to the hotel bar alone. And it's partly true. I go to meet people and talk or I'd stay in my room. After a couple of drinks, men start looking better, but so far I'm holding the line. That could get to be a low-life way to live. Worse yet, with all the new diseases, sex on the road, unless you're with a work mate you already know is at least fairly okay, can be fatal.

I'll put it this way. If it comes down to drinking—or occasionally more—with a married man I know from the company, or a stranger who says he's single but may not be anyway, I'll take a chance with the devil I know.

Men, of course, have been on the road longer. From Willy Loman in *Death of a Salesman* and onward, their foibles are a part of the American culture.

A management counselor from Pennsylvania says:

Although there are no corroborating statistics on the subject, I know from my own practice that almost no men tell their wives when they're traveling with women who work with them. That seemed sad, because most of the men said it was all strictly business. Who knows? It may be true or they may think I put what they tell me in their personnel folder.

I tried a technique I thought would help. We introduced

wives to female managers in a series of small social events. It made it much worse. The managers were attractive and their conversation was more worldly and stimulating than that of the housewives. Wives who worked outside the home could hold their own, but didn't like the thought of potential single rivals any more than the women at home did.

It will take years before that situation is demystified or resolves itself. Every time a traveling pair missteps, it all goes back to ground zero. It's difficult to blame any one person or group because out-of-town travel does present the most danger of all work and play situations.

A married working woman, who travels occasionally, sees the conflict from a broader perspective, decides, "I think that men and women traveling together for business is fine . . . Just as long as it's not with my husband."

Go with what works for you is the advice many educated women were given. At work and at home, being female carries its own set of mixed signals. Nature provides sex as a female's most important bargaining tool. It is the basis for the continuance of life itself. Whether or not she decides to put it on hold as she fights for her economic security in the workplace is a fairly recent innovation.

For women, sex is more apt to be channeled to socially acceptable limits than to reverse its goals entirely. How sex at work affects women in their business interactions with one another is the current dilemma. As long as some are using sex as a business tool, it's safe to assume that all are indulging—emotionally, if not physically.

Sex is insurance for those who have married and made it. It is a weapon for those aspiring to join their ranks. These are the wars within the Uncivil Business War in every white-collar office.

The woman's war zone is a minefield of sexual tactics. Professional women battle one another to make the most of the full range of what may be a fleeting command.

13

When a Woman Is Boss, It's War

Reaching the top of the corporate ladder is the all-American woman's professional dream. As she fights her way up, promotion by promotion, at least half her coworkers will be fighting to push her down at every rung of her climb. If competition from men trying to climb up and over her weren't enough, she has to contend with still more. From women.

On the basis of a 1985 survey at Baylor University in Texas (reported in *Weekly World News*, November 19, 1985), Dr. Kris Moor concludes, "Women in general are the greatest detriment to the success of other women . . . there is a repeated lack of cooperation by female employees with newly promoted female supervisors and managers."

Qualifications, credentials, and comradeship notwithstanding, it's Women vs. Women when the female aims to lead. Whereas the woman on her way up has no problem fantasizing herself into the plush corner office with subordinates scurrying at her behest, she has more than a little difficulty in seeing herself as the worker busting her back on behalf of a female boss.

Working women would adore being the boss lady; not many would care to work for one. The dilemma that these women must

ly ponder is: If so many employees are unwilling to accept
ses, why should companies create them?

e fun side of reigning is irrefutable. The Careerist, and
even the Balancer and the Homing Pigeon, would enjoy the executive glamour spots, at least for a short spin.

Many women are qualified, on paper, to rise above the midlevel, white-collar jobs they have held for five to ten years. Yet
they're not being tapped for a proportionate number of leadership
roles.

The glass ceiling barring females from senior corporate positions may exist in part because of the attitude of the women below
them on the promotion ladder. Psychologist Virginia Schein says,
"What they praised in men as crisp, efficient, logical behavior,
they interpreted in women as cold, mean, and uncaring. Women
are still judged more harshly than men in equivalent positions,
even though their behavior may be exactly the same."

Women say they hate to work for other women because female
bosses

    are jealous of the achievements of others
    bring their personal lives into the office
    withhold helpful information
    are unfair, impersonal, overbearing, vague, unqualified *and*
      unprofessional
    won't provide subordinates with opportunities to advance

And this list could go on ad infinitum! When women occupy
positions of corporate command, the battles become heated. Survey after survey supports the contention that women cancel each
another out of the leadership sweeps. A national poll reported by
the *Los Angeles Times* is typical. It shows that 47 percent of the
women who responded said that they would prefer working for a
man, and only 18 percent said they would rather work for a woman. Men—44 to 30 percent—said their bosses' gender wouldn't
matter.

As part of a study released by the University of Michigan in
1986, analyst Harish Tewari reports that women's images suffered
from low credibility with their employees and that 80 percent of

the males and females polled said they preferred men over women supervisors.

One area has improved for women who aspire to leadership. Two surveys, one in 1965 another in 1985, in a study at Baylor University show a change in male workers' attitudes toward female bosses. In the original sampling, ". . . 41 percent of the males had a negative attitude toward women executives, which dropped to only 5 percent [in 1985]. Men are now much more likely to accept women in positions of authority."

But the complaints women make against one another in the office show little sign of diminishing. They continue to run the gamut from petty annoyances to accusations of counterproductive leadership. A female statistical manager with 14 employees reporting to her says, "I think women are generally more forgiving and less critical of male bosses. They expect to survive by supporting and manipulating male bosses in ways that seldom ring true when applied to other women."

Many women who work for women vow never to do it again. Their dissatisfaction stems from their belief that women bosses "get on your case and stay on your case." Women bosses are consistently portrayed as more demanding and less sympathetic than male bosses.

Female bosses seem over-motivated to prove themselves, even at the expense of others. The management styles of female bosses fall within several major categories.

The *Queen Bee* is most likely a token executive put in her position by male management to meet a quota. Her attitude is that she doesn't ask anyone to do anything she herself wouldn't do.

From her standpoint: Sometimes a female subordinate won't ask questions when I lay out the assignment. She just nods and walks away. I have to ask her later how it's going. She smiles and says she didn't understand some parts of what I wanted. I go over it; she nods again. I have to follow up, and eventually she hands me a slipshod piece of something that isn't even close. When the deadline passes, I eventually take over and just do it. When it goes on my own month-end report, she pouts. And that's typical.

Responds the subordinate: She hired me for my skills, but it seems that if it's not her way, it's not the right way. I do the research, she polishes it a little, and turns it in to her bosses as her own. She's afraid I'll get noticed if she shares credit. She says to get to it when I have time and always asks about it the next day, even when she knows I have other deadlines.

Another determined Queen Bee observes that in her opinion women prefer to work for men because they can get away with more. Pure and simple.

From her standpoint: They come to me with tales of needing time off for PMS and sitter problems and I know I just stare through them until they finish. One part of me is focusing on my own cramps and sitters— and that I take pride in getting the job done on time anyway. And if I allow one gal a privilege, five minutes later, a similar request comes in the door. They compare notes and all want what one gets. Sometimes I get roped in, but I'm usually sorry. It's like the old saying, "No good deed goes unpunished." They find something else to complain about.

The employee responds: Not only does she think she's superwoman, but she thinks that everyone admires that and wants to be just like her. As far as I know, no one does. The guys don't mind her as much because they get away with a lot by flattering her macho opinion of herself.

Many of the most successful Queen Bees alienate other women by the sheer force of their personalities. They assert themselves with confidence. They see it as a reward for their status. When interviewed about their methods of leadership, most high achievers take pride not just in doing it all, but in doing it *their way*.

One female executive vice president says: "When you're the boss, you can express yourself emotionally to your employees. I like to yell when they're wrong and give out big hugs when they're right."

Another states, "Every day I am determined to make whatever seems impossible be possible."

Some women with command positions incorporate their assertiveness into all aspects of their lives.

At a business luncheon one irate female executive caught the waitress's eye. "Take back this parfait," she snapped. "The ice cream is far too cold served prefrozen in the dish."

When the Queen Bee stings, men tend to accept it with a smile and proceed to change the subject. Women on the other hand, tend to treat it with a chilled reserve that isolates the offender. One employer of a Queen Bee commented, "I would label her behavior 'compulsive.' She tries to create a world of perfection we don't buy into."

The *Tougher-Than-Thou* executive forms the second category. She is often a scarred fighter.

One Tougher-Than-Thou executive explains herself: I'm not one of those women who have it all. My goal was to reach director and I'm proud to say that I got here. I gave up a home life as such after my marriage lost out to my work. No one helped me get where I am, but I love my career and if the cost was high, it was worth it.

The minute I open my eyes in the morning I think about the job ahead. By the time my feet hit the floor I'm anticipating specifics at the office. In the shower I'm detailing items in my mind's calendar. I plan as I drive to work. When I open my office door, it's as though I'm midway into my work.

I don't expect the people who work for me to do that, but I really do expect to see them on time and ready to go. Usually, they drift in 10–15 minutes late—right to the brink of getting by without my comment—get breakfast from the machines, catch up on chitchat, and by then their phones ring and they're off on some tangent without even getting to the top item on the day's agenda. So they're unprepared and behind.

I try to understand, but usually their train of thought is beyond me. They don't seem to care about their work. Women have this laissez faire attitude far more than men do.

The Tougher-Than-Thou's subordinate responds: I instinctively lower my voice two octaves and stop smiling when I'm summoned to her office. I know it's trouble ahead. Otherwise, she stays in there alone.

I feel like a kid called in to see the principal. Even when she tries to smile, it's a major effort. Her face doesn't change, there's just this phony crocodile grin on it. It's like she's gearing for a fight over anything less than perfect.

Says another subordinate: I've learned to survive by remaining impersonal. I stick to the issue, compliment her work whenever I can do that sincerely, and get away from her as soon as possible. She takes pride in being a workaholic, so I let her see the side of me that appreciates her guidance on my top projects. I back away when she snips and turns cold.

The woman in the *Uncertainly Yours* category isn't quite sure how she got to a position of prominence, even though she appears qualified. She remains focused on the difficulty of maintaining her "lucky" promotion break.

An Uncertainly Yours executive explains herself: Try this theory. Even paranoids have enemies. I'm the first woman to have a regular seat in the boardroom and I love it and am afraid of it at the same time. The men seem to be reserving judgment about what I can do; the women who work for me give me the impression that they wouldn't mind so much if I fail.

Women who work for me consistently ask my boss questions I could answer, as though what I would say would be less true because I'm a female. It diminishes my authority in his eyes.

I don't have a woman who's already been in my place to emulate, so I'm cautious. I feel pressured and don't want to misstep. I don't want anyone to witness even my small failures.

The employee responds: She's so insecure she seems to think that those below her rank are lesser beings whose lack of status might be catchy. She's so distant I hate to ask her anything.

Another subordinate states: I never get a sense of my lady boss trusting me or my judgment. She responds better to men's suggestions, even if I said about the same thing in other words.

Another female category is the *Ageist*, who can be Older, Younger, or In Between. Generational lines are often a part of female boss/employee confrontations.

An Older Ageist Boss explains: I came up the hard way. My route was the secretarial pool and night college classes. The young women I hire try to grab my job instead of learning it. They're hunting careers. They assume I live to mentor. I think they'd learn a lot about office politics and feelings if they were secretaries for a year. They tend to be brash and insensitive.

The Younger executive responds: I had an opportunity to replace an older woman who had created a small department and was unqualified to take it past a certain point when it grew. It needed the technical degree I had. She did everything she could to undermine me with the staff. She'd come around from the department she was transferred to and offer suggestions within hearing of the other women. Then, behind my back, she'd tell them I was unqualified and hinted that I had unseated her because I was young and pretty. She gave everyone the impression that she was the brains behind the throne and I was her employee.

Another young employee provides a different perspective: Older female bosses have all of the characteristics of older male bosses, but more so. If you don't hang on every word, they remind you they went to the school of hard knocks. Actually, a lot of women stayed home to raise their kids and then came back. They resent our formal education and drive and keep us back whether we're good or not.

A Younger Ageist Boss explains: What older women below me fail to see is that I'm not an enemy. I just have a little more power than they do. The hierarchy has the real power and we should cooperate. Instead of being jealous, they should work with me.

I didn't expect so much hostility, and I want to prove to my boss that I can handle it on my own and still get the work out. What I get on a good day is passive resistance. The bad days are near mutiny. My MBA impresses them about as much as a bowl of alphabet soup.

An older employee responds: When I was introduced to my boss, who is younger and a woman, I was stunned. My first thought was "What could she possibly know?" I tried to be friendly and help her out with work suggestions, but I don't think she likes women. I'm not sure she knows she is one.

A Same-Age Boss states: This is a tough situation. Whatever I try to make things work with me and the woman my age who works for me is taken wrong. We may seem the same to her, but we're not. I got the job without having the benefit of a college education and have worked twice as hard to do a terrific job. I'm capable, but some women in particular put politics and stress in my way.

I'm just going on, usually doing my work and everyone's who won't work. What I should do is let those who won't perform fall and document a case to fire them. But if I do that, it could look to my bosses like I'm jealous of other women.

A same-age employee responds: I didn't really want to work for a person so near my age. We both started here together and have ten years of experience. But she got the break to move up when I was out on maternity leave. I came back to work and took it on myself to go back to school nights and get a college degree to advance myself. I now know how to manage this department better than she does and believe I should have a chance to do more than work for her to help her look good.

I may have to bide my time. She said her husband may transfer out of town. So things could change. But her type wouldn't help a woman to replace her. A man had the job before her and I think she'd want to show it's still important enough to go to another man after her.

What's the true role of the Female Boss? Women bosses are somehow thrust alternately into the roles of mother, sister, wife, friend, date. A female leader isn't often seen simply as a professional manager there to get the job done.

One female boss explains: I must come across as a parenting type. I keep getting thrown into role playing I don't ask for. Young women try to get me to protect and mother them, which is the furthest idea from my mind. The ones nearer my age pull the sister bit, which feels nice and comfy until it backfires in a work and personality conflict. It's hard to know how to react and keep the peace.

Men especially feel the need either to be my dad, my brother, husband, or some variation of semi-lover.

Then they react to everything that happens at work according to roles. They seem to denote my woman's place.

A male employee gives his point of view: In the actual work context, I don't mind working for a woman. After all, she's there because management thinks she's qualified. But personality is something else. She either lectures like she's a mother and I'm a naughty boy or acts like a giggly date. My ego cringes most when this happens at meetings outside the office and I have to introduce her as my boss. My wife hates me working for a woman worse than I do. She feels it's a loss of professional status. I'm taking a hard look.

A female employee offers another perspective: Sometimes she gets us to confide in her and then everything is used against us. For petty control. Or to show her bosses she knows everything that goes on in the department. And she plays favorites. Usually she has one or two pets and everyone else is left out. Then we kind of take it out on each other, although we know it's stupid. She gets us acting like a bunch of kids looking to mommy for approval.

Management styles consistently separate the men from the women. Although men certainly fall into behavioral categories according to personality types, these are perceived as more "normal" within the Business Rules.

When a Woman Is Boss, It's War

Women who bring their own personalities to the ex
suite are often damned if they do and damned if they don'
women who do not work and have never held a job outside the
home are uncomfortable with the concept of taking orders from a
woman. They don't like it for themselves and they don't like the
men in their lives to do it either. It conveys a comic-strip sense of
being henpecked.

In a 1986 *Wall Street Journal* survey of 722 female executives,
more than one-third conveyed deep feelings of resentment for the
way their careers affected their personal lives.

Another recent study, this one at the University of Texas,
found that, of 1,500 male and female MBAs, the women had a
divorce rate three times higher than the men. This indicates that
high achievement and leadership bring problems to the more traditional male/female roles.

Feelings between women and those they would lead seem beyond casual dislike. Even those who profess not to discriminate
against female bosses prefer not to be governed by other women.

The "boss lady" has few role models and little notion of the
likenesses and differences between herself and those she hopes to
lead, and often acts against her own—and other working wom-
en's—best interests.

In Margaret Atwood's insightful best-seller novel about wom-
en's situation in the near future, *The Handmaid's Tale* (1986), she
explores the issue of women ruling other women. In a segregated,
protective time, when women are taken care of in the best interests
of society, they live within severely controlled boundaries. One
class is the "aunts," who control the daily lives of large groups of
young women. Their rule is effective only if there is "policing"
within the group.

One aunt explains that ". . . no empire imposed by force or
otherwise has ever been without this feature: control of the indig-
enous by members of their own group . . . when power is scarce,
a little of it is tempting."

This may be the issue when women in today's work force
clash in employer/employee relationships. They fight one another
to a standstill; as a result, the number of women in management
is automatically kept to a minimum. In Women vs. Women, bosses

are corrupted by fear of other women's capabilities and, at the same time, by their lack of confidence in their own business acumen.

If women do want to gain corporate leadership—and there is evidence of ambivalence in that matter—they like to do it in an environment controlled by men. "Natural" roles are taken when men defer to women on small issues at the lower levels and bide their time to win more complete control later on. Women fight to achieve lone leadership roles under the protection of male power.

14

The Political Animal

The realm of politics offers women a supreme opportunity to demonstrate their feelings for each other. This they do. Across the board, it's Women vs. Women in the political arena.

The similarities in the ways women react to one another in business and politics are strong. In business, women have reached management only in recent times. But in politics, women have occupied mid- to upper-middle level party and government jobs since the beginning of the century.

In both arenas, however, the number of female leaders does not come close to matching the percentage of women in the population at large. Most significantly, those who reach the top do so largely without the support of other women.

The women of America seem to have a logical goal: A solid political base, from local government to the White House, staffed with strong female leaders pledged to represent the bread-and-butter issues of middle-class working women. Whereas educated and presumably world-wise women consistently look to the government for support on issues they say are vital, they also reject uniting with other women to secure enough power to bring these goals to fruition.

Women have voted in larger numbers than men in presidential elections for at least 20 years, yet women hold relatively few elected or appointed offices at higher levels. Women's caucuses and political activities work mostly at the grass-roots level.

After the 1986 national election, there were only two women in the U.S. Senate, Nancy Landon Kassebaum of Kansas and the newly-elected Barbara A. Mikulski of Maryland. Only three women serve as governors and only 23 are in the House of Representatives.

It would seem that serious women should support candidates who pledge to work for their issues. Elected officials who owe their seats to the votes of women should lend an ear to their goals on issues such as child care and equality in the workplace. Whereas men have been known to rally round the old-time promise of a "chicken in every pot" or a lighthearted pledge of "free beer for the working man," women go the opposite route. They reject any good that could come to them as a result of pulling together. Do women purposely reject unity and the prospect of success? The attitude of women toward one another in both business and politics—and the business of politics as well as the politics of business—raises the distinct possibility that women do not crave independence.

Women, divided by age, social class, religion, ethnic background, and hundreds of other factors, would rather be placed in any demographic classification other than "female." Each heeds her own siren song and inevitably supports traditional loyalties. For the most part, these have remained unchanged over the years.

When suffragettes first began their fight for the right to vote 138 years ago, naysayers claimed, "No point to women voting. They'll just vote the way their husbands do anyway." Those who believe it today could muster the same arguments as their predecessors.

Women got the vote in 1919, but in the intervening decades they have yet to use it to advance the cause of financially independent women. Instead, those who vote generally cast their ballots in support of special interests closest to their hearts.

One interest close to the female heart is Mother's Rule of not letting other women push ahead. This means anywhere—from the buffet line to the ballot box. How do women get female approval to advance to the head of the queue? Very slowly.

Women elected to office in American politics are rare enough to remain in the exceptional category. Some widows have inherited the offices of their spouses. They are usually selected by the party more for the continuity of name and ease of control than in recognition of the wife's political or administrative aptitude. These and other abberations occasionally swell the ranks of women in public office.

Most women in office do as credible a job as any man, so gender is not the determining factor. Since being able to get elected is no guarantee for doing a good job, ability is not the most crucial issue. These days, most contenders, both male and female, boast advanced degrees and considerable experience.

In 1964, President Lyndon Johnson made a historic statement in his State of the Union Address. It was intended to signal a bright, new future. He said, "I believe a woman's place is not only in the home, but in the House and Senate and throughout the government. One thing we are insisting on is that we not have a stag government." As an astute politician, Johnson may have made this statement in an effort to court this bloc of prospective supporters. Few remnants of his Great Society plan remain in the political climate of today.

A staunch Democrat who voted for Johnson remembers: "I know I went to a rally and bought an apron that said, 'Women's place is in the House . . . and the Senate,' but I really don't remember that anything came of it. No more than the buttons and balloons."

Whatever inroads were made during that Administration were dissipated by 1984, the era of women's giant steps backward. Reality had proved that there was no reason for politicians to believe in the existence of a homogeneous "women's vote."

The evidence became clear in the candidacy of Geraldine Ferraro. When Democratic presidential candidate Walter Mondale selected Ferraro as the first woman to be the vice presidential candidate of a major party, there were high hopes for a historical breakthrough.

A 50-year-old, three-term congresswoman from New York, Ferraro had worked actively for women in business since 1981. She introduced bills to recognize marriage as an economic part-

nership and to make provisions to give benefits to women leaving
for maternity leave that would match those of men in the military
service. She also drafted a bill giving two-year tax credits to employers for hiring displaced (divorced or widowed) homemakers.

When these individual bills faltered, they became a part of a
major piece of legislation (in 1983) called the Women's Economic
Equity. The package included bills by other female legislators,
including: providing IRAs for homemakers and tax relief for single
heads of households, tax credits for child care, nondiscrimination
in insurance, eliminating federal rules and regulations hampering
women in business, and a stronger system of child-support enforcement. Over a period of years, Ferraro banded together with
female colleagues to fight for this package.

Personality, appearance, political and party affiliation aside, it
would seem that Ferraro's work would appeal to a considerable
number of female voters, if only to give a woman of this calibre a
chance and to see if any good would come of it.

The Mondale-Ferraro ticket will be most remembered for carrying only the male candidate's own state. To put it mildly, neither
men nor women supported the ticket. Reasons abound, but one
fact remains. Enough women did not band together in any one
part of the land to put a woman in the nation's "senior management" arena.

Whether or not women would have preferred some other female candidate, the fact remains that Ferraro was the one in the
lineup. Women did not use her as a symbol to send a message that
the concerns of females were to be reckoned with.

One female independent recalls, "It's not that we didn't want
a woman. For one thing, the National Organization of Women
(NOW) said they could 'deliver' the female vote. I didn't want
anyone to think they spoke for all women. Not for me, at least."

A Democratic party worker adds, ". . . And the men were
against Mondale for caving in to a special interest group and being
naive enough to believe NOW could make a difference."

As for NOW, they could indeed be credited for delivering the
female vote because women turned out in droves. CBS exit polls
suggested that record numbers of women voted, perhaps because
Ferraro was on the ballot. But the women voted for Ronald Reagan

and George Bush, and added *no* female candidates to the House or Senate.

A single woman in her twenties says, "Politics isn't a regular topic at work when I talk to the gals. We discuss other things. But I never heard anyone of us come out against women. In fact, the night after Geraldine was in the TV debate, we did mention that she stuck up for herself really well. The other guy, Bush, did that 'overpolite' bit that women get here at the office as a put-down. And she shoved it back at him. But none of us discusses who we're actually going to vote for."

A married, middle-aged woman says, "My husband and I talk about going to vote the night before the election. We discuss things like when we'll go, before work or after, and who we'll vote for. We think for ourselves, but usually don't cancel each other out. Of course, in the privacy of the booth, we could go any way we want and not even say."

Says another married woman in her early thirties, "If one or the other of us has a strong preference we try to sway the other. But it's pretty casual. We each vote what we believe in."

A slightly angry, middle-aged woman concludes, "Just because we're women doesn't mean we're for women's lib. I believe in their stand on equal pay and that's about it. I don't believe in ERA or strikes or abortions or any of it. My religious beliefs and my family mean more to me than what they say is right. I'm not a libber and I don't much care for those people taking for granted how I'll vote."

There were reasons galore for the across-the-board trouncing suffered by the Democratic duo. Some even say that having a female candidate caused the loss. Ferraro said the experience was a positive one not only for her (benefits include a line in the history books, a $700,000 advance for her memoirs, and a lucrative Pepsi-Cola TV commercial) but notes that she has paved the way for the next female candidate.

A male Democrat muses, "I wonder when that will be? We're still trying to pick up the pieces. For whatever reasons, our white male voters also went Republican and we've somehow got to get them back again."

Obviously, the Republicans, who also needed the female vote, went after it in different ways. They gave the matter serious thought and came up with more palatable candidates and platforms for female approval.

Republican pollster Richer Wirthlin discussed the winning strategy in a *Wall Street Journal* interview. Republicans decided to avoid the feminist agenda. They divided women into 64 different categories and went after their votes with media focus keyed to female's personal concerns and life-styles. Ads addressed single issues such as nuclear war and inflation.

This approach worked. Women were more comfortable with broader issues such as peace and prosperity rather than areas keyed to their individual benefit. For women, there was a hint of "divided we stand." Perhaps they fear "united we fall."

Female politicians, in the wake of their lesson of 1984, have backed off from issues that smack of feminism. After all, they've been severely rebuffed. Geraldine Ferraro did not run for the Senate seat she was considering. (Of course, her decision was tied to many aspects of her political fall-out.)

Democrat Lieutenant Governor Marlene Johnson, former board member of the feminist National Women's Political Caucus (NWPC), says, "People ask if I'm a feminist. It's like being asked if I have a disease." In 1985, seven members of the NWPC ran for one Wisconsin legislative seat—and lost to a man.

Concerned that "women's issues" could get in their way, women in the Democratic and Republican parties decided to restructure their approach and try for issues with wider appeal in 1985. Cleta Deatherage, a former Oklahoma state legislator who became the general counsel of a bank, says she burned out after fighting for the ERA for eight years and will run again after a stint in the private sector.

Missouri state legislator Karen McCarthy pursued a business career while considering a future race for state auditor. She says she was advised "to distance myself from this woman's thing and get into a business persona."

Women are sending confusing signals to one another. In September 1986, the League of Women Voters (LWV), for the first time in its 65 years, decided that their new leader would be a man. After interviewing 120 qualified final candidates, the League awarded their highest administrative position, executive director, to a 45-year-old corporate lawyer.

Grant Thompson, feminist and son of a feminist, fondly recalls stories of growing up with his mother's league involvement and says, "Frankly I get kind of a zip out of telling people I work for the League of Women Voters." This is lovely. But consider the message to the 110,000 members of the largely volunteer group. The LWV, outgrowth of the suffrage movement, has 105,000 female members.

Even if Thompson is a strong LWV supporter and member, has impeccable credentials, and will perform competently, one thing is clear. Many members wrote to complain about this obvious point: A male member was judged a superior choice for one of the few paid professional positions in the League of Women Voters.

One woman, a midlevel supervisor, shakes her head and says, "It reminds me of the time I started as a secretary and was working my way up. The best paying, most prestigious clerical job opened. It was for an executive secretary to the CEO. The company went outside and hired a male. Then they sent a memo around tying this decision to a feminist stance. Like, '. . . see, men are secretaries, too.' A man got the plum job and the company used it to make a political statement of open-mindedness and equality. Extremely puzzling. And frustrating."

What do women want in the current political arena? The question is rising to the fore while plans are made for the 1988 presidental election campaign. The women's vote is seen as crucial.

The gender gap has been studied and restudied since it was discovered in 1980 as a vote-getting factor. The Democrats have determined that their appeal to women's own special financial and personal interests was a failure. The Republican's appeal to individual social issues fared far better.

On one level it appears that women fear the independence that would grant them total opportunity. Freedom can be frightening. There were homebound slaves who refused to be set free after the Civil War to make their own way. The uncertainty was too crushing a prospect.

Even today, many middle-class women think it's safer to be

taken care of and would rather leave the country in the control of male providers. Women can turn their political attention to less personally threatening, although undeniably serious big issues. A caring stance on issues of national and global concern places "warm-hearted" women in strong yet "feminine" roles that set women's concerns above the more mundane economic interests of the menfolk.

Taking the high road on moral issues and maintaining a hands-off reserve at the polls is in the interest of many women. The stakes are high. If through some extraordinary transformation of the body politic, women were elected to top government positions in great numbers, they could pose a danger. Suppose these elected officials were to take women at their word and give them the equality that many have been demanding?

Once in effect, this new policy might eventually make it possible for middle-class women to earn their own keep, from high school graduation to retirement, with little possibility to take time off for personal activities and family concerns. Something akin to what working men experience. This, of course, would be a disaster, and wholly unacceptable. Entering and leaving the white-collar world is easier to rationalize when women remain largely on the lower rungs of the corporate ladder.

Ethel Klein of Columbia University, who has specialized in analyzing the gender gap, sheds a soft light on female sensibilities. Klein says that women are an unusual special-interest group in that their special interest is the general interest. Women see self-interest as selfish, fear selfishness, and will reject it at the polls.

Using this guideline, candidates, male or female, Democratic or Republican, are advised not to favor women or call attention to their gender. They are often counseled to avoid promising to represent women if they are elected. Candidates are reminded not to even mention women's issues, and instead label these with the euphemism community issues and responsibilities.

The Democratic party has been conducting focus groups to discover how to appeal to women. They are finding that women "are more likely to favor government involvement and doing things collectively." Voting women seem to favor not only *caring* but

being taken care of. This produces a difficult obstacle for women
who hope to lead.

Fund raising is the name of the political game. It has been
observed that women are more comfortable "manipulating" funds
for their use than coming right out and asking for money on the
basis of the usual give and take of politics.

A group that refuses to recognize itself as a group makes it all
but impossible for first-time female candidates to gain financial
support. It would be natural for women to turn to their own and
work toward common goals. Women lose at the outset by declining
funds earmarked for the female cause.

The Los Angeles Women's Campaign Fund (LAWCF) explains that women supporters aren't used to writing checks. The
bipartisan group brought Oregon Republican gubernatorial candidate Norma Paulus into town in September 1986 to help raise
funds. She explained that even in Oregon, the only state to ratify
the ERA twice, where polls showing that 85 percent of the elec-
torate would vote for a woman, Paulus was being outspent three
to one by her opponent.

Paulus explains that being a woman candidate has built-in
problems, sometimes tied to other women ". . . like Phyllis
Schlafly. She's liberated herself, but she doesn't want anyone else
to be free." The LAWCF pursued its fund-raising efforts, mainly
for candidates in state races, by encouraging "first-time" activists
to be involved in women's politics—by writing a check.

The "typical" American voter has changed. Democratic
pollster Pat Caddell explains. In the 1970s, the typical woman voter
was an Ohio housewife in her forties. In the late 1980s, she's under
40, hails from the South or Southwest, works outside the home,
and is conservative on economics but liberal on social issues.

Women have the profile and the potential, but the attitude
remains doggedly unchanged. Their reasons for fighting and holding one another back revolve around every issue but the real one.
Middle-class women back away from any threat of legislative help
that can stand them squarely on their own two feet and establish
them as adults responsible for their own financial well-being. Fearful of falling a socioeconomic notch or two and being in the posi-

tion of their working class sisters by losing the economic opportunity to depend on men, they would rather vote against measures that would grant women greater employment opportunities.

Instead, women consistently thrust men into Big Daddy roles, and government is the biggest daddy of all. And women maintain a childish insistence that the government can make everything better. Fighting the frightening idea that they are strong, and capable, they refuse to join together and win the elective offices that would put women in the driver's seat as the nation's problem-solvers. It's more comfortable for women to break up their majority by refusing to vote for anyone who threatens to prove that that majority even exists.

Women fight any women who dare to put their heads above the crowd and say, "We can solve women's problems in the workplace and provide the economic opportunity that will enable women to function in true equality with men." If women can do this, they must be responsible for the success of their own lives.

Careerists, Balancers, and Homing Pigeons would be expected to march together. Excuses of male prejudice and the up side of expecting men to take on the bulk of financial responsibilities would be null and void. Men would no longer be shamed or coerced into being the major breadwinners for the majority of middle-class women.

To paraphrase Pogo, "I have met the government. And she is us."

Women dread the day when other women will force them to take on equal responsibility. They'll fight one another to the ground before letting that happen. Politics is a prime arena for battlefronts of the Uncivil Business War. As long as women can keep one another from attaining positions of high power, they can remain dependent on individual men or the male collective in government. As long as they can remain barren of power in the political arena, they have longer-term hopes of remaining impotent in providing for themselves financially in the work world.

15

Motherhood vs. Work: The Waterloo of Feminism?

The feminist battle cry of the 1960s—"equal with men in every way"—is rising to haunt the movement and women in general in the 1980s. Women vs. Women is a battle among furious females who are finding that the American dream seldom combines business achievement with the nurturing of a family. The current fight, most often played out in the business office, pits maternal instincts against the need or desire to work outside the home.

All factions embroiled in the Uncivil Business War direct their bitterness, disappointment, and anger toward the powers that be in government and the corporations where they work. Women who expect more in the way of personal support find that business is business.

Their lowered self-esteem in the face of setbacks in the work force and being overburdened at home prompt women to seek help and assign blame. Many of their disappointments center on their battered dream of feminism. In the 60s, women were ecstatic to be liberated from society's traditional roles and welcomed an era of sexual freedom and individual autonomy. Feminism provided an opportunity to fulfill their hopes and dreams.

The next wave of working women accepted freedom as a given and expected even more from the movement. They wanted enlightened social legislation and personal support systems to accommodate women's many roles at home and at work. If feminism could not provide solid help in those directions, it was written off as antifamily.

In the early days of the National Organization for Women (NOW), its identification as antimale and prolesbian posed a major problem. One faction of leaders wanted to distance the movement from these stances to avoid keeping feminism alien from the mainstream of American middle-class women. The decision not to abandon those at the outer edges has often risen to haunt the rank and file, although attitudes have since mellowed.

An early NOW worker says:

> Today's women don't understand. We couldn't just ask for equality in a single sector, like fork over the same pay as men get. It had to be women are equal to men in every way in order to come up with the major reforms such as equal pay for equal work that provided a better financial picture for working women. The next step can be to carry on and ask for additional measures, such as benefits for the family.
>
> We couldn't rally support with a slogan like hire women on equal terms, but they want flex time, day-care, extended maternity leaves . . . and you name it. We'd have been laughed out of existence.

Another early feminist agrees. "We put women in position to gripe or go for refinements to fine tune their desire to have it all. We supplied the fire and the drama that got them in gear. I see little evidence of gratitude. Or even understanding."

Many frustrated working mothers now view women's benefits in European countries as better. Although few Europeans champion the American feminist credo, European women seem, to American eyes, to be more accepted in the work force. Perhaps they are less than equal in some social aspects, but they receive more support and benefits for their families than typical American working women.

A young American woman combining motherhood and work says, "I'd like to turn in some of this so-called equality, including the 60 cents or so I earn to my husband's dollar, for some subsidized support. My ego can handle it being called enlightened social legislation and if the feminists want my vote, they can take turns babysitting and I'll burn my nursing bra. Get real. Feminists are more entranced with the rhetoric of equality than with where to find time to get to the grocery."

"Motherhood is the problem modern feminists cannot face," according to Sylvia Ann Hewlett, PhD, author of *The Myth of Women's Liberation in America*. Modern corporate America is structured to offer them success only if they remain childless. Extended maternity leaves, convenient and well-functioning nurseries, and job guarantees are things that the feminists have said must be sacrificed in the name of equality with men.

Hewlett, economist and mother, says the result of this attitude is a troubled society in which middle-class working women are penalized for having babies while the less competent are compensated by the state for reproducing. She says, "Liberation will mean little for either men or women if women enter the men's world on men's terms."

A midlevel manager in her early forties offers another perspective:

> These professional mothers—not mothers who are professionals—are driving me crazy. Who elected them to speak for me?
>
> I'd probably be further along in my career if I hadn't juggled my daughter and her schedule with my husband and chores at home. Many a time I gave up lunch to run errands and many a time my husband fit a dance class car pool into his day. I consider myself a feminist, although I don't belong to any group. They did inspire me to maintain a level of credibility at the office and move up the corporate ladder just like my husband did.
>
> Now a young woman on our floor keeps badgering our bosses about every benefit in the book to make her life as mommy easier. Well, I don't need it and I don't like it. She

doesn't know, or care to know, what a feeling of equality
means or the fight some of us had to sustain it. I want management to see me as totally dedicated. I am. I don't want my
interests and perks to even be seen as bundled with hers.

It is in the business office where the consequences of this
combative thinking unfold. Pregnant women often find it easier to
leave the work force than to return to their jobs, leaving management dubious about hiring and training other prospective mothers
as their replacements. Feminists feel that they are put at a disadvantage in hiring and promotion.

One female critic notes that new mothers who must return to
work are endlessly ". . . coming in late, taking time off, and in-
terrupting work for constant emergencies of one kind or another."
This behavior generates hostility and resentment among co-workers who have to pick up the slack of the distracted mom on a
regular basis.

A woman who recently entered the work force says, "I can
spot a libber a mile away. They have an attitude, brassy and strident. Yuck."

The voice of a displaced homemaker sounds a death knell for
feminism for another reason. "Women's lib. I'm closer to a cry
than a laugh on that one. I was divorced—might as well call a spade
a spade, I was dumped by my husband after 35 years—and had to
become a clerical. For me, equality meant no alimony. But I was
unequal and unprepared. I've managed, but the rabble-rousers
weren't thinking of women in my position when they rallied to
make divorce no fault. There's fault all right and it's theirs. My
income went down 60 percent and my ex's went up 40 percent. If
the ERA is dead, you won't catch me shedding a tear."

Another young office worker fresh off the campus says, "I
don't want to be independent. I want men. To me, feminism is a
form of indentured servitude."

The history of feminism in America is the story of strong
women who gained positions of leadership in their communities.
As far back as the 1880s they struggled for women's rights with
motherhood. *Mothers of Feminism: The Story of Quaker Women in
America* by Margaret Hope Bacon tells how women such as Lucre-

tia Mott, Susan B. Anthony, Angelina Grimke, Abby Kelley Foster, Elizabeth Cady Stanton, and Alice Paul contributed to the reform movements that led directly to modern feminism.

From the beginning of modern feminism in the 60s to the demanding 70s, it somehow fell short as a symbol for the goals and aspirations of the broad spectrum of working women. In the late 80s some women still identify feminism with equality, but others equate it, negatively, with troublemakers.

More than a few working women wonder if any group composed primarily of women can solve their problems in today's workplace. On one side are those who applaud the efforts of the movement which have helped them land high positions in today's corporate structure. Others hate the mess they find themselves in—trying to be all things to all people at home and at work—and would cheerfully strangle the feminist leaders who got them into all this.

Women's feelings about feminism range from indifference to appreciation to resentment. Many young entrants in the office sweeps, who came of age post-Vietnam and post-Watergate, give feminism little thought. The older Baby Boomers, whose ideals were formed during the 60s rights movements, believe that feminism put them in position to achieve their goals and confirm their ideals. Older women often feel that feminism dealt them a hand that combined the worst of all possible worlds. For some, NOW is a snaggle-toothed dinosaur that accomplished little and annoyed many. They thank the group for equal pay, known in the movement as the-part-I-agree-with, and watch from the sidelines as NOW battles those who would send women back home in defeat.

The feminist movement takes a stand on issues such as abortion rights and reviving the spirit of the defeated ERA. For Careerists, being able to make independent decisions about life choices and enjoy equal rights remain vital points of interest. Balancers and Homing Pigeons often feel that these matters are far less important than leading a well-balanced life.

Feminists write off what they consider nonissues, e.g., the importance of marriage and family, leaving wide-open gaps for their enemies to move into the fray. By reassuring women that their desire for warmth and a man's devotion are more important than the feminist goal of self-sufficiency, they are in line with Mother's Rules. In retreat from the grueling demands of the workplace, apple pie and motherhood offers an intriguing way for modern women to try to go home again.

The conservative fundamentalist movement, composed primarily of evangelical Christian women's groups, are pushing and praying hard to pick up the slack and convince women that they can lead them in the right and only way to the truth. Two rival, but nearly identical, groups vying for attention are the Concerned Women for America (CWA) and the Eagle Forum. Both oppose abortion, and the ERA, and are against equal pay for comparable work. Both had their start in the early 70s and both tally their supporters by their subscriptions to their newsletters.

CWA president and founder Beverly LaHaye believes she is qualified to speak for the American family because she's been married for 30 years to a fundamentalist Baptist preacher, Reverend Tim LaHaye. (He runs the American Coalition for Traditional Values that advocates that the government hire a 25 percent quota of Christian conservatives.)

A CWA follower and disenfranchised feminist says, "I had to have a better job than my man when I was a libber and it nearly did us in. I was nothing to love when I was only thinking of myself. God gave me humility and I'm a satisfied woman at home with my two wonderful babies." Another says, "I'm in the group that loves men. And adores fathers."

Eagle Forum's founder and leading spokesperson, Phyllis Schlafly, also defines her group as profamily. It was originally called "Stop ERA" in 1972. The major issues of the Eagle Forum revolve around the revision of educational philosophies and textbooks to reflect "traditional roles for people and elimination of secular humanism." Eagle is supportive of the movement toward educating children at home.

A Schlafly follower says, "It would be the joy of my life to win the Full-Time Homemaker award from my state at our next convention. I'm praying I can make that dream come true."

A NOW leader says, "Schlafly is a liberated woman who went to law school in her middle years. Without our group, she probably wouldn't have gotten in. She draws the line at other women accomplishing what she has. She's a professional. As a working woman, it's extremely doubtful that she'd follow the limitations she advocates for others."

Eleanor Smeal, past-president of NOW, refutes the claim that the two conservative camps represent the majority of women. She says, "That's an outrage. How can this puny group of bloated figures be compared to all the major women's organizations in this country? We all have rules for membership, we stand for elections, we pay dues, have public meetings, and file reports. Our numbers are not make-believe."

She cites the feminist stands of organizations such as the National Education Association, the American Association of University Women, the League of Women Voters, the National Women's Political Caucus, the American Nursing Association, and the United Methodist Women in her roll call of supporters.

Whether any of these groups represents the majority of working women is up for debate. Perhaps one of the contending groups will refocus its platform to appeal to middle-class working women in the throes of re-evaluating their lives.

One new idea coming to the force is "neofeminism." It represents a grass-roots idea that there should be more to life than work and independence. It seems to give voice to the poignant call of the exhausted working woman: "Is this all there is?"

The neofeminist catch phrase is "equal but different." Without giving up equality in the public sector, particularly the workplace, it attempts to place the responsibility for the family squarely in the laps of private corporations and on the government. Feminists may well agree to disagree with the neofeminist idea of the source for the money to provide the massive budget that will provide the perks they crave.

There's more than a hint of anger in the voice of an employee who works at a plant that provides subsidized day-care for mothers and fathers. Here's another aspect of the Uncivil Business War. She says:

> People come from far and wide to work here since my company offered to pay half of child care expenses. A nursery was created right here on an extension at enormous expense. Since

no Santa appeared with funding bucks, guess what? All grade levels were reviewed and the pay scale re-evaluated.

Surprise. My company now pays employees far less than other comparable plants in the area. They still can compete for top-drawer management and show a profit on their bottom line. A new-hire male engineer with a choice of spots came here because they have birthday parties for the kids and daddies are invited. A new-hire female director came for the warmth and caring shown by allowing her to leave work to nurse her baby.

I'm 45 and I don't blow candles or nurse, so I can't compete with the available talent hanging in at the high end. They won't resign at any inconvenience, injustice, or stagnation because they wouldn't dream of changing jobs and shaking up junior. Even if I didn't mind working at frozen wages, which I do mind, I resent otherwise intelligent working people who think they're getting a free lunch when we're all getting ripped off.

Neofeminism is rooted not only in the difference between men and women, but separates Careerists, Balancers, and Homing Pigeons as well. Women trying to balance the merits of their choices find that social expectations contribute to the mayhem.

One woman captures the ambivalence clearly. Americans "have so arranged life that a man may have a home, a family, love, companionship, domesticity, and fatherhood, yet remain an active citizen; a women must choose: either live alone, unloved, unaccompanied, uncared for, homeless, childless, with her work in the world for sole consolation, or give up all world service for the joys of love, motherhood, and domestic service." This comment from the battlefront came from Charlotte Perkins Gilman in 1897, and it could have been written today.

The fastest growing segment of today's work force includes the eight million mothers of preschool children. Half of all women with children under three years of age are working outside their homes. Once they're in the work world, they report feeling torn and trapped by priorities of home and office.

Women who do not have young children also feel torn and trapped by ramifications of the bailout by former feminists with advanced degrees who get tired of the rat race and cheerfully join the downwardly mobile. The newly demotivated enjoy approval and envy from their peers, while their still-toiling sisters experience a deep sense of frustration.

The concept of a "caring" workplace is fast becoming woven into the fabric of the corporate attitude toward equal pay and opportunity. Women find it difficult to mesh the new feminism with the old value system.

Syndicated columnist Mary Anne Dolan comments on the feminist movement. She says, "Women, most notably those who grew up during the feminist revolt, are having babies. About four million babies will be born in 1987 and 43 percent of them will be firstborn children. The needs of those children and of the families who are responsible for them, whether unwed teenagers or wealthy adults in second or third marriages, will dramatically refocus all social efforts—particularly the women's movement."

A puzzled professional says, "I'm really getting confused. I gave up any realistic hope of having my own family for a single's life and my legal career. Now everyone's doing an about-face and seeing liberation in terms of marriage and children. The reel is running backward, or I got it wrong in the first place. It's too late for me to say 'whoops' and start over."

A working woman in her early sixties says, "My life was changed by Betty Friedan. Instead of being revered as a leader with wisdom to offer the new generation of working women who wouldn't be there without her, she's been mocked for revising her point of view. I think she was banned for being old and ugly. Youngsters didn't identify with her."

On a college campus: "The only feminist I've heard of is the pretty one with the long hair and big glasses. I forget her name, but she's the only one who smiles. And is sexy at her age. I truly do admire that and hope I can be like her."

In her book *Feminism on Trial*, Ellen Hawkes used the Ginny Foat murder case as a platform for examining feminism in the 80s. Foats, president of California's NOW, was indicted in 1983 for a 1965 murder. Her arrest provoked controversy over her possible guilt, and personal and political dialogues that continued throughout her trial and vindication. Hawkes explores the schisms between gays and straights and middle-class and working women. The book poses the question: Is feminism a political commitment or a psychological need? As women battle one another's loyalties and lifestyles, the possibility of enticing these women to work together for a common good seems remote.

Exploring the psychological side to feminism, Patricia McBroom, in *The Third Sex*, asks, "What does an equal society offer, other than the equal right to kill yourself for achievement?" She explains that the culture of male/female expectations of the previous century still affect us. She suggests using the knowledge gained from the study of primitive cultures to become a more equal and humanistic society.

A woman who remembers the 60s says, "I loved it. We were proud to strip ourselves of makeup and frills. It was a way to take off the outside masks we were trained to show the world. It gave us hope for our futures."

Erica Jong shares her thoughts in a *Vanity Fair* magazine article, "The Awful Truth About Women's Lib" (April, 1986). She tells of being so deeply depressed by participants at a feminist poetry festival who booed when she read her poetry about new motherhood that it dried up her "dwindling supply of milk" and ended her career as a nursing mother.

Her analysis of feminism today is, "When the dust had settled . . . women had infiltrated certain professions where they were previously not welcome. In publishing, in advertising, in television, some became visible and highly paid. But they failed to reach the very top in corporate, financial, and political arenas . . . it became apparent that the world would be lost for the want of a competent nanny and that the workplace did not take kindly to milk stains on the silk blouse or the canceling of meetings because of sick children."

Jong feels that had feminism concentrated on "the pragmatic problems of working mothers, it might not have alienated the millions of women . . . the issue that might have built a cohesive nonpolitical feminist movement, a coalition of left and right, of men and women—was the issue of liberated families, liberated child-rearing: how to be a mother, in short, without getting screwed."

The mother of feminism, Betty Friedan, denies that she has backed down even a little in her book, *The Second Stage*. The first stage focused on winning equal rights and sometimes casting men as the enemy. She now advocates that men and women work together to ease the burdens on both. She says, "It's not either/or, it shouldn't have to be a choice between career and family." Because younger women "don't face the same nameless frustration that older women did," Friedan feels they can put the rights older women gained into practice. In an interview in the *Los Angeles Times*, she says, "Some of these women do take their rights too much for granted . . . They're happy to benefit from sacrifices others made, but are unwilling to pay their dues, to work for women who still need help. They ought to have their bottoms spanked."

Friedan spoke of the future of feminism when she toured college campuses: "The women's movement will never look like it did ten years ago, and it shouldn't."

In today's work world, feminism takes a backseat. Women trying to make it happen fight one another, and seem unlikely to rally round together. The pendulum swings toward home and family and away from the politics of social change. Feminism seems to be suffering a backlash that began with the defeat of the Equal Rights Amendment in 1982. It seems to be in a lull under ongoing debates of human life amendments and the current administration's opposition to affirmative action for women.

Feminism may be in a stupor, like a watchdog drugged with an overdose of complacency by its caretakers. It may growl when a stick is thrown at its head and it's taken to task for its sins of past behavior. Yet it's tethered and fairly benign. Like the American Civil Liberties Union, it is vilified until it is needed to defend an issue that no one else will touch. Feminism may rebound when women in the workplace need to reach out to one another for support.

For now, many close-to-middle-aged women are dreaming of homes and babies at any career cost, while their juniors and seniors have little choice but to remain focused on earning their way. As mixed messages abound in the office, Women vs. Women takes on an individual and group strength that works against the feminist core that would preserve a measure of hard-won financial and social equality.

Just as women may only speak once (twice is labeled nagging), the feminist movement may be experiencing burnout. For now, its message may seem a twicetold tale. Feminism may rise again from its ashes, or remain crushed by the barefoot-and-pregnant fervor sweeping today's workplace.

Unless they reconsider, working women today may be leading the feminist movement to its ultimate Waterloo.

16

The Stressmobile Express

Janine J., age 39, owns a big-city public relations agency. She says:

> It seems strange that I got an abortion at 29 just so I wouldn't miss a beat in my career. My meaningful other would have been supportive. As it was he kind of drifted away in the fog of our mismatched expectations. Now I have no one and what I do have doesn't seem to matter. I match man and baby against freedom, condo, and business, and it's no contest. I made a mistake.
>
> It's almost too late, but I'm getting a partner in the office and taking off for a long vacation. I want to find a mate. Every time I see a woman in blue jeans in the park with a toddler, it literally sets my teeth on edge. I feel sick.

Vickie P., age 24, is an entry-level trainee in a medical office. She uses drugs to soothe her frustrations.

> I snort in the morning before I leave home, in the car at lunch, and a few times at breaks. Some of the old women would die if they knew, but the doctors wouldn't. They do it. Some nurses, too. It gives me incentive to go back to school, so I can follow in their footsteps. They earn enough for an extra

toot and access to some other goodies to make the day go by.
The nurses who don't do drugs cluck ain't-it-awful about those
who do, but they cover for doctors who abuse the prescription
drugs. They think doctors are godlike beings and have an
excuse because they're supposedly overworked and "under all
that pressure." And the biddies have their own addictions.
One of them is a jealous mouth always ready to get the younger
girls in trouble by telling lies.

Cora is in her early fifties. She is an assistant superintendent
of schools in Iowa. She comments:

It took most of my career just getting here. There were no
other women who got this far in my school system. One thing
that held women back was the two female supervisors who
undermined women every chance they got over a period of ten
years. I was much older than the men in the position when I
finally became a principal. Those supervisors would come into
the building and stir the pot.

They'd ask the predominantly female staff leading questions like, "Do you feel she keeps order at all times?" They'd
give the impression that a negative answer would bring smiles
of approval. And they'd ask my male peers in other buildings
to "keep an eye on her" and "offer help."

To top it off, they'd go back to the central office with
sighs about needing to visit my building more often than the
men's and build everything they unearthed into a major problem where none existed. Everytime they'd walk in my office
my blood pressure would zoom. They finally retired, but I
had to hide my feelings for many years, so I wouldn't be seen
as a malcontent. I always thought that the male superintendent knew more about the true situation than he let on, and
that helped a little. Now my stress comes from trying to hurry
and get one step further along before the retirement age
catches up with me.

Endlessly weighing personal choices and trying to second-
guess themselves about the best route, working women commute
daily on the Stressmobile Express. Fueled with nervous female

energy, it's a vehicle that runs relentlessly over the hopes and dreams of other women.

The engine of the Stressmobile Express is fear of failure. Chronic stress is more likely to be brought on by lack of career success than by anything pertaining to the work itself. Failure is a cause of stress. Small wonder so many women suffer from it.

In *Executive Essentials*, Mitchell Posner suggests, "Success and what comes with it is one of the best methods of reducing stress. Many of us like to think that everything is not rosy at the top, that success has its drawbacks: powerful and wealthy people must, underneath it all, be unhappy. Well, it just ain't so. Most successful people experience less frustration on the job, have high self-esteem, fewer financial worries, more freedom, and find greater pleasure in their jobs."

Every day, those under pressure, says Posner, "ingest over five billion doses of tranquilizers to calm ourselves, five billion doses of barbiturates to help us unwind and sleep, and then three billion doses of amphetamines to make us feel perky."

While women struggle at the office over commonplace problems like the need for more money, a better job, and a nicer office, they also fret about personal choices, responsibilities, and desires. Their needs generate internal conflict, and their attempts to meet their needs produce open conflicts with co-workers. Women become embroiled in internal and external wars of nerves: The Stressmobile Express is always on time.

The strain is made worse by the realization that they could ultimately fail, not only at their careers, but at their plans for life. If the pressure isn't handled properly, stress can lead to illness, disability, and under extreme circumstances death from a stress-related disease. Dr. Hans Selye, specialist in stress research, assures us that our bodies are built to handle and even thrive on various types of stress. He calls the good, competitive stress *eustress*, and the excessive, prolonged, and bad stress *distress*.

The medical community claims that physical stress is easier to deal with than emotional stress. That's not much help to women who suffer stress in the workplace. Stress there generally means distress.

Stress is a prestige ailment in a world rife with socially ac-

ceptable diseases. The distress of work-related unhappiness is
shared by men and women alike. Men drink and take drugs when
they are frustrated with their lot in life. So, how are women different? Curt B., 43-year-old Illinois personnel director, gives the
question deep consideration.

> Aside from the obvious differences, men are less frazzled.
> They seem to know where they're headed and have a fair idea
> of how to at least try to get there. If they come in with symp-
> toms of being stressed out, they give me the impression that
> it's a temporary byproduct of hard work, like a string of tight
> deadlines. We discuss things like hiring additional support for
> them, or scheduling in more physical leisure activities, like
> the company softball team.
>
> Senior management uses access to business and social
> clubs or takes time to take incentive trips with the salespeople
> to give everyone a needed boost. If there's an alcohol or drug
> problem, we steer them to formal help programs and work
> with the man who's trying to kick bad habits. If they're hav-
> ing an emotional setback, like divorce or illness in the family,
> we can't suggest much but offer understanding that this too
> shall pass.
>
> By and large, midlevel managers and above are extremely
> interested in preserving their jobs. That's their priority, and
> we work together to salvage their career and control stress
> symptoms. They realize they need to do that.
>
> Being frank, with women it's less easy to pin down. Some
> want help to get through a bad time, but some seem to be
> asking for an excuse to take home so their husbands will tell
> them to quit. Or, they say they're under too much stress, but
> they don't pin it down to what the matter is or how the com-
> pany can be supportive. Their complaints are vague. They're
> less likely to admit alcohol or drug problems, although it's
> often been brought to our attention by others before they come
> in. Usually, it's pretty emotional. And we may be less helpful
> than we'd like.

Men tend to pinpoint the source of their problems. Cause and
effect part company when women have problems at work. Women
imbibe heavy doses of bad and good stress. They attribute many

of their problems to lack of time, love, and money, and fight the women who seem to have more of any or all of these commodities.

One woman's show of calm is enough to generate a suspicious anxiety among her female peers. Instead of asking to share her secret, their attitude is more likely to be "What's she trying to prove?" *or* "Who's she trying to kid?" *or* "Wonder what's she's up to?"

The word *stress* was once used solely to measure an amount of wear and tear on a body or a beam. Alvin Toffler's description of the effect that work tension has on the human body (in his best-selling book *Future Shock*) popularized stress as a modern medical ailment. *Future Shock* is the human reaction to the constantly accelerating rate of change in the lives of ordinary people. These rapid changes challenge men's and women's ability to adapt to the demands of their environment.

Women riding the Stressmobile Express confront an internal struggle produced by the memory of their war dancing in their brains. Mother's Rule—do unto yourself before other women do unto you—instructs her daughter to find someone to take care of her before the good men are gone.

A case of nerves is understandable when Mother's Rules are in play. The "love" Band-Aid is prescribed to chase the boogeyman of reality from her door. And there aren't enough men just like the man who married dear old mom. It's nerve-racking for the middle-class working woman to realize the portly male caretaker is gone. The caring, sharing nerd in the warm-up suit whom she ostensibly prefers has as many doubts and questions as she has.

It may be a cliche that women reserve the right to change their minds, but there is truth to it. Indecision and fear become a double-edged sword of unsettling choices. As battlefront warriors get tangled in ambivalence, they constantly clash with women who do it "their own way" in the office. At home, where a fair division of responsibility never really caught on, the result is often distress.

Clinicians in the field of stress-related disorders tell us that the physical self can adapt to almost any daily inconvenience in uncomfortable or even mildly dangerous work conditions. This includes small, crowded, noisy offices with polluted air or excessively high or low room temperatures. They confirm that it's more often the psychological factors that grate on the human nervous system until they reduce workers to masses of quivering uncertainty.

A sense of failure combined with the old home remedy of "mother's little helpers" may explain why women often appear nervous and strung-out as they indulge in the Uncivil Business War of nerves. Opposing one another has brought them dismay and frustration. The fear of rebuffs in the office and the prospect of failing to have a career or realize their happily-ever-after dreams lead to distress. As an entire generation of women engages in these hostilities, they suffer the symptoms of soldiers in battle: fatigue, illness, paranoia, and exhaustion. There is even a decrease in the number of years by which women outlive men. Distress is an equalizer.

Heart disease among women is on the rise. Eating disorders and associated complications are near epidemic. Drugs, absenteeism, and sloppy work habits are the order of the office day. War, women have discovered, is indeed hell.

Elizabeth J., a 35-year-old midlevel technical training manager, shares her chagrin.

Now I drink. That's different from my previous pattern of having a drink on social outings with friends. This is evenings in, erasing the warts of my day.

After being with the same company for over ten years with two promotions and cost-of-living increases, I seem to be bumping my head on the glass ceiling. So, I toast my best friend in college, who didn't go this route.

She majored in getting her old-fashioned Mrs. degree and worked just until she had her first baby. Her years at home with two kids equal my years here. She waited until they were in school and she got bored before she considered a job.

Her husband knew someone who knew someone and she got something similar to mine. Her starting pay is just a little less than what I'm earning now.

Need I say more? Part of me is happy for her. A small part. The rest is a primal screech for the lost years I left my babies home with a sitter to enjoy just six weeks after they were born. I was crazy to think I'd get anywhere here or that it would make up for missing the kids' first steps. I toast my failure. And that income that mattered so much at the time . . . I don't even know where it went.

Helene K., age 34, midlevel support communications worker, says, "After being away from work for eight years, let me tell you, most of these women are fierce. What hurts is they acted friendly when I hired in. I was glad to enroll my little one in school and get back with adults. But, although they're nice to me to my face, they resent that I just started to work. It would be easier for me if they just right out told me I was unwelcome. What's hard to adjust to is constantly trying to be accepted, but getting the cold shoulder and not being exactly sure why."

A downhill runaway ride on the Stressmobile Express is the course for many fighting women. They worry and fear that further miscalculations about work and personal goals will plunge them into being unloved relics. They are afraid that life will pass them by.

A Tennessee women in her midforties comments: "I'm working two jobs—at the office and home. Both require full-time commitment. I'm constantly reassigning priorities and feel I'm doing neither job very well or making much progress."

A contemporary of hers says: "I work part-time. The other women resent that I have more time for myself. I don't see it that way. By the time I dress and drive to work I might as well stay and earn more and maybe get somewhere. But they still put me down."

A woman in her midthirties who lives in Washington, D.C., claims: "Women here are separated by their personal priorities. Those like me, half on the work side of the fence and half on the family side, end up not much of anywhere. I'm lukewarm on life. I sleepwalk at home and work. I don't feel I have much control over anything. Gals here all want to be married, but no one respects homemakers. We're the ditchdiggers of the universe."

A newly married 30-year-old city worker and suburb dweller in Missouri asks: "Will someone tell me how a woman can decide between a power lunch and rushing home to try to be there for a repairman? I speed across town and they don't show up half the time, anyway. I end up feeling like a helpless victim."

Younger women embroiled in the Uncivil Business War are sometimes amazed at their inner turmoil after a short time in the work force. They enter eager and confident, and observe the women around them jockeying for position and agonizing over the frustration of their jobs. They either react with determination to change it all, or find themselves pulled down by the tension of the women around them. Seldom do they escape the galloping stress.

Gloria B., age 26, is a laboratory technician: "I can't believe that Big Brother has come to work. They're going to do drug testing. Which will affect just about everyone our age. I take a little of whatever I can get to cool out. Now I'm not sure what I'll do. They'll have to have someone stand there while they take the sample, or everyone would get around it. The idea is wrecking me and it hasn't even started. I could face tapering off to only weekends—maybe—but stuff stays in your urine."

Rozene G., age 26, is a clerk: "The girls here hate me. I just want to drift and party for a while. I got divorced this year and don't have anyone to care. Sometimes I come in a bit distracted and they freak if I slough off. This job is so easy, it doesn't matter. I'd quit doing it if I was running the company."

Women who are a few years older often rely on prescription medicine to soothe their work and personal woes.

Says a 43-year-old in Michigan, "I was never told my nerve medicine was habit forming. Evidently it is. I take more now than ever, even though it makes my mouth dry and I get drowsy."

A contemporary from Colorado shares symptoms: "I can do my work okay. Sometimes I slur my words by the end of the day. I get tired and frazzled. The doctor says I need help to relax to get through the office day and evenings with two teenagers."

A woman in her late twenties asks:

How do I deal with stress and tension? I jog in the morning and go to a health club after work. I try to keep positive thoughts. What gripes me is that I'm not moving up any faster than the women who drug out and always complain about being tired.

The chief provider of stress in my life is the older woman who works with me. She hates me for having been hired as her equal, which is absurd. Like I should have insisted on less money to satisfy someone I never even knew existed. Her health isn't so hot, but it seems convenient. She has hypoglycemia, so she keeps leaving her desk to snack.

Her other biggie is hyperventilating. Then the boss runs out of his office and puts a bag over her head. If I told you how I react to that you'd call me catty. Her nervous diseases do nothing to stifle her appetite. The fatter she gets, the sicker she gets. The more she annoys me, the more miles I jog.

Vicky P., a woman in her early thirties from Oregon, says, "My stress comes from frustration. Because I'm in what's known as child-bearing years, the older women drop lines in front of our male bosses like, 'You'll be getting pregnant and leaving us soon' when there's talk about future opportunities. It's not one comment; it's their attitude. I'm not sure it's meant to be serious, but it is to me. It builds up a wall of words against me being equal to them."

Baby Boomer women nearing the witching age of 40 share their nerve-racking frustration over the gap between expectations and reality. Midlife crisis is a quick ticket to a ride on the Stressmobile Express.

Laments one: "The babies in here bat their eyes and are content to slack off at the bottom until they catch a man."

Another says: "My frustration is with women who lie and complain to get by and get ahead better than I do with honest effort."

A word from the East: "I get nervous in traffic before I get here, trying to be on time. Then I get upset because no one else is even at their desk half an hour later, even when a meeting is scheduled. No one else seems concerned and I get more upset."

"When something else comes up, like school calling to say Jody has a fever and I should come get her, I literally start to tremble. At least once a week my married boss ducks out for a nooner with my chief rival and I have to cover for a woman who's trying to do me in. My stomach churns and I can't even eat. I just drink more coffee. By evening, I'm too burned out after the day and commute to key down. Usually, I'm a confirmed grouch and go to sleep right after the kids are in."

From the Midwest: "Stress. Yes. I've been called too intense and too gressive all of my career. I've been told I've been passed over for being too opinionated and too tactless. But I've always been given harder jobs to do than all the other women combined. The bosses know I get the work done.''

From the Northeast: "It's the new technology like the damn computer that spells stress in my life. We had to learn it or die on the vine. Now I'm its slave. I'm in charge of a department that now uses the computer as an excuse for every mistake. When it's down, which is frequently, the gals just fold their hands and chat. It becomes like a holiday. The idea of work goes out the window. Then everything piles up and there are more mistakes.

"Okay, not only is my job the same boring mess it was five years ago, but I'm personally busier picking up the slack for those who have given up, but still show up.

"Those about my age have problem kids or problem husbands. Everyone is dieting and jumpy. They bring every woe to the office and we all pay. No one dumps on the men. They wouldn't put up with it.''

A step beyond those forty-ish Boomers are the older set, working women in their fifties who have achieved a measure of management success, yet express high levels of frustration. They sense that they approach goals that are consistently a step beyond their grasp. The nightmare of elusive success, after making choices which favored their careers over their personal lives, accounts for the resentment and nervous energy that make these women souls in near torment.

Sara J., from Pennsylvania, is a group management director in her late fifties:

It's baffling. I know I'm being excluded from decision-making in my company. There seems to be an in group, and I'm on the outside, like a kid with her nose pressed against the candy store window. Part of the good ole boys prestige in the Philadelphia area comes through private club membership. Two of the main clubs exclude women and two have recently opened their membership. There's one for women only and it excludes men.

It all sounds childish, I guess, but it matters at my level. There are people I need to meet in my reach for a vice presidency. That can come casually in the right environment.

Clubs will open, but not in time for my career to benefit.

Some women, wives of executives here for one, defend the
men having their own place to go and relax without women
around.

It's nice that they view me as a threat to their husband's
libido, but a better career will happen for some young snip if
not for me. She'll reap the reward of my groundwork. Stress?
That's a mild word for it. If I read about it in the old folk's
home, I'll have a stroke and die then and there. Just kidding.
I hope.

Women of every age group haven't moved up as far and as
fast as expected. In the current political climate, the heat is off on
the discrimination issue. There is little impetus for change from
the federal top. Flamboyant firsts for women seem to be a thing
of the past. Stress is the result of no success.

Many qualified working women have struggled no further than
midpoint, while most earn less in a society that doesn't value their
contribution. In fear and frustration they devalue one another and
create stressful working conditions to stop any one individual from
advancing even a small step beyond her sisters.

For women who perservered and made it to senior management, the many women who enter the scene makes them more
vulnerable. Their self-serving instinct to keep their positions rather
than help other women to join them suits their needs. But failing
to help advance the cause of female power may also leave them in
solitary distress. In any event, there is less and less room at the
top for women.

On the other hand, there are now only 439 females on the
corporate boards of the top 1,000 companies. They are more visible than ever. Although small in number, this group has still nearly
tripled over the last decade. The token woman is less needed and
less protected than ever before. There is a great deal of stress in
the current senior management picture. For one thing, it's getting
easier to get rid of women without suffering undue repercussions.
In 1980, women represented only 4 percent of fired clients served
by Henchey & Co., a New York job placement consultant agency.

In 1986, that figure quadrupled to 16 percent. Susan Walker,
the firm's executive vice president, reported to the *Wall Street*

Journal that "it will continue to increase in the next few years."
She explains that with corporate downsizing and mergers, women
"have the same vulnerability (to firing) that goes along with success."

Corporations that once hesitated to fire top-rung women have
now taken off the kid gloves, she says. In their firm, "the average
age of fired clients is 40, with an average salary of $47,000, both
lower than averages for men." In reflecting about personal attitudes, Walker says that fired women take longer to heal and
"grieve a little bit . . ."

Some women are retreating to the home as others rejoin the
work force. Fully packed Stressmobiles steer women to the edge
of daily tension and frustration. Women devalue one another at
every level as they skirt the fine line between personal success and
career failure.

Seldom do they halt their nerve-racking daily struggle long
enough to evaluate the toll stress takes on their bodies and minds.
Few take the time to try to manage stress; few come to terms with
the sure long-term effects of chronic stress. Women deal with one
another in terms of their emotions about failure, indecision, and
ambivalence about the wisdom of their life choices.

Middle-class women speak of many nerve medicines. No pla-
cebos on the horizon can bring the serenity that would result from
women working together toward common goals. Instead, the ca-
reening Stressmobile Express ensures little eustress, while nearly
guaranteeing a consistent barrage of distress.

PART FOUR

Cease-Fire

Are we approaching the end of a yellow brick road? Like the characters in Frank Baum's book, are we in search of heart, brains, and bravery? In *The Wizard of Oz*, the Tin Man, the Cowardly Lion, and the Scarecrow sought to better themselves, but Dorothy was only looking for a way to go home.

When Dorothy first left home she managed to take her house with her, only to land that house right on top of a wicked witch—the first female fatality. The dead witch's wicked sister hated Dorothy for killing her favorite sibling and swore vengeance. Later, young Dorothy killed this bothersome older woman also.

Dorothy's goal was to do whatever it took to get home again. There were witches in her way—one trying to stop her, another trying to help. Dorothy killed the bad witch on the assumption of "kill or be killed." But after the bad witch was dead, the good witch told Dorothy that she had to get home on her own anyway. In fact, the good witch let her know she never needed any help. She could get what she wanted all on her own, but she had to put her mind to it. The good witch thanked Dorothy kindly for doing away with her bad sisters.

All the men wanted was courage, brains, and heart. So much more simple. Dorothy wanted to help them achieve their goals, and they in turn encouraged her in her quest.

Is there an inner voice waiting to guide each Dorothy from the confused land of mind trips so that she can become her own best mentor? Won't her independent will help her overcome the wizard within?

Part Four acknowledges what most women already suspect—we're not in Kansas anymore. Like modern Dorothys, many women yearn for the magic it would take to go back home to more simple times.

Some women have tried to find answers through the Oz of the powerful male hierarchy. Many, like Dorothy, find only an unsure human using an amplifier to make his voice authoritative enough to mask his own insecurity.

Upon this discovery, Dorothy's sisters may be emotionally ready to say, "Thanks, fellas, we can take it from here." Women may be poised to take on their own economic destiny. They may be ready to stop battling one another and create their own magic.

The situation of Women vs. Women has never been more in need of an across-the-board cease-fire. Now's the time to slip into Dorothy's ill-gained but lucky slippers and get real. The Uncivil Business War will not end with a whimper or a bang. The remedies are self-reliance and the rewards of hard work. Part Four offers ways to evaluate and begin this process of separating fact from fantasy.

17

Peacemongers "Take It Personally"

Women vs. Women crept sneakily from the home to the workplace without anyone noticing the cumulative negative impact. Like a raging forest fire ignited by unnoticed sparks, the Uncivil Business War began small—with typical girl-on-girl rivalries. Now the conflagration has grown; women's independence and their economic futures are at stake. Only women strong enough to say "I, for one, take it personally" have the power to initiate a cease-fire.

Historically, women have been the most vocal advocates for peace during times of war. Never before has an individual's willingness to "do what she can" offered more direct opportunity to bring about change. To do her part, a woman must be a Peacemonger.

Peacemongering is an activist form of peacemaking. Women who now fight one another are in perfect position to take this giant step. The immediate goal is to create a cease-fire by bringing about a measure of harmony that will in time displace and overpower the war mentality pervasive in modern business offices.

Peacemongering is not easy to begin. It requires a willingness to rethink and modify the behavior that has created obstacles through years, behavior that has become second nature for millions of women in their transition from the home to the work world.

Good campaigns often begin with good slogans. In the case of the Uncivil Business War, "Take It Personally" fits the bill. Why? Fighting women dismiss the damage they've done with a shrug and the refrain, ". . . but don't take it personally." But it *is* personal.

The Uncivil Business War is the concern of every middle-class woman who might work, is now working, or may have daughters who will work. That's about as personal as an issue can get. So, do Take It Personally.

Perhaps a review of how the fighting started will give women an idea of how to work toward a cease-fire. The objective is to look at the current situation, evaluate its effect on the future of working women, and then begin to redirect goals.

Peacemongering is a physical, emotional, and intellectual effort; it requires strength, courage, and skill; it has a beginning, a middle, and an end. Like any fitness regimen, it can be understood and mastered if it is considered in terms of three basic parts: the warm-up, the activity, and the cool-down.

As in any sport, the warm-up is crucial to success without injury. Enlisting unused muscles can cause anything from strain to headache. It's best to follow the tried-and-true format of working on each section in order. Beginning Peacemongers need to slowly stretch and awaken their minds in preparation for the deceptively simple action that lies ahead.

The first mind-stretch is to take a long-range view of the entire Women vs. Women issue. A good place to start is with business signposts. In 1986, Karen Nussbaum, executive director of the National Association of Working Women (also known as Nine-to-Five), reported that an increase in part-time and temporary workers is creating a less stable work force, a true threat to the U. S. economy. This should signal a warning.

In an article in the *Los Angeles Times* she said, "Some see the trend as an answer to women seeking to balance both job and family, but it comes at the expense of workers left to cope with lower pay—part-time workers earn an average of 57.7 percent of the hourly full-time wage—and few fringe benefits." Peacemongering women must consider how this erosion of the work force will affect their future, as well as the futures of their qualified daughters, who will have to compete harder for fewer rewards. Consider that a 1986 report from the Bureau of Labor Statistics states that 62 percent of all temporary workers are women. (Only one out of five of the temporary jobs are held by part-timers needing full-time jobs.) Women who prefer temporary or part-time work destroy their power base in the work force.

Rather than ignore news about the economy that does not affect them at the present time, women should study and understand the economy. They must learn to appreciate the larger financial impact of their individual work decisions.

Interpreting news is well within the intellectual capabilities of Peacemongers and serves as a cerebral "muscle flex." When a woman decides to go home, with a vague plan to return to the workplace at some undetermined future date, and then only to work when it is convenient, she might stop to ask herself, "How might this affect my future? Will a job that I want be there when I want it? Does my casual attitude about work cause employers to distrust other women?"

The president of a Milwaukee-based personnel firm says that many women in their early thirties who worked, then stopped to have children, and reentered without seeking permanent jobs enable employers to budget for hiring only when a specific project or workload demands new employees. This means planned usage of "temps" to erode full-time staffs. And, it is noted, temporary help is no longer mainly clerical. Today's available women have a "richer education and background." This enables employers to hire "marked-down" talented women.

The peacemongering female must acknowledge that this situation discounts the value of her expensive MBA. She should ask, "Is there anything I can do to protect my investment? Am I contributing to this situation?"

Peacemongering women need to consider how the increasing emphasis on part-time work may affect their futures. After all, most employers consider contingent employees "a secondary work force that carries no benefits."

A woman who quits work and retreats home is not freed of her obligation to be a Peacemonger. Even if she opts not to work full-time, she must give serious thought to the battle she leaves behind. Can Homing Pigeons or part-time workers devise strategies to lessen the damage to the future of working women? It's a question millions of women should ask themselves. It's one of a million possible questions.

For instance, as a woman prepares to peacemonger, she might ask herself, "Do I play office games?" *Every* working person, male or female, plays office games. But how often do women ask themselves, "In choosing to do this, am I hurting other women, and ultimately myself?"

Peacemongers in the midmanagement work force full-time can confront themselves: "I'm slipping into Women's Rules (*get her before she gets me*) on this one." They can discipline themselves to make a practice of asking, "Does this make good business sense?" The name of the office game is survival, but women don't have to automatically sacrifice other women to stay alive.

Many pressured and threatened women do not believe this. Instead, they strike out at the women they envy. When financial, professional, and personal lives are uncertain, a fight mentality is understandable. But all-out war is excessive.

Given the economic realities, Peacemongers must classify each aggressive tactic according to its appropriateness. Consider "social" and "professional" behavioral categories. Once a form of behavior is put in its correct context, the fight can be confined to its proper place.

The warm-up is nearly complete. The heartbeat is beginning to accelerate at a slow but steady rate. Ready for action, Peacemongers can fortify themselves with a few salient facts to hold them true to their course even when they feel like heading for the locker room. For example, when wages are frozen, women still earn less than men, and living expenses are just as high. At difficult moments, the Peacemonger can remind herself of the consequences of continuing the folly of Women vs. Women. Such knowledge can help her to sustain her mission and persevere.

Peacemongers can review previous chapters of *Women vs. Women* and relate them to their lives. Even after dismissing circumstances that don't apply to their real lives at the moment, they can focus on the situations that *do* apply to them now or may sometime in the future.

Remember to keep the long-term picture in view. Can you say you'll probably never be divorced? Underqualified? On your own? Without adequate funds? There are still some areas of concern. For instance, few can say they'll never be old, ignored, or ill. In any case, focus on realities.

Is a single-parent household a possibility? Stretch the mind. They are on the rise and are most often headed by a low-earning woman.

Can you see yourself as part of a second family? Imagine the concerns of mix-and-match varieties of his kids, her kids, and their kids—and young adults who return home with financial problems and broods of their own.

What if you become a man's second or third wife? What if your mother does? Wives may be unexpectedly expected to help provide such items as tuition, braces, or cars for youngsters in the extended family. Such circumstances could require the new wife to stay at work.

Some family trees are as complex as biblical begats. Peacemongers who never thought they'd be a part of this intricate scene could become involved. Expand your thinking to consider all the possibilities.

Whether or not women genuinely love their female friends, they have no choice but to regard other women as rivals on all fronts. Girlhood skills allow for outdoing even cherished friends, when necessary. It's now necessary. Many women put themselves first, at home and at work. Peacemongering demands only a fair fight. That may allow Mother's Rules at home but it should be Business Rules only at the office.

Peacemongers aren't required to be perfect. Many of those who left the home front for the excitement of the wild ride in the fast-paced world of business ended up with the car broken down at the side of the road. The option was to get greasy and try to fix it, or don mother's well-preserved dainty white gloves and call for a man to come to the rescue. Those who didn't accept (or failed at) that ploy resent those who compromised. It isn't productive to criticize other women's mistakes or emulate what worked. Peacemongers should now Take It Personally. This concludes the warm-up portion.

The next order of business is to work up a burning sweat—and act. And the first act in peacemongering is merely to stop fighting.

Once the fighting has stopped, it's time to consider a list of what to do. Every woman in midmanagement knows that the basics aren't easy. "Do unto others . . ." or "Pay three sincere compliments a day . . ." are important, but the mental jog is what counts. Stop to think about how your present conduct will affect your future.

Here is an overview that could be embroidered in needlepoint but should be put in the busiest time manager's appointment book every day.

1. *Tolerate the objectionable.* Peacemongers need not judge other women. Women do strange things. So do men. But when women do them to other women, they seek revenge. For now, hate the sin. And feel free to hate the sinner, but separate feeling from acting. The word *tolerate* may seem condescending. So be it. During office hours, social ungraces must be ignored and never copied.

2. *Respond intelligently.* When in doubt, think first, be emotional later. Peacemongers who have fought their way to midmanagement have a lot going for them. A woman with a rational mind who showed up for classes, took exams, got that first job, and made her way through roller-coaster years of joy and fatigue is likely to be a successful Peacemonger. A clear decision that the present situation is not working is the groundwork for change.

3. *Learn.* Discover what's going on in the office just below the surface. Peacemongers need to cultivate a sense of how it really goes. In addition to paid work, what else is going on? What are women doing? Who's going where? Who isn't? Who's helped them get their last promotion? Who pulled for someone else? On what grounds? How did those who missed react? What did they do?

Reread the policies and procedures book and department job descriptions. Decide who's following the rules, who's doing fine without, and who's mired in the mud. Peacemongers rule by unwritten but enforced office laws. The road map may not be in print, but it is available in some form, perhaps verbally, recorded in memory, part of a ritual some know and some do not. The real road to the top is marked. Peacemongers can illuminate the misleading detours.

Peacemongers can train themselves to become more aware. Who's chatting in the morning? How loud? About what? Who's in earshot? Do male bystanders seem to enjoy the "girly" byplay around them? Are they sometimes played to as an appreciative audience? Are they really nice about time being taken away from work? Why? How could this affect the way women are perceived? Does anyone realize this could be a problem? Why not? Is work behavior like social behavior? Who-all got promoted this year?

Tolerate, evaluate, and learn. Can peacemongering be effective if based on anything that elementary? It sure can. More than one self-help group has modeled itself on the world-famous Alcoholics Anonymous. They advocate accepting the problem and dealing with it just for today. The today philosophy could make this cease-fire do-able. Peacemongers need to make the commitment to Take It Personally.

In aerobics parlance, this active section could keep the heart rate at a pace guaranteed to open the glands and produce a full sweat. Peacemongering should be conducted at a pace that brings about more than a ladylike dew. The goal is to go for the burn.

Although there are similarities, peacemongering is less dangerous than aerobics. Overdoing produces little physical stress, and the emotional rewards remain intact. Positive exercises banish depression—brooding and working out are almost impossible to do simultaneously—and both aerobics and peacemongering can be done only by the individual. There's no way to hire another to do either.

Peacemongers accept mistakes in judgment, assuming that all do the best they can at the time. This need not convey approval.

Even Peacemongers with a strong work ethic and fairly decent jobs will be discouraged some of the time. Women know that all work can become mundane. Whether you're a night shift janitor or the president of the United States, a job is a job is a job. Some parts of it become routine. For those with less pay and less prestige, the days grow long. The journey to retirement lacks glamour. The brave new world can be a real drag. And a plodding bore of a job seems to be the new reality. Peacemongers need to add enthusiasm for creative work to days when only "girly" tricks and activities liven up the party.

Peacemongers can position themselves for a fight for the slightly better job that offers a bit more money and a few more perks. A complex economy grounded on two incomes—63 percent of today's families are running on two paychecks—may be a situation that is all but impossible to halt. Most women—figures place the number at seven out of ten—work not by choice, but to survive. Active Peacemongers may be the most comfortable; they're doing what they can to make it better.

It behooves Peacemongers to accept the fact that they may be in the workplace to stay, and to spread this idea among coworkers who treat the office as though it's a temporary way station.

Even Peacemongers who do have a choice must remember that circumstances change. Even the aristocracy takes a tumble every now and again. Relationships crumble, fortunes fade. Illness or new tax structures may change a family's finances.

An unpredictable change of fortune is always possible. Consider what happened a few years ago in the small nation of Israel. To halt runaway inflation, the Israeli government decided, without prior warning, to take a zero from the currency of its citizens. A person could go to bed one night with $100 in the bank and wake up the next with a new balance of $10. The lesson: In today's electronic economies, financial security may be altered with a push of a button. History shows that work is destiny. It behooves all women to plan for the job they may one day need.

Is there a way for the next generation of women to prepare for a work world of real opportunity? Will the daughter of a corporate dropout find a welcome mat at the door of tomorrow's senior hierarchy? Is escape a solution to the problem of lack of equality in senior management? A wartorn office offers little hope for tomorrow's women. But keep in mind that it's not necessary to love one's fellow women in the white-collar work world. In fact, that prerequisite could set the cease-fire back a dozen more years.

Now comes the best part. The important cool-down. Tight muscles have been loosened, used hard, and are now ready to bend and sway, accompanied by a feeling of emotional well-being. Not everyone enjoys aerobics and not everyone will take on peacemongering as a way of life. The point is to give it a try and decide if there are benefits to the three-part peacemongering exercise. Here's the cool-down portion.

Working women can become immediate Peacemongers by employing the wisdom found in the straightforward Hippocratic Oath, which guides physicians in the healing arts. The credo directs "First of all, do no harm." In the parlance of Eastern philosophy, "There is action in inaction."

Women should reassess their attitudes toward working for one another and consider how a change in their biases might open the way for more female executives—perhaps the Peacemonger herself. The cause of peacemongering could be aided by withholding criticism when a female colleague goofs in a big way at work. Clenched teeth and a ready sense of humor may save the day when a female colleague behaves unprofessionally—attends meetings in gimmicky costumes and flashes red-taloned fingernails in a bid to be noticed at any cost.

Working women need not try to love the crazy-maker who giggles at the end of each remark and turns every sentence into a question. They can merely tolerate the meekness of the woman who apologizes enough to drive everyone up the nearest wall, or the one who insists on initiating inappropriate personal conversation within earshot of others during the day.

Women can cling to the thought—and the chair if need be—that there are also men who goof up and are ignored or casually categorized as people who won't advance. There will always be worst, better, and best.

Peacemongering silently tosses a daily pebble of mutual acceptance into the work pool. Peacemongering creates ripples of ongoing waves that women can ride all the way to their personal goals.

This is a halt-and-cleanse action, designed to recognize and counteract women's almost instinctive inclination to keep one another at the same, or a lower, level. Peacemongers accept that most women are in the workplace to stay and that mutual success is the goal. The methods are meant to tackle the most flagrant injustices. No attempt should be made to fix anything that's already working.

Just as there are periods of limbo between cease-fire, peace talks, and a genuine cessation of hostilities, there must be a quiet time in peacemongering. Patterned more on Gandhi than Genghis Khan, the aim is to instill an atmosphere of trust and a whisper of reason. Calm, tranquility, and acceptance can be helpful tools.

In the closing cease-fire sections of *Women vs. Women,* peace is declared. Ways for women to work together are explored further, with emotional considerations set aside. It is not for us to judge whether women deserve tolerant treatment in specific instances when they're trying one another's patience as well as souls.

Peacemongers should keep their early expectations at a reasonable level. Each hour may not be intense enough to burn hate. But if they're not adding fat to the fire, they're continuing positive conditioning. This keeps the muscles in good tone.

During the cease-fire, all women will be assumed peacemakers, with the potential to elevate themselves to become Peacemongers. Women will then be in a position to advance. The first step is to Take It Personally.

18

In Distance
There Is Hope

Peacemongering and Taking It Personally have an element of "something old and something new. . . ." The next step is "something borrowed, something blue." It's called Trial Distancing.

Trial Distancing has its basis in the practice of trial separations (for marriages) and parental "Tough Love." The premise is similar. Those who are having problems withdraw from each other, physically and emotionally, for a period of time. Creating a space provides time for contemplation and breathing room. Rather than antagonizing each other, individuals can break the endless cycles of action and reaction.

When married couples separate, they move away from one another physically, while they attempt to sort out problems. Sometimes circumstances prevent a change of residence, but the idea is to initiate a cool off in as many ways as feasible.

With Tough Love, parents distance themselves emotionally from their troubled children. These young people may use drugs or exhibit other socially unacceptable behavior, and then return home for help when they're unable to function on their own. Tough Love advocates that parents remove themselves from this dependency cycle until the troubled kids take action to stop their self-destructive behavior. Withdrawing support—food, shelter, and funds—from ill and needy kin is difficult, but this method has proved successful in changing behavioral patterns. It was found that attitudes changed more quickly when negative actions elicited neither warmth nor comfort. Love doesn't end; it just goes into a holding pattern.

In both types of separation, time is given to a discussion of the problems that led to the crisis. Whether or not there are legal or financial matters to settle, all parties involved agree to disagree. They decide, formally or informally, to back off and examine the relationship in all its aspects. Relationships are dismantled in order to find which parts work and which falter from day to day.

The purpose of Trial Distancing is also to initiate new ways of thinking and start patterning in a new direction. Physical distance isn't at issue here. "Cease and desist" is the imperative.

Friendship in the workplace has caused more harm and fanned more winds of war among women than anything else, including economic considerations. Since trial separation and Tough Love are solutions for solving troubles among people with close emotional ties, Trial Distancing could prove invaluable in bringing about a cease-fire.

To begin with, Trial Distancing calls for a total separation of business and social interaction. Most women consider socializing at work as a given. It's generally assumed that most "nice" women at the office will form at least daytime friendships. Possibly because there are fewer women in management, or because a presumption of "just girls" prevails, these bondings are expected to transcend rank and business functions.

Office friendships among women follow a full set of Women's Rules, which are devoid of the restrictions placed on the etiquette and ethics of commonly accepted (male) Business Rules.

Female office friendships can grow as complicated as office romances. They interfere with business and interfere with business decorum. They place restrictions on the "strictly business" aspects of advancing up the promotional ladder. Contradictory expectations fuel the flames:

If she was my friend, she would never expect . . .
Why is she going . . . when I'm not. . . .

She thinks she can . . . , but I know, in her own home, she's
not even able . . .
I only said it for her own good
Of all people, she should know why I had to . . .
She should have taken into consideration how I felt
about . . .

Qualities that make fine friendships can directly interfere in
the frenetic pace of the work day. Enjoying the warmth of good
friends at work is an indulgence women can ill afford when they're
deeply engaged in all-out business competition.

Survival in a crowded workplace precludes the distraction of
Women's Rules. At present, women are afraid of letting one another out of their work sight, for fear someone will step ahead and
leave them behind. If they weren't such good friends, they
wouldn't be threatened by each other's success or failure.

Trial Distancing is a direct challenge. It's a cold-turkey
change. Disengage the friendship clutch at once. Stop. Now.

Initiate one discussion to explain Trial-Distancing limits to coworkers, and it's time to begin. Other forms of behavior modi-
fication will take up the issues of Women vs. Women and help
restructure the ways women interact at work. This stage is yet
another vital cool-down.

Trial Distancing is like a traffic stop sign. Temporarily stop
lunches, personal calls, coffee breaks, after-hours socializing, and
office confidences about anything other than business.

The terms of Trial Distancing should be in effect for at least
one full business quarter in order to give the concept enough time
to take effect. Discuss the terms upfront in a light but firm manner. "Hey, I quit smoking this way. It might help. I'm going to
give it a try. Let's confine ourselves to business only, from tomorrow until . . ."

Most likely, defining the terms will lead to good-natured, or
possibly ill-natured, teasing. Or both. The agreement may be verbal, but it can be formalized in a written affirmation, such as a
contract declaring "From this day forward . . . Betty Smith and
Jane Doe agree . . ." Contracts can be between two women or
among colleagues on an entire office floor. Whatever is workable.

A matter-of-fact approach and sense of humor sets the right tone. Again, as at the beginning of a marital or parental separation, evidence of deep trouble is apt to surface. This has a good, if painful, purging effect. Uncovering hidden problems is like shock therapy.

Dark resentment can emerge in Trial Distancing, as some resist the need for the concept. It also offers the serendipitous way to break out of habitual mental sets.

Although silence on the subject of women fighting women might be easier on the individuals involved, it does not help the situation. Discussing the unmentionable is awkward at first. It was that way with the difficult issues of sex, race, and money. Why should this subject be less—or more—sensitive? It may bring blushes to the maidenly countenance, but no permanent psychic damage should come of it.

It's possible to take part in Trial Distancing without being convinced it will do any good. It's also permissible to be uncomfortable with—or even dissapprove of—the concept. Unwilling partners may choose to withhold discussion or approval. It doesn't take a unanimous vote to stick to business at work. If some need to take this time to giggle in the opposite direction, that's their problem.

Each woman in Trial Distancing is only responsible for the words coming out of her own mouth and for the social events she chooses to skip or to attend. If she's the only one actively participating, she's still making others stop and think about what she's doing, and why.

In many separations, one partner is more interested in the method than the other. One group may be getting more out of the status quo than the others. In marriage, one partner may want to continue as is, while the other yearns for change. In parenting, the abuser may prefer to know there's a place to return when he or she is strung-out and broke. It's to the advantage of the weak to fight any change that will inconvenience their lives. It's to the advantage of the family to encourage the troubled child to live an independent and responsible life. These opposing desires will naturally make sparks fly.

The most unwilling participants are generally most in need of the program. But they cannot be expected to lead the parade. However, this cannot excuse their lack of participation. Even those who don't care to talk about it—or approve of it—should be included anyway. Their resistance is understandable. They're allowed a choice—to like it or not to like it.

As women disengage at work, they will have an opportunity to assess whether familiarity does indeed breed contempt. They can step back and decide how much energy was used to accommodate one another and apply that energy to their professional career goals. They can separate their goals from those of their office neighbors.

Women can judge the impact of being morally free to conduct themselves in a more formal, strictly business way during office hours. They can examine the advantages of competition according to Business Rules without the guilt of a social demerit. Women can experience and weigh the liberating effects of not competing in popularity contests. Without social judgments to pressure or influence them, women can experiment with the ways the new business-only office rules make them feel different. They can test the subtle changes in their self-images.

Does Trial Distancing sound easy? Do women who fight one another really care about lunch and swapping recipes? Are they concerned with one another's fight/flight plans? Do they care about daily bonding through an exchange of personal information? Are they really interested in the weekend activities of rivals and comparative strangers? Do their inquiring minds want to know who did what to whom and where? The answer to all of the above is yes.

Females are programmed early on to place a high value on popularity and peer acceptance. And to know as much as possible about what their enemies, as well as their personal friends, are doing and planning.

Separation will be one of working women's toughest chores. If their relationships were not so complex, the need would not have arisen. Women are curious, for better or worse. There is no natural cut-off point.

In Trial Distancing, women may at first need to look over their shoulder to copy the ways their male colleagues keep business and social interactions clear. For example, there may be an office bowling league. That's business, although it takes place out of the office and is fun.

As with golf or poker, the purpose is to get to know co-workers off-site and participate in a function as an extended family. That's all a part of the Business Rules. More social exchanges—such as pairing off and trading personal confidences—can veer off into Mother's Rules.

After-hours meetings should lead to a few moments of general chitchat. Business Rules do not dictate coldness or snobbery. A planned shopping excursion with female co-workers, however, would be verboten. That would stray from business limits and slide right into Mother's Rules.

The concept of distancing is easy, once the overall purpose is absorbed. For most men, its business application is as natural and lasting as riding a bike. Most know when they traverse from the casual to the personal and proceed with career caution.

Trial Distancing should naturally provide the technique that will become second nature to women as well. It will be easier for women to interact on business terms if there is a social space between co-workers on equal, higher, and lower rungs on the work ladder.

Announcing department or companywide participation in Trial Distancing, perhaps with a kicky flyer or two, would remove the Mother's-Rule stigma of being heartless and uncaring, unacceptable for any reason. It could be seen as a positive action, rather than just being—horror of horrors—unfriendly.

What a burden would be removed if women could only laugh or smile when they really felt like it. They could stop ''nicing'' one another to death at work. Removing the burden of false ''caring'' could free up a lot of work time. Friendliness would cease to be a female mandate.

A model for the new relationship among women could be copied from the one now in place between men and women who work together. What is needed is the measure of natural reticence built into those interactions. These may evolve into the personal, but they generally don't start that way. For example, they don't begin

on the first day of work by going to the bathro
compare notes.

Between men and women, there is no expectat
job will be done in a professional way. Men and
pected to cooperate at work, respect one another':
compete as appropriate. In office relationships between men and
women, there is a business interaction and a conversational reserve. An invitation is required for anything more intimate. A wall
of professional respect results from holding back on personal confidences. This is an important basis for the success of Trial Distancing. Sharing gossip may later be approved if that becomes
appropriate.

The boss is always the boss, and he is usually a man, so the
respect that enables him to see that the work gets done remains in
place. His title sets him apart from those who report to him. Right
or wrong, the boss has the final say—if employment is to continue.
He looks like the boss; he acts like the boss. There may be com-
radery, but the fine line is drawn. That it is not crossed is always
understood.

With women bosses, it doesn't always work that way. She
doesn't always look like the boss and she doesn't always act like
the boss. It's a muddy line between friends. "Just us girls" is a
heavy burden for executive women.

Trial Distancing is an affordable way for women to let one
another off the smiling-cheerful-friend hook. It's a good time to
form the habit of open communication, rather than party talk.

Business competition can then be "gloves-off" within corporate confines—with no hard feelings. Building distance into office
interactions automatically puts Business Rules into effect.

Absence may make the heart grow fonder, but then again it
may not. Either way, it is productive. But if nonfriendship benefits
women at work, it must be done.

Trial Distancing may be viewed as a special diet, or even a
fad diet. It may work; it may take more than one try to stay on it.
It may only work for a while.

But there is a chance that a quick start can provide immediate
success and evolve into a solid, practical regime.

Few problems in life or love are immediately solved for all time. Life is a learning experience. In interaction, among women, as with all else, it's two steps forward, one step back. Habitual problems return now and again.

Trial Distancing can provide a large step forward. It can comfortably end when appropriate business expectations among working women become natural. Less demanding office friendships can be initiated under career-oriented guidelines that assume women are in the office to succeed.

Like trial separations in marriage, Trial Distancing can go one of two ways. The result can be a stronger relationship—or a definite assurance that divorce is the answer.

Comparing Trial Distancing with Tough Love, adult women may have to leave the comfort and protection of the nest and risk being thrown into a competitive environment that can bring independence or failure. Working women must become fully grown self-managers. The sink-or-swim, fly-or-die traditions also carry over into the business world.

If women can live through divorce, surely they can bear a daily separation from the women they fight with tooth and nail.

If parents can face the need to take a tough look at their family and pinpoint problems that can be improved only by withdrawal, the work family can also look at its problems in a cool, analytic way.

Trial Distancing is the second—and perhaps the strongest and most meaningful plank—in the platform of cease-fire. There is hope in distance.

19
Follow the Leaders?

Wars end when leaders command "Cease-fire!" This would be a terrific time to call upon female corporate leaders to move into the spotlight and advocate an end to Women vs. Women. Where are the role models—the leaders, the proven-by-fire Moses figures to guide their followers to the Promised Land? Where are the voices of women dedicated to pursuing the corporate climb? The Uncivil Business War is concentrated in the offices of corporate America, but unfortunately there is a decided absence of management-level achievers who are in position to command across-the-board respect.

The truth of the matter is that there is no Top Ten consortium of corporate businesswomen to help end war among women. In a workaday world, there are few easily recognizable female leaders. Women have simply not allowed their kind to rise and lead.

As a result, women have fought their daily fight without any measure of guidance from an experienced, mature leadership that might help pave the way to advancement for all women. The war must be stopped, yet there is a dearth of professional women who have risen above the crowd and might serve as the core of a cease-fire movement. The situation requires a search for new beginnings.

Who can take the lead in stopping Women vs. Women and ending the Uncivil Business War? Must female role models evolve naturally, or can they be created? By whom? When? How? What is the value of celebrity role models admired for feminine charms, mate's title, or entrepreneurial success, as opposed to women who inconspicuously try to advance in the corporate world? The problem with well-born, well-married, well-buried, or otherwise entrepreneurially successful women is that they are not at the center of the trouble. White-collar working women need leadership from those who fight the fight daily in the business office.

To begin, women will have to improvise proper role models to fill in for the lack of women in senior management. Here's a profile of the ideal corporate role model who goes about the business of her life, does not seek public recognition, but is willing to help women in any way:

She works in her chosen field, and came up through the management ranks independently. Her achievements over a decade or more have elevated her profession and her employer. She radiates contentment with her lot in life. She is dedicated to humanitarian causes, is always willing to help others to reach their highest potential, and has gained recognition over the years. She would be, in short, the corporate world's equivalent of Mother Theresa. It is entirely within the realm of reason to suppose that there will be a need to settle for less.

Creating a role model where none exists is a practical alternative to waiting for one to emerge naturally. This "ideal" woman has come to terms to some extent with her lot in life and her role in the business community, and is willing to give a small measure of time to sharing her experiences.

She is somewhat akin to presidential wives. They are certainly somebody all the years before their husband's election, but only as First Ladies are they turned into role models.

At that point, they are encouraged to choose a promotable cause of some general benefit—such as conservation or drug abuse prevention—and to focus their public activities around it. Midmanagement women are already active and somewhat successful in their chosen work; some must be in prime position to become role models within their orbit and may be ready to mount a public platform to serve in an inspirational role.

Role models—natural or synthetic—may be thought of as diamonds in the rough, hidden in some unearthed corporate niche. Where might they be? Think small. Look around your home and office. Everyone lives in a small village, even in the heart of a huge metropolis. The boundaries are home and work, and the hubs of daily life. Ignore the city lights where the stars glitter beyond the reach of most more ordinary citizens.

Consider the women who share professions, interests, and bus schedules. Role modeling will be newer to them, and easier logistically. Everyone can learn the ropes together as they begin. This is a bootstraps program.

Is all of this really necessary in the full days of modern women's lives? It seems so. Doesn't the day go better with leadership? Isn't inspiration a part of achievement? If role models are important, aren't there enough already? Not really, and certainly not enough of the kind with whom most working women could identify—the office pro.

Although issue after issue of women's magazines are filled with admiring articles about women who are successful, the featured women have not become role models. Many of these are women who succeed at small businesses. Some start with kitchen enterprises, and receive help from their families in covering overhead expenses. Others start services and boutiques with enough financial backing for a trial period. Some are widows in a position to look through windows of financial opportunity.

Their smile-for-the-camera faces fade long before they have become household names or moved into positions of leadership. The fleeting stars shine briefly in four-color print and disappear. For most working women, the lives of such successful women have no relationship to their own daily lives.

The path of female entrepreneurs is not much hindered—and may even be enhanced—by reliance on Mother's Rules. Even when they play with the big boys, it's within an accepted social context. There remains a vast difference between their modus operandi and that of women in the corporate structure. This is why so many white-collar women would adore owning their own business, where they could function more comfortably and be their own boss, in command of their own time.

The methods that work for women in small businesses can actually confuse the situation for corporate working women. The paths of entrepreneurs provide little practical help for midlevel career women trying to learn interpersonal management skills that are nothing like the rules they learned as girls. They need leaders and role models in the know.

Catalyst, an organization that works for the advancement of women in business, estimates that there is "only a small pool of women—perhaps 250—at the threshold of national corporate leadership." They note that "few Fortune 1,000 companies have more than one woman, if that, on their boards."

For that reason, the rank and file population of middle-class females are on their own. Women do not know group strategies that can advance the greater good. The result is an unsure, rudderless Women vs. Women. Few leaders have come forth and proclaimed the macho "Lead, follow, or get the hell out of the way" approach to problem-solving.

This situation can be remedied. While peacemongering is taking hold and Trial Distancing is underway, the time is ripe to add another vital link: the creation of role models.

A local, garden-variety top-ten consortium is the key. A few good women can be instrumental in creating this group, one step at a time. Cultivating successful women would provide outlets for positive social interaction. It could replace the professionally detrimental infighting. As with the other cease-fire projects, this one won't be easy. This clarion call can be, "Take action to create positive role models in your business community."

Societies traditionally elevate strong and admirable individuals to role model status, and all benefit by encouraging the young to follow in the inspirational footsteps of the more experienced. Leaders create realistic goals for others to reach and try to surpass. Heroes are an important part of almost all cultures. Female corporate heroes are few and far between.

Although there are not many executive women at the top of large companies—fewer in 1986 than in 1982—there are some. By virtue of their scarcity, women who have attained senior management through promotions in their fields are to be valued and respected for their experience and insight. Midlevel working women should regard them as a step above national treasures. They are the elder stateswomen of the business world.

Living, breathing role models are rare enough to be spotlighted now and again in the national media as freaks. And with the rough road they've had to hoe, some "perform" in an eccentric way. They may seem odd at first glance.

Peacemongers must learn to identify women who—on their own—have achieved some measure of corporate success. Peacemongers can begin by scanning the local papers and trade journals. They can look around the table at staff meetings and auxiliary business functions with an eye to their mission. A notebook should be open and handy to list possible candidates, their work, and any relevant personal information.

Let's discuss some general guidelines to begin the search, and then follow through with specific plans to elevate potential candidates to modified stardom.

Peacemongers have their work cut out for them. They are most qualified to undertake this strange mission. Elevating other women to a status above one's own is a task foreign to those trained by Mother's Rules to knock potential rivals. For most, this is an entirely new mind-set.

Peacemongers who Take It (the War) Personally shouldn't mind if they feel awkward at first. They need only persist.

Peacemongers must target women of any age, education, and personality who work in corporate settings and rose through the ranks. Those holding the title equivalent to vice president or above are appropriate candidates. Be they physically attractive, personally objectionable, or even social hermits, these are designated for role model stature.

Personal attributes should not enter into the selection of individuals. Men and women alike laud Lee Iacocca, controversial Chrysler spokesman, as a role model. It's doubtful that this approval is based on either his looks or quiet charm. These are not important. Candidates need not parade in swimsuits, be congenial, or exhibit social skills. Most admired folks exude power, a more difficult quality to commend in a female, although a plus for the purpose of leadership.

Women who are vice presidents (or the equivalent) will be

among the busiest in the universe. Probably middle-aged or older, they've lived with superwoman as a part of their cosmic package. Most have been complimented for their businesslike (or masculine) demeanor.

They keep their priorities, are often very organized, and guard their time and energy. These characteristics have enabled them to survive in the corporate jungle.

There's a wall around their private lives. Friends are precious and few. Family time is a guarded treasure. They work long hours and combine business, sport, and leisure activities. Vacations are planned not only as rewards, but to protect the good mental and physical health that enables them to sustain their frenetic pace.

These working women are generally under heavy stress. They're in the big time. In order to get where they are, most have to be self-reliant, confident, independent, assertive, decisive, and super-busy. They're take-charge people at home and at work, in control of their destiny.

How can these titled, highly motivated women have impact on the average midlevel woman's career? Assuming that top management women are serious Careerists—with a latent longing to be Balancers at least part of the time and possessing Homing Pigeon instincts buried deep within—can they be expected, coerced, or influenced to take on a leadership role for working women?

The feminist movement doesn't play a daily role in their lives. Nor does networking. Senior management women do not react as one of the girls. They've never allowed themselves the luxury of these activities and should not be expected to give hands-on help to the female masses struggling at lower levels.

Elite women can at first be expected to serve only as ceremonial role models. They are to be put on a pedestal and elevated into models of inspirational value.

The new attitude must be that eventually, in the near future, those who emulate winners will themselves be inspired to rise. Step by step, through their own business acumen, they will attain levels closer to the role model's own. At that time they will be in position to interact with—and become one of—the Top Ten. Queen Bee could take on nature's most positive meaning.

This idea is a spoonful of strong medicine for midlevel women to swallow. They will need to remind themselves to award star status to those a step or two above them, just to be sure they're operating according to Business Rules, rather than Mother's Rules.

The Elder Stateswoman is a business breed all but unknown in the corporate office. This class of classy woman could play a vital role in accelerating the peacemongering process. What would entice such senior management businesswomen to want to be recognized as community elders—even if the word "stateswoman" is used? What's in it for them? This is an important consideration. It should precede an exclamation about "how good this would be for all women."

The hard, cold truth is that the potential role model achieved her present position without much assistance from other women. Odds are that other women didn't promote her or help her rise. Just like other women, she grew up with her own full set of Mother's Rules.

In spite of all this, she has—at least on some level—made it; she's a success in the male-dominated world of business. As such, she's above most of the girls and must be paid her due in order to enlist her cooperation. She's earned the right to hang tough and to act by her own standards.

One vice president of a midsize temporary agency says, "I don't trust people who say they're here to help me. That's as bad as those who say, 'trust me.' I always say, 'I don't trust you. I don't even know you. Let's get down to business—real business to do us both some good.' "

Needless to say, this type of woman would not step forward to be honored at a PTA bake sale. There has to be something of real value to entice the Elder Stateswoman to come forward. The offer must be a formidable one. A position of honor. Women in top management respond to requests for their time in the same manner as their male colleagues. This rationale must be used as the standard: In our community, prestigious men will give their time to . . . Fill in the blanks and the deed is begun. Important people—especially the most important—will help a worthwhile business or charitable cause. But in deciding on the best use of their time, value judgments are made. Top-level people respond to top-drawer requests.

Almost everyone welcomes community appreciation. Senior management women surely crave the knowledge that they are lead-

ing their lives wisely, that their inspirational words are appreci-
ated. Their elevation to role models could create a powerful class
of peacemakers and possible Peacemongers.

There are many local opportunities to explore. If Peacemongers across the country begin their individual efforts, the movement will take on a life of its own. Once the idea is in actual
use—even in a small way—it will expand. Here's a way to begin.

Middle-class women can find a local need and fill it through
a fund-raising event. The event can be supported and sponsored
by business or the community. Many charitable groups seek service projects to keep their membership active and interested. Try
to find a special niche. A Hollywood star was advised to gain re-
spectability by backing a cause. She studied the situation and
moaned, "But all the good diseases are already taken!" However,
there are always new needs waiting to be addressed.

A prominent speaker is always included on such occasions.
With or without an award, a prestige event can easily promote a
role model. Local media coverage appropriately records the event
in the community. Given momentum, both the cause and the
spokesperson gain recognition. It doesn't take much; the newspaper mills and the business press must be fed. They welcome local
news.

Because this is a new undertaking, it will be necessary to use
male role models as a measuring stick in selecting causes and events.
To be on the safe side, use a man a level above the woman. Consider
a male CEO to decide on an honor for a female VP. Would the
award impress this man if it were given to him? Would you ask the
top gun in your business to speak at this event? The award or speech
should in no way be given to the honoree because she is a woman,
but in recognition of her contribution of time and effort.

The event should be modeled on the community standard for
first-class benefits. Nonprofit opportunities on behalf of charities
and the arts abound in every town and city. The local newspapers
offer a who's who of active movers and shakers in their social
columns.

The political arena is also a prime spot for attention-getting
community functions. Perhaps a female political leader would be
amenable to working on a project that could include a spot for her

on the podium. This would cultivate a healthy one-hand-washes-the-other attitude that women so sorely need to learn.

The creation of a single role model (think small at first) should involve a take-charge midmanagement woman as chairperson and committees of busy businesswomen to help at every stage. Each woman who is involved automatically becomes a Peacemonger.

This exercise should benefit the super-busy woman and bring all her creative efforts to bear. She will have to seek a deserving recipient just as Diogenes sought an honest man.

She should offer the platform to a woman who is not a personal friend. Someone she may not even know. If the Peacemonger comes up with a woman who has risen in business by no-holds-barred methods she cannot condone, or if the prospective honoree is a woman the Peacemonger has heard of and doesn't have much use for, she's on the right track. If the soon-to-be-elevated has conducted her personal life by dubious standards—short of anything punishable by a jail term—it's a good sign.

If this monumental effort is of some professional value to the planner, fine. She is not to feel guilty if she meets higher-ups in filling the podium with a star-studded guest list for a truly worthwhile occasion.

She is not to feel guilty if these social and business contacts prove fruitful to her own career on some other occasion. It does not diminish, but rather enhances, her unselfish contribution to the cause of women in the corporate work world.

Anything that accomplishes the goal of allowing a senior management woman to receive recognition from other women will do. If it proves to help the underprivileged or becomes an annual event because it is successful, these are additional gains. Much good to the general public comes about exactly this way.

The honoree may at first be doubtful or even cynical about being approached for a civic honor. Especially by a female stranger. This is natural. It doesn't happen every day. Or hardly at all. But given human nature, she'll probably rally from the shock in time to perform dutifully.

The clue is to treat her exactly as you would the male role models she has emulated in her rise. No corsage and probably no lipstick kiss on the cheek. For openers, play it straight. Model the event on a similar event in your community. Check around. Enlist the help of people—such as those who work with nonprofit agencies and charity benefits—who regularly pull off these events. Do not, under pain of death, do not include a fashion show in any way, shape, or form. You have a grander vision.

Some homework is needed before approaching prospective role models after they're spotted. Consider where she's coming from. As a rule, she probably has only a limited number of hours to devote to causes and people outside her immediate area of concern. It is likely that she is unknown to the general public. Such women do not yearn to get involved with strangers below their level. They have reasons beyond those of limited time. They've been buttonholed at cocktail parties by women wanting their secrets and whatever else they can pry loose.

Unmentored by women, they are not likely to volunteer counsel. They don't need to.

Female corporate leaders don't indulge in "girly" activities, but they will respond to an appeal to their personal interests and favored charities. They have to understand the big picture as well as their own roles in bringing about change.

How will anyone know if this process is successful? Ultimately, success will be manifested in a turnaround for American women in the ranks of midlevel business. Victory must go to those who plan to stay, work toward consistent business goals, and advance as high as their expertise can take them. It must go to those who value independent financial incomes.

The long-termers in today's workplace must evolve as pacesetters for the drive toward excellence. Careerists who came to play ball are forerunners of the new truce.

Busy Careerists may consider this time-consuming effort a project to do someday. Keep in mind, however, that the problem exists now. The news about corporate working women is not presented in glowing terms that will allow them to break free from the midlevel glut.

At present, the Uncivil Business War is afire. Would it be fanciful to suggest that fanning the flames is a conspiracy to encourage the huge number of qualified midlevel women to quit and go home? Could the male CEOs of Fortune 500 companies have met behind closed doors to ferret out a potential female take-over? Is it possible they resolved—in James Bond style—to eradi-cate women rivals by destroying every ounce of female credibility?

For the past decade, the news on white-collar women in the work force was nearly all upbeat, modeled on "First woman to . . ." themes. Women were not a threat, just tokens. As women moved up a bit, the atmosphere changed. The honeymoon was over.

At present, leaderless women are fighting isolated battles against one another without an inkling of the overall damage being done. Without intelligent, capable, and qualified role models to articulate the real problems of working women, malcontents have been featured. Many repeat the theme—"Happiness is at home. Women begone." Women are allowing themselves to be lulled to sleep once again. Women are being prepared, or are preparing themselves, to cash in and check out—as soon as they can find the financial route to do so.

On the surface, psuedoleaders appear sympathetic and con-cerned. These spokespeople are portraying today's women as rein-carnations of Betty Boop. Where are the real experts—local and national—who can be interviewed on the nightly news when the issue is corporate women?

At one time, this role was coopted by the feminists. But hav-ing led women through 20 years of wandering in the desert, this group has lost its credibility. They don't always speak for serious working women.

One feminist faction insists "women are equal but different, because we bleed every month and men do not." This double standard replaces the former theory of equality: Men and women have natural physical rhythms to deal with over the course of their lives.

Betty Friedan offers mellow reassurances: "How little we started with. I know what can be done." This is hardly a rousing call for excellence.

Spokeswomen seem to leave their future to circumstance, rather than planning a clear-cut course of action.

There is a dire need for new role models to lend reason to the current divisive scene. If there really is a Big Bad Boy conspiracy, or a resurgence of the diabolical Stepford Wives plot to replace thinking women with brainless robots, there would be no practical solution. But if the problem is that only a few airheads are finding their way into the limelight, there is hope.

The challenge to Peacemongers: Always ask the busiest people to take on the big jobs. They'll usually rise to accept an important task.

Next: Follow the leaders. Then be one.

20

Hatred Management to Truce-Time

It's time for a truce. This could be the beginning of the end of the Uncivil Business War. Maintaining a cease-fire in the war now raging among women in America's offices will be about as simple as trying to keep the peace in the Middle East. Yet, if women are to survive at a professional level in today's economy, there is no other choice but to make it happen.

Peacemongering offers a strong beginning and can generate the momentum needed to follow through with Trial Distancing and creating role models. The next step is one more solid thrust toward changing the status quo.

Call it Hatred Management. This idea is based on the management development programs under way in corporate America. Hatred Management could be taught as part of a course on managing interpersonal relationships, complete with analysis of individual and group behavior, awareness of self and others, planning strategies, and confirmation feedback on how women are meeting one another's—and the corporation's—needs and expectations.

As with other methods, success depends on the individual. However, programs of this scope require the full support of management. To be successful the program must involve senior management and include all employees.

At some point down the line, the male corporate hierarchy must be enlisted in the grass-roots cease-fire movement. Here is their opportunity. They can use cohesive methods implemented by a competent human relations or personnel department to bring about a solution to a grave problem. It must come from the top down to reach those who have remained uninformed and uninvolved.

Corporate decision-makers shouldn't help out of altruism. This issue is of critical importance to them because the battlefield mentality in effect in the office wastes talent and money every working day.

The economic devastation caused by the Uncivil Business War is incalculable. America women earn $500 billion annually and their influence on the economy is profound. So the wasted time, irregular work hours, substandard performance, excessive stress-related absenteeism and sick days resulting from women in turmoil cost American business dearly. In business, the bottom line is at the heart of the matter. Bankrupt companies can't help workers.

Managing the hatred that fuels the Uncivil Business War begins with a truthful acknowledgment of the problem and calls for restructuring attitudes about women's place in the work world. Both men and women need to reconsider many of their cherished beliefs about what working women should expect from the companies that employ them and what those companies should expect in return. There must be give and take.

Recent rhetoric in the press about what corporations can do for women has had little to suggest about what working women can do to help pay for additional benefits, such as extended maternity leave and on-site day-care centers. As humanitarian as these services seem, there is little practical discussion of how women can help offset the enormous costs of these programs through increased cooperation and productivity.

Hatred Management can stop female war games and make it financially sound to promote women to upper management. A well-planned program, properly implemented, will explore how the benefits for one faction may work against the interests of the others, and examine the impact on the company.

Hatred Management can help individuals acknowledge that they may like or dislike one another and still not wage war in the workplace. Such a course can explore the specifics of women's office battles and the effect these have on management.

Corporate management often steps in to accept challenges that affect the performance of workers and, ultimately, the bottom line. Women fighting women is such an issue. It invades every white-collar workplace and interferes with the performance of trained and qualified women over the long run. It's a legitimate corporate concern that a large number of skilled and trained workers regularly leave their jobs at the level at which their know-how begins to pay back the firm which provided the training. It's also a concern when experienced personnel seem content to stay at entry level or midlevel without bringing something more—such as increased efficiency—to their work.

In other words, when employees' real life concerns are elsewhere during the work week, the company gains little from their fragmented efforts. It certainly is not provided with talent to utilize or promote. As women stagnate, they begin to realize that they're failing in their original goal to earn their own way. Their ambivalence proves a distraction and eventually becomes a self-fulfilling prophecy. The result is often not only the fear of failure, but failure itself.

Consider subsidized child care. Women with young children naturally favor it. Women without children generally do not. Men are somewhere in between, but child care is often not their main responsibility, or interest.

Mothers say they could work with freer minds if their employers provide on-site child care or benefits that help pay for good quality off-site care. Nonmothers feel otherwise. Companies that have initiated on-site centers cite the tremendous costs involved. There are considerations, such as: (1) the hiring, turnover, and quality of staff; (2) the ratio of staff to children; (3) mothers taking additional breaks during the day to nurse, check on, and visit with their children, and sometimes bringing along coworkers; and (4) ill and contagious children showing up at the workplace.

What impact does this enormous perk have on those who do not need or want the service? Does the participation of large numbers of mothers using this benefit translate into dollars and cents returning to the company? Does it lower the pay scale for all?

Would government funding help? Where would this money come from? Who would be taxed? How would the benefit be offset for those who do not use it?

This is a topic of concern to all workers that should be discussed openly. Although there may be no quick and ready solution, it would be helpful if those who advocate such programs could understand how the company and other workers feel about the costs and merits involved.

Hatred Management can be a vehicle to turn unnamed fears into a recognition of the problems which build resentment among women. Exploring issues such as child care in an open forum can unearth anger and bring out opinions that could be debated in a reasonable way.

When Careerists and Balancers turn into Homing Pigeons, or when Careerists perform like Balancers, the corporation's investment is often shortchanged. Those directly involved (members of the work force) remain ignorant of the impact of these forces on them. The slackened or halted productivity of qualified personnel is a hidden price tag that translates into diminished opportunity for all women.

Peacemongers can flip the price tag so that the numbers show. By initiating a program of Hatred Management, the business community can begin to directly address the issues. The Peacemonger should not view her mission as altruistic. A female leader who understands the problem and is motivated to take action could view this as an opportunity to spotlight her expertise before senior management.

Rather than seeing it as a do-good activity, a woman should consider a Hatred Management program a showcase for exhibiting her talents for organization and leadership. For this to be the case, the program should be good for her company, good for her own career, and good for other working women. Her professional attitude should be forthright.

The overall strategy to change work behavior should be modeled on formats for problem prevention, rather than tackling specific issues. Action plans that have been effective in altering workers attitudes and have brought change to the office can be used as guidelines for this issue.

Some authorities say that workers of the 80s will believe only top management and only accept decrees directly from them. Any less credible source is downplayed or ignored. Of course, planning comes from other professionals and is presented to conclaves of senior staffers. A sponsor will likely be "volunteered" from the senior level, as is the general practice for company support activities.

Cynicism at Work, written by Philip H. Mirvis, associate professor of organizational behavior, and Donald L. Kanter, professor of marketing at Boston University School of Management, makes this claim: "Many workers—particularly Baby Boomers and newcomers—have developed insatiably high aspirations . . . and chafe in jobs that don't meet their needs for self-actualization."

The authors remind those who would change behavior patterns that their data show ". . . 43 percent of the working population fit the profile of the 'strong' cynic, who sees selfishness and guile as the dominant part of human nature."

Bob Rayfield and David Pincus, of California State-Fullerton's Department of Communications, are the authors of a study called *The Emerging Role of Top Management Communication: 'Turning On' Employee Commitment*. They say: "Employees want a relationship with their corporate leaders that is separate and distinct from that with their immediate supervisors. [From the top] They want to receive information . . . they believe can affect their future . . ."

This provides behavior modifiers with guidelines. According to Rayfield and Pincus, "Today's work force is (1) more educated, (2) more independent, (3) more worldly and knowledgable, (4) less awed by authority." They want key elements involving their future to be presented as a part of the big picture. In formulating a plan to alter thinking patterns, there must be a forum for open and public communication.

The most efficient way to present a plan is through a written proposal to senior management, incorporating specific time-dated schedules for action, complete with a budget. The main points within each section should include: building trust by a high level involvement, the dissemination of pertinent information, the active involvement of women, and forums for feedback at each step.

The following points must be considered:

Trust must be built through internal communication. Without it, messages will be rejected.

Two-way communication is vital. If there already are structures in place at the company—such as quality circles, newsletters, or other participatory vehicles—they can be enlisted in generating feedback on this topic. Short surveys, Management By Walking Around (MBWA), or any informal one-on-one can bring this subject to open discussion. The subject is, by definition, a business concern, even when it's presented in a "social" context.

Media involvement can help. Generate reports on corporate progress, senior management participation, and women's approval at each phase. This can create a snowball effect for internal programs. It's positive, newsworthy coverage for the corporation.

None of this is an abrupt departure from the ways in which other sticky corporate personnel problems are handled. To be effective, the program should have sufficient authority to ensure that it becomes a policy that reaches the entire female staff. And the men who must promote them.

A written proposal should be planned to meet the needs of the specific company. How many women are in midmanagement? How long have they worked there? How many have come in over the past decade? How many have left? What were the circumstances? How many women are in upper-level management? What is their profile? How do the female fight/flight patterns at that workplace translate to the financial bottom line? These statistics explain the overall picture.

How quickly can a plan of action be implemented? As corporate people know, a plan approved by senior management is placed on an agenda. Even when driven by a concerned faction, the issue takes its place alongside other vital business concerns.

While all reasonable procedures are followed to track the time frame and progress of each step of this major undertaking, other more individual—and speedy—approaches can be initiated. With management sanction, the communications and personnel departments could begin a program to build awareness of the situation of Women vs. Women. Specific women's issues in company publications might tackle factual (rather than cheerleading) news of the financial situation of women in the white-collar workplace. It's not too soon for middle-class working women to recognize that they can't stay put without an automatic downward spiral in their livelihood.

The fight for financial well-being may begin at entry level for the newcomers, but they mean to set their sights upward. Most of the jobs they hope to enter into and grow with are now being—or will be—held by someone else. Jobs as yet unknown will also beckon newcomers. The future promises a free-for-all. It's a practical time to begin working toward planned progression for experienced working women in line for promotions.

Never underestimate the power of a Peacemonger. It's well within her midmanagement expertise to appoint herself a Hatred Management initiator. The cease-fire process begins with peacemongering. Trial Distancing can be a part of a woman's work day from day one. Researching and creating role models will require a few months to get the first candidate and program off the ground. Hatred Management will take the longest to bring about positive results.

Corporate leaders must understand the duration of the cease-fire process and its component elements. This will help them understand that Hatred Management is a good long-term investment. It will require great perseverance, yet offer untold rewards for leaders and supporters.

Considering that large corporations offer employee courses on telephone answering techniques, managing one's time, and personality interactions, there is much to be gained in offering a program of Hatred Management to personnel departments whose purpose is to broaden employee horizons and to help them toward better performance.

To begin, the course of action is: (1) Review material in this chapter for procedure. (2) Write a proposal that follows the guidelines in this chapter. (3) Enlist the support of your immediate supervisor. (4) Submit a written plan to the manager of personnel/human relations and request an appointment to discuss it. Ask for procedural techniques on how management training programs are initiated at your company. (5) Schedule short meetings with appropriate managers—complete with written agendas—and offer some new information at each meeting. (6) Issue one-page progress reports to all who might or should be concerned at each stage.

To be effective, Hatred Management should be well-planned and formulated to reach out to as many staff members as possible. Peacemongers will need to reread and study—in textbook fashion— to bring the theory to fruition. Each step should suggest and lead to the next.

Hatred Management is a formal management program and is a giant undertaking for the Peacemonger to initiate. But individuals have used more time for less reason. If the question is "Why me?" the answer might be "In order to experience change within my work time."

Success will be manifested in a turnaround for American women in the midlevel corporate ranks. Victory must be the exclusive reward for those who plan to stay, work toward consistent business goals, and advance as high as their expertise can take them. Success belongs to those who value their financial independence.

The long-termers in today's workplace must evolve as the pacesetters in excellence and the new truce.

As with their male colleagues, fulfilling personal lives must be melded into the fabric of their professional world. Although it might as well be assumed that women will always have the larger share of responsibility for the creation and care of the family, this cannot be a primary consideration of the corporate business structure. In order to be paid and promoted as equal, personal priorities must mesh with the company's vital concerns.

Free Americans have choices. Women who decide to try for economically subsidized lives may do so, but their standards must be separate from those who have made the choice to depend only on themselves for financial sustenance.

Women who elect to stay home must realize that their freedom to swing their fist ends where their sister's jaw begins. They must make the mental adjustment to their trade-off. They are basically homemakers who make occasional forays into the job market as their situation demands. Euphemisms and self-deception about the depth of their commitment destroy the credibility of those in the game who play strictly by Business Rules. Mother's Rules must stay at home.

Women who have decided not to adhere to the career path must matter of factly take their place in the backseat, out of the running. Understanding their choice, they should not denigrate themselves or worry about being judged failures by society. Their part-time mentality should be brought to the forefront as they enter and leave the white-collar world. This would allow them to present themselves as a back-up resource that functions completely separately from the financial negotiations of the more dedicated, full-time female work force. This self-acceptance will help them and other women.

Careerists need the support of Homing Pigeons and Balancers to maintain corporate credibility and move forward. Careerists must remain spokeswomen for the professional community and not be compromised by the goals of the homemakers-at-heart. This will benefit all three group—and the next generation—in keeping the spirit of equal opportunities for working women alive.

Women must give full professional concentration to career goals while they're in the office. The alternative is to accept support positions that require less than total dedication.

Mother's Rules were misleading. There is more than one way to be a good girl or a bad girl. And there's no innate stigma attached to certain individual life choices, unless those choices cause damage to women who choose a different road.

Midlevel Balancers and Homing Pigeons must adjust their attitudes toward Careerists who single-mindedly aim for the top. They deserve acceptance and moral support in their persistence— even when they bypass some of the social niceties.

Peacemongers should be given the benefit of the doubt as they initiate the first round of cease-fire changes that may bring discomfort to many. In a cooperative atmosphere, Peacemongers can roll up their corporate sleeves and take hold. In the battlefields, any gains for truce and progress should be lauded by peacemakers who watch and wait. Positive efforts should be accepted, if not applauded, by bystanders.

With a four-level plan of action in play, some success for working women who decide to Take It Personally should surface in a fairly short time. For those who accept the challenge at its inception, change should be visible in office corridors within the year.

"Cease-fire" is a strong command. It offers a balm of truce to the wounds of Women vs. Women—and a time to heal. The Uncivil Business War can take its place alongside other painful upheavals that have led to eras of higher achievement and understanding.

Truce can provide the salve of independent economic possibilities to middle-class working women. Women may recall having heard the admonition, "Someday you'll get what you deserve." They now have the challenge of deciding what it is they really do deserve.

Index